LUTHER ON WOMEN
A Sourcebook

Martin Luther contributed extensively to the sixteenth-century "debate about women" with his writings on women and related subjects such as marriage, the family, and sexuality. In this volume, Susan Karant-Nunn and Merry Wiesner-Hanks bring together a vast selection of these works, translating many into English for the first time. They include sermons, lectures, pamphlets, polemic writings, letters, and some informal "table talk" recorded by his followers. The book is arranged into chapters on Biblical women, marriage, sexuality, childbirth, and witchcraft, as well as on Luther's relations with his wife and other contemporary women. The editors, both internationally known scholars of the Reformation and women, provide a general introduction to each chapter, and Luther's own colourful words fuel both sides of the debate about whether the Protestant Reformation was beneficial or detrimental to women. This collection will make a wide range of Luther's works accessible to English-speaking scholars, students, and general readers.

SUSAN C. KARANT-NUNN is Professor of History and Director, Division for Late Medieval and Reformation Studies, University of Arizona.

MERRY E. WIESNER-HANKS is Professor of History and Director, Comparative Study of Religion Program and the Center for Women's Studies, University of Wisconsin-Milwaukee.

LUTHER ON WOMEN

A Sourcebook

EDITED AND TRANSLATED BY

SUSAN C. KARANT-NUNN

AND

MERRY E. WIESNER-HANKS

CAMBRIDGE
UNIVERSITY PRESS

CAMBRIDGE UNIVERSITY PRESS
Cambridge, New York, Melbourne, Madrid, Cape Town,
Singapore, São Paulo, Delhi, Mexico City

Cambridge University Press
The Edinburgh Building, Cambridge CB2 8RU, UK

Published in the United States of America by Cambridge University Press, New York

www.cambridge.org
Information on this title: www.cambridge.org/9780521658843

First published 2003

A catalogue record for this publication is available from the British Library

ISBN 978-0-521-65091-5 Hardback
ISBN 978-0-521-65884-3 Paperback

*In love and loving memory to the women of our families,
by birth, marriage, and spirit.*

Contents

CHAPTER I

Introduction

It is hard to imagine that any aspect of Martin Luther's ideas or life is understudied. There are countless biographies in many languages, specialized analyses of his ideas about various theological, political, and intellectual topics, and journals and book series devoted completely to him. The five-hundredth anniversary of his birth, in 1983, saw academic conferences and church-sponsored lectures all over the world, and interest in his ideas and the Protestant Reformation that resulted in part from them shows no signs of abating.

It is also hard to imagine, given the last twenty-five years of women's history, that the ideas of a man who wrote so much about women and who was so clearly influential would not have been analyzed to death. Educated men's ideas about women are one of the easiest things to investigate when exploring the experience of women in any culture, as they are more likely to be recorded than women's own ideas. For someone who lived, as Luther did, after the invention of the printing press, they might also be published and thus widely available, not simply found in a single private letter or archival record. The sixteenth century was a period in which men – and a few women – argued often in print about the nature of women, whether they were good or bad, human or not human, whether they had reason or were governed by their passions. These debates – often termed the "debate about women" or in its French version, the *querelle des femmes* – have been very well studied by historians and literary scholars.[1] The writers central to the debate about women, such as Giovanni Boccaccio, Christine de Pizan, Heinrich Cornelius Agrippa von Nettesheim, Juan Luis Vives, Desiderius

[1] Joan Kelly, "Early Feminist Theory and the *Querelle des Femmes*, 1400–1789," in her *Women, History and Theory* (Chicago: University of Chicago Press, 1984); Constance Jordan, *Renaissance Feminism: Literary Texts and Political Models* (Ithaca, NY: Cornell University Press, 1990); Pamela Joseph Benson, *The Invention of the Renaissance Woman: The Challenge of Female Independence in the Literature and Thought of Italy and England* (Pittsburgh: Pennsylvania State University Press, 1992); Margaret Somerville, *Sex and Subjection: Attitudes to Women in Early-Modern Society* (London: Arnold, 1995); Ian Maclean, *The Renaissance Notion of Woman* (Cambridge: Cambridge University Press, 1980).

Erasmus, and John Knox, have been analyzed and their works issued in modern editions and translated into English.[2]

Luther took vigorous part in this debate, and his thoughts about women and related subjects such as marriage, the family, and sexuality emerge in every type of his writings. It is thus very surprising that there continues to be relatively little scholarship on Luther's ideas about women. Calvin's ideas about women have seen two book-length studies in English and a large number of articles, and the ideas of Italian humanists and English Puritans extend to many articles and a number of books.[3] Though there are articles on Luther's opinions about women and a few books on his ideas about the family, there is as yet no book-length study of his ideas about women in any language.

We hope that the present book will help to begin to fill this odd gap in the scholarship on both Luther and women, by making available in English translation a good share of Luther's writings and statements on women, marriage, and sexuality to an audience that may not be fluent in New High German or Latin. (Our source citations should also make it easier for specialized scholars to find these passages in their original languages.) It strives to open the floor to wider discussion of the significance for women of the religious and associated institutional changes of the sixteenth century. We acknowledge that this discussion must take place within our modern frame of reference; our perspectives cannot coincide with those of the women involved in the Reformation.

This is a book that we have long hoped someone else would write, for neither of us is a specialist in Luther's ideas, and we are both trained as historians, not theologians. Over the last several decades, we have both explored different aspects of women's lives during the Reformation period,

---

[2] Over the last ten years, the works of many continental women writers and men who participated in the debate about women have received excellent editions and translations in the series The Other Voice in Early Modern Europe, edited by Margaret King and Albert Rabil, Jr., and published by the University of Chicago Press. See also Erika Rummel, ed., *Erasmus on Women* (Toronto: University of Toronto Press, 1996); Joan Larsen Klein, ed., *Daughters, Wives and Widows: Writings by Men about Women and Marriage in England, 1500–1640* (Urbana: University of Chicago Press, 1992); Susan Gushee O'Malley, ed., *Defences of Women: Jane Anger, Rachel Speght, Ester Sowernam and Constantia Munda*, The Early Modern Englishwoman: A Facsimile Library of Essential Works 4.1 (New York: Scholars Press, 1996); Suzanne W. Hull, *Women According to Men: The World of Tudor-Stuart Women* (Thousand Oaks, CA: Altamira Press, 1996); Renate Blumenfeld-Kosinski, ed., *The Selected Writings of Christine De Pizan: New Translations, Criticism* (Boston: Norton, 2001).

[3] See, for example, Jane Dempsey Douglass, *Women, Freedom and Calvin* (Philadelphia: Westminster Press, 1985); John Thompson, *John Calvin and the Daughters of Sarah: Women in Regular and Exceptional Roles in the Exegesis of Calvin, His Predecesors and His Contemporaries* (Geneva: Droz, 1992); Margo Todd, *Christian Humanism and the Puritan Social Order* (Cambridge: Cambridge University Press, 1987).

fully expecting these to be joined by analyses of the ideas about women of the most important Protestant Reformer. This has not happened to the extent that it should, and we finally resigned ourselves to choosing, assembling, and translating the words you find here.

THE TEXTS

Luther wrote a huge number of works, some of them published during his lifetime and some of them not; scholars of the Reformation sometimes comment that he seems never to have had an unpublished thought. Many of his works went through multiple editions during his lifetime, some of which Luther approved, but many of which were put out by enterprising printers who simply copied an earlier edition. By the nineteenth century, scholars began several series of what they hoped would be complete and accurate collections of his works, comparing various editions of many works to arrive at the best version. Of these, the fullest and most highly respected is the series *D. Martin Luthers Werke: Kritische Gesamtausgabe*, published at Weimar from 1883 with a number of different editors; it eventually totalled more than one hundred volumes, and remains the authoritative version used by most scholars today. The publishing house Böhlau is currently issuing a comprehensive reprint that is made up of about 117 volumes. This is the text from which most of the translations in this book have been made; it is identified as WA, which stands for "Weimarer Ausgabe" or in English "Weimar edition." The edition is subdivided into four parts, the primary and largest of these containing lectures, sermons, and formal writings, the second the German translation of the Bible, the third Luther's letters (*Briefwechsel* [BR] in German), and the fourth the "table talk" (*Tischreden* [TR] in German) – informal and spontaneous comments made by Luther while sitting at the dinner table or other places for conversation, devoutly recorded by his admiring students, friends, colleagues, and others.

English translations of Luther's writings also began to appear in the sixteenth century, and, like German and Latin versions, their quality and fidelity to the original varied. The most authoritative English translation of many of his writings is the fifty-five-volume *Luther's Works*, published from 1955 by Concordia Publishing Company, Muhlenberg Press, Fortress Press, and Augsburg Publishing Company, also with a number of different editors and translators. *Luther's Works* includes Luther's major theological and political writings, much of his exposition of the Bible, a selection of his letters and sermons, some of the table talk, and other writings the editors judged to be especially important or interesting. It contains many works that discuss women, marriage, and sexuality, such as the treatises on marriage and the 1535–45 lectures on Genesis. We have included excerpts from this edition here, identified in the text as LW. (This material has been reprinted with the kind permission of the Augsburg Fortress Publishers and Concordia Publishing House, which now hold the copyright to all of *Luther's Works*.) Many of the works that we excerpt are quite long, and reading them in full in *Luther's Works* will give you an even better understanding of Luther's ideas.

The most difficult decision we had to face in preparing this book was what to include, for, in the same way that Luther's writings in general are very extensive, his writings on women and on topics related to women are voluminous, certainly enough to fill several long volumes. His thoughts on women appear in every genre of his works: Biblical commentary, sermons, polemical tracts, the Bible translation, lectures, letters, and the table talk. They appear in Latin and in German, and in works such as sermons that move from Latin to German and back again several times in a single sentence. Thus we ultimately chose to include a balance of works, favoring those that had never appeared or were not easily available in English, but including some segments from major writings that had previously been translated, because to omit them entirely would have provided an incomplete picture.

Our second decision was how to handle the translations themselves. Luther, like all sixteenth-century writers, did not use paragraphs, sentences or punctuation as modern writers do, but staying with his usage would have made many of the texts very difficult to follow. Thus, like most translators, including the many who prepared *Luther's Works*, we have added punctuation and occasionally repeated words or used paraphrases to allow Luther's points to emerge clearly. We have not included the large critical apparatus about variant editions and other issues that is found in the Weimar edition, and have limited our explanations of disputed or confusing points to those we found absolutely necessary. We have also tried to capture the vibrancy of Luther's language, which in some cases includes blunt, slanderous, anti-Semitic, and scatological terms, as well as irregular spellings.

Our third decision was how to arrange the material, and we chose to do this by topic rather than by chronology or type of text, as this seemed the best way to see the range of Luther's thoughts on an issue. As you are reading various selections, however, it is important to pay attention to when a piece was written or a sermon delivered, as Luther's ideas at the end of his life on some issues may have been quite different than they were when he was beginning his career as a reformer. It is also important to think about the audience for a particular work, as the way he expresses things in a formal lecture in Latin delivered to his students and colleagues – all of them male – may be quite different from the way he expresses them in a letter written to a noblewoman or to his wife, and different again when he is talking informally to his dinner companions. This attention to the setting and the audience is especially important when you are reading the table talk; the comments they record were often made after people in the Luther household had all been drinking the excellent (in Luther's opinion) beer brewed by his wife, and were chatting about current events or gossip they had heard. Some of Luther's most colorful statements about women or sex appear in the table talk, but these may not reflect his most considered opinions.

WOMEN IN THE SCHOLARSHIP ON LUTHER

As we have noted, Luther specialists have been slow to take up the subject of Luther's relations with and attitudes toward women. That is, Luther biographers have lightened the heft of their theological analyses and their accounts of the Reformation as apocalypse-laden conflict with the Roman Church with depictions of the Reformer's marriage and ultimate wedded bliss. For the most part, such treatments have been interludes, structurally placed between the crises of the early Reformation years culminating in the Peasants' War and Luther's decade of theological maturation and elaboration. Katharina von Bora could hardly be omitted from the story. A biographic segment on Luther's domesticity moved Roland Bainton to write in the 1940s, "The Luther who got married in order to testify to his faith actually founded a home and did more than any other person to determine the tone of German domestic relations for the next four centuries."[4] Ewald Plass proclaimed a decade later, "Martin Luther's influence on marriage was profound and permanent."[5] These assertions remained to be proved.

The 1983 quincentenary of Luther's birth witnessed an outpouring of books and articles. Martin Brecht's three-volume biography uses Luther's marriage and home-life in much the same way as earlier scholars had: as an episode revealing devotion to principle and simultaneously the great man's humanity. At the end of nine pages dedicated to this subject, Brecht remarks, "That Luther was able to concentrate on his manifold tasks in

---

[4] R. Bainton, *Here I Stand: A Life of Martin Luther* (New York: New American Library, 1950), p. 233.
[5] E. Plass, comp., *What Luther Says: An Anthology*, vol. II (St. Louis: Concordia Publishing Company, 1959), p. 884.

such an atmosphere deserves our respect."[6] A prominent account from the still-separate realm of East German (Marxist) scholarship took very much the same approach, as did the charming diversion of a Catholic scholar.[7] A two-volume set of essays, edited within the ranks of East German Christian historians and purporting to include every salient facet of Luther's career, gives no attention to Katharina von Bora, much less to any other woman.[8]

Heiko Oberman's biography, which is psychological as well as theological, brings the findings of Ian Siggins concerning the bourgeois provenance of Luther's mother to bear on her son's mentality. Margarete's expectations that sons should be educated, accompanied by the means and connections to achieve this, were as telling as father Hans's post-peasant ambitions. Both parents were strict, and to each of them Luther later attributed thrashings when he misbehaved.[9]

None of the major biographical studies has assessed Luther's attitudes toward women or considered what effects either his teachings or his life might have had upon social conventions. Researchers touched by the feminist currents that swelled from the late 1960s quickly perceived the possible value in considering whether Luther, whose religious and political consequences were alleged to have been dramatic and enduring, had also influenced the relations between women and men. Roland Bainton's and Ewald Plass's throwaway assertions begged for scrutiny. Steven Ozment affirmed the principle that, in the wake of the Reformation, women's dignity and place in society rose. Those of his sources that are pertinent to this discussion were Luther's treatises in favor of marriage and against vows of celibacy.[10] However, several women experts on the Reformation took a more inclusive look at Luther's numerous utterances, of both pen and mouth, concerning women and presented in articles a more differentiated – which is to say in part a negative – picture.[11]

[6] M. Brecht, *Martin Luther: Shaping and Defining the Reformation 1521–1532*, trans. James L. Schaaf (Minneapolis: Fortress Press, 1990), p. 204.
[7] Gerhard Brendler, *Martin Luther: Theology and Revolution*, trans. Claude R. Foster, Jr. (New York and Oxford: Oxford University Press, 1991), pp. 302–10; John M. Todd, *Luther, a Life* (New York: Crossroad, 1982), pp. 260–67.
[8] Helmar Junghans, ed., *Leben und Werk Martin Luthers von 1526 bis 1546: Festgabe zu seinem 500. Geburtstag*, 2 vols. (Berlin: Evangelische Verlagsanstalt, 1983).
[9] H. Oberman, *Luther, Man between God and the Devil*, trans. Eileen Walliser-Schwarzbart (New Haven: Yale University Press, 1989), pp. 86–94; Ian Siggins, *Luther and His Mother* (Philadelphia: Fortress Press, 1981); Erik H. Erikson, *Young Man Luther: A Study in Psychoanalysis and History* (New York: Norton, 1962), p. 64.
[10] S. Ozment, *When Fathers Ruled: Family Life in Reformation Europe* (Cambridge, MA: Harvard University Press, 1983), especially pp. 3–25, and *idem, Protestants: The Birth of a Revolution* (New York: Doubleday, 1992), pp. 153–64.
[11] Merry E. Wiesner, "Luther and Women: The Death of Two Marys," in Jim Obelkevich, Lyndal Roper, and Raphael Samuel, eds., *Disciplines of Faith: Studies in Religion, Politics and Patriarchy*

LUTHER IN THE SCHOLARSHIP ON WOMEN

Most considerations of women and the Reformation go off in one of two directions. The first explores women's actions in support of or in opposition to the Protestant and Catholic Reformations and looks more broadly at women's spiritual practices during this period. The second focuses on the ideas of the reformers and the effects of the Reformations on women and on structures that are important to women, such as the family.[12]

Analyses of Luther's ideas about women, marriage, and sexuality have been part of this second direction, and they, too, have tended to divide into two groups. As noted above, older studies of Luther's and other Protestant thinkers' ideas about marriage and the family, often written from a clear confessional viewpoint, frequently describe Luther as rescuing marriage (and by extension women) from the depths of dishonor created by the medieval Catholic championing of virginity. These studies are joined in their largely positive evaluation of the effects of Luther's ideas on women by newer works written primarily by church historians trained in Germany, who also emphasize the honor accorded the role of wife and mother in Luther's thinking; because the vast majority of women in early modern Europe *were* wives and mothers, this respect worked to improve their status and heighten their social role.[13] Luther took great care, they note, to highlight the important role women played in both the Old and New Testaments, and specifically and vociferously attacked the scholastic denigration of women. For Luther, women were created by God and could be saved by faith; spiritually men and women were largely equal.

A second group of scholars, most of them social historians and literary scholars trained outside Germany, have viewed Luther's ideas about women and their impact more negatively. They point out that elevating marriage is not the same thing as elevating women, and that, by emphasizing the centrality of marriage, Luther and other Protestants contributed to growing negative opinions of the 10–15 percent of the population who never married,

(London and New York: Routledge and Kegan Paul, 1987), pp. 295–308, and the works listed in note 14 below.

[12] For larger bibliographies on women and the Reformation, see Merry E. Wiesner, "Studies of Women, the Family and Gender," in William S. Maltby, ed., *Reformation Europe: A Guide to Research II* (St. Louis: Center for Reformation Research, 1992), pp. 159–87, and the bibliographies in Merry E. Wiesner, *Women and Gender in Early Modern Europe* (2nd edition; Cambridge: Cambridge University Press, 2000).

[13] Gerta Scharffenorth, "'Im Geiste Freunde werden': Mann und Frau im Glauben Martin Luthers," in Heide Wunder and Christina Vanja, eds., *Wandel der Geschlechterbeziehungen zu Beginn der Neuzeit* (Frankfurt: Suhrkamp, 1991), pp. 97–109; and Luise Schorn-Schütte, "'Gefährtin' und 'Mitregentin': Zur Sozialgeschichte der evangelischen Pfarrfrau in der Frühen Neuzeit," in Wunder and Vanja, eds., *Wandel*, pp. 109–153.

and restricted women's proper sphere of influence to the household. They note that though Luther denounced the ideas of Aristotle on many things, he accepted the Greek philosopher's idea that women's weaker nature was inherent in their very being; this inferiority was deepened by Eve's actions and God's words in the Garden of Eden, but was there from Creation. Women's faith and spiritual equality were not to have social or political consequences, and the Biblical examples of women's preaching or teaching were not to be taken as authorizing such actions among contemporary women.[14]

As you will see in the texts included here, there is plenty of ammunition in Luther's words for both sides of this debate, often expressed in the strong language that he favored; he is self-contradictory, but never ambiguous. Because churches today – both Protestant and Catholic, as well as Jewish, Muslim and other religions – are still wrestling with the balance between men's and women's spiritual equality and social difference, his words, like those of other authoritative religious writers, are not simply matters of historical interest. The contradictions found in Luther's writings are also found in the central books underlying the world's religions, of course – Hebrew Scripture, the New Testament, the Qur'an, Buddhist and Hindu spiritual texts – so that these, too, are easily mined for statements supporting nearly every opinion that could be held about the relative worth of and proper roles for women and men.

LUTHER ON WOMEN

An excursion into the Wittenberg nightingale's opinion of women must include his intellectual analyses as well as his correspondence and the table talk. Luther's periodic sermons and commentaries on Genesis, and especially on the first three chapters of what he usually called "The First Book of Moses," yield much on the establishment of marriage as the first estate ordained by God, on the innate qualities of women (and men), and on

[14] Lyndal Roper, "'The Common Man,' 'the Common Good,' 'Common Women': Reflections on Gender and Meaning in the Reformation German Commune," *Social History* 12 (1987): 1–21 and *The Holy Household: Women and Morals in Reformation Augsburg* (Oxford: Clarendon Press, 1989); Susan C. Karant-Nunn, "Continuity and Change: Some Effects of the Reformation on the Women of Zwickau," *Sixteenth Century Journal* 13 (1982): 17–42; *idem*, "The Transmission of Luther's Teachings on Women and Matrimony: The Case of Zwickau," *Archive for Reformation History* 77 (1986): 31–46; *idem*, "The Reformation of Women," in Renate Bridenthal, Susan Mosher Stuard, and Merry E. Wiesner, eds., *Becoming Visible: Women in European History* (3rd edition; Boston: Houghton-Mifflin, 1998), pp. 175–202; Sigrid Brauner, *Fearless Wives and Frightened Shrews: The Construction of the Witch in Early Modern Germany* (Amherst: University of Massachusetts Press, 1994).

the proper relations between the sexes. Luther tends to accept Eve's primary blame for the Fall of humankind, yet he does not ignore the grave responsibility of Adam, too, as the one who was more rational and who personally received and understood God's commands. Adam ought to have rejected Eve's offer of the apple. Eve's punishment was, he thinks, properly more severe, but he praises God for a quality of mercy that left the possibility of salvation open to both sinners. The consequences for both were drastic and explain prominent aspects of women's lives: they had to suffer in childbirth, and they were to be obedient to their husbands in all things. Notwithstanding, husband and wife were to love and console one another.

We need to measure the degree of Luther's commitment to these penalties as binding characteristics of life in the world by examining not just other treatises – which themselves bear witness to the Reformer's ongoing theoretical persuasion – but also evidence of his efforts to enforce these abstract precepts in his own life. Here is where his relationships with his Katharina von Bora, his mother, his daughters, his friends' wives, and many other women from the expanding circle of his acquaintances and unknown devotees take on greater importance than they possess in simply revealing the celebrity's humanity. Actions speak as loudly as words. In his loving and flexible deeds Luther may gain a certain redemption in the eyes of modern and independent women who from their twenty-first-century milieu react viscerally against this man's insistence upon Everywoman as the totally subordinate housewife. In the abstract, Luther envisioned each woman's and girl's confinement to the home, where, in pious mood, she labored efficiently and frugally. He regarded even the domestic sphere as under the direction of the paterfamilias, who, if he trusted her sufficiently, could, *saving only his right*, delegate to his wife the day-to-day authority over the household. When we shift our gaze to Luther's own experience, we see him closely bound to, and dependent upon, his Käthe. Indeed, he admits his subject status, even as he engages in word play and flirtation, when he addresses her as his lord, as *Herr* Käthe. Because of his need, he has wittingly exchanged the masculine role for the feminine. Nevertheless, to his way of thinking, the decision to do so lay with him and not her.

We ought to assess Luther from the dual perspective of theory and practice. We are fortunate in having considerable access to his practice. John Calvin, by contrast, was thoroughly reticent. Although a book-length study remains to be written, we can offer a summation of Luther's conservation and innovation. The German Reformer preserved and transmitted many of the tendencies of high- and late-medieval thought. He regarded females as lower than males in the hierarchy that made up the universe. They were less rational than males in a scheme within which rational equated with better; they were more inclined toward emotion. Like Eve, they could be more easily led astray than men. Their reasoning faculties were less engaged than men's and were less capable of high development – although women could occasionally render good advice. Little girls did not require and could hardly master higher learning, and their limited schooling should train them in piety, housekeeping, and upright motherhood. Nonetheless, for these practical purposes girls' schools should exist. Certain Biblical figures, such as Anna the prophetess and Mary Magdalene the preacher, were extraordinary, but their like did not exist in Luther's time, when women were firmly enjoined not to prophesy or preach. Luther heartily supported this prohibition. He objected to his wife's loquacity in the dining room and admonished her to be silent. All women, in his view, were inclined toward gregariousness and chatter, from which their husbands and fathers should dissuade them.

For Luther, women's anatomy bespoke their destiny as mothers rather than thinkers. He describes women's broad hips as suited to giving birth, and their narrow shoulders as symbolic of their lack of weight in the upper quarters, that is, in their heads. Women ought to nurse their infants. Here he shares medieval and humanistic opinion concerning the transmission of traits of character through breast milk. Wet-nursing was not as widespread in Germany as in Italy or France, however. Luther adheres to the persistent view that women's experiences – including unpleasant scenes that they happen upon – will misshape their fetuses.

Luther's advocacy of marriage for all women has sometimes been taken as progressive, particularly by scholars who share the Reformer's bias against the monastic life. It is true that throughout Europe, children far too young to consent were placed in convents and monasteries; and we regularly hear of those, like Erasmus and Katharina von Bora, who were discontented there. It is essential to bear in mind, however, that nuns as a group were more adamant than monks in refusing to violate their commitments, leave their orders, and marry. Many women preferred their lot, whether it had been freely chosen or initially imposed by relatives. Late-medieval women from the pertinent social echelons *did* have a choice between marriage and monasticism; and others, despite stereotypes to the contrary, were able to remain single, in the world, and respectable. Luther's insistent promotion of marriage together with the abolition of monastic houses in lands that became Evangelical are rightly seen as narrowing the choices of women. In combination with the stern articulation in wedding sermons to broader audiences of women's inborn inferiority, marriage could be seen as a means of shielding society from the deleterious effects of Eve's vices.

However, we must not overlook another dimension of this message: the reciprocal love and forbearance that preachers also advocated more intensively than before. The Reformation in many respects is most novel in its selection, combination, and intense dissemination of ideas that were available earlier. Among themselves and for the reinforcement of their own vows of celibacy and chastity, Catholic clergymen had written and spoken harshly against the corrupting influence of women. Among the laity for whom they carried out the cure of souls, they regularly held forth in tones of praise in support of marriage, including the consolation that spouses were to afford one another. Late-medieval lay society was clearly grounded in marriage. Luther rejected the clerical mode, and even made St. Jerome the target of harsh criticism; he retained and stressed the lay mode. In addition – and this is crucial – he was so lacking in restraint within his own wedded bond that he became a living, and later a dead, exemplum of loving mutuality and appreciation. This is so, even if neither his ideology concerning Eve and her "daughters" nor his condescension toward Käthe appeals to us. He was a man of his day and yet a creative one.

Martin Luther's theories of sexuality were quite close to what we are able to divine of his practice, and certainly to what he recommended to others (with the main exception of Landgrave Philip of Hesse) about practice. He retained the clerical prejudice against lustful demonstration as sinful. The sex act was of course sinful outside marriage, but it continued to be so even within the "unspotted" marriage bed. Adults married as a "remedy against sin," as Luther saw it, but after reading his commentaries on Genesis, we see the need to insert the word *worse*: marital sex is a remedy against *worse* sin. Spouses engaged in intercourse cannot think about God. They behave as though they were having an epileptic seizure. This is the unhappy result of the Fall. In His mercy, God covers over the passionate embraces of the Christian pair so that He Himself cannot see them. For the sake of His Creation and the continuation of humanity, He chooses not to count these as sin. This position is quite in keeping with Luther's doctrine of justification by faith.

In order for marital sex to be an effective antidote, it ought not to be overly circumscribed lest during prohibited periods partners vent their desire in some non-condoned way. Married people could now engage in sex during pregnancy, menstruation, and Lent – no clergyman was peeking even figuratively into the bedchamber. Nevertheless, Luther thought that pious couples should exercise restraint. They should not disrobe for sex, they should not try to arouse one another unduly, they should not turn the marriage bed into "a manure heap and a sow bath" by resorting to unusual techniques and positions. Once again, we see in the Reformer a combination of the old-fashioned and the liberating.

Martin left us fleeting glimpses of his and Katharina's bedroom. He observed how strange it was, in the early months of marriage, to find a pair of braids on the mattress beside him. Within the hearing of his dinner guests, he told his wife how pleased he was with her gravid condition; she underwent pregnancy, he said, to honor him. Martin may well have expressed this feeling to Katharina in their times of intimacy. Most direct of all, he wrote to her on his final journey, a week and a half before his death, concerning his impotence. He knew that his inability to make love to her would be hard for her to bear; he would love her if only he could. He advised her to consult Philip Melanchthon, who would know what to say, perhaps partly on the basis of his personal experience. We can infer here that until nearly the end, sex had been a regular, binding part of the Luther's marriage, one presumably not curtailed by the ecclesiastical calendar. We gain a sense of the Luthers' living out the Reformer's convictions concerning marital sexuality.

We see, too, in his life as in his writings, his understanding of the equal need of both sexes for gratification of the flesh. Although he does not argue against the widespread clerical view that women were more highly sexed than men and were often responsible for men's falling into sin, Luther implicitly redistributes the onus of desire until it is borne proportionally by both genders. From our perspective, this accords more nearly with reality than the former and persistent stance, still echoed in the stereotyped witch-images of the century after Luther's demise, that women were "carnally insatiable" and formed pacts with the devil partly in the hope of sexual gratification.[15]

We today are justified in regarding the great Reformer as a force for tradition rather than an innovator. He may have thought that he was a partisan of women, but some of us cannot entirely share his view. His condemnation of witches reverberates in our minds, and his denigration of women's nature and capacities repeatedly presents itself to our gaze. At the same time, we should not overlook the positions he took, such as the reduction of marriage to a civil transaction with its concomitant possibility of divorce, that generations after his career was finished might

[15] Heinrich Krämer and Jacob Sprenger, "The *Malleus Maleficarum*," in Alan C. Kors and Edward Peters, eds., *Witchcraft in Europe 1100–1700: A Documentary History*, p. 127: "All witchcraft comes from carnal lust, which is in women insatiable."

find a liberating resonance with that new era. In his own day, regardless of his opinion, marriage went on being sacred and very nearly indissoluble. Although he disapproved of wife-beating, he did not categorically condemn it if no other means of discipline sufficed. Women were to be pious, quiet, and submissive. Luther shifted monastic values into the domestic sphere and strove to inculcate them in the whole of society. The household was the little convent – but in it heartfelt affection was to mitigate the monastic rule. The domestic community was to be immune to the misogynist rantings of ancient and contemporary seers as collected by Sebastian Franck.

Actual practice seems invariably to depart from norms that are prescribed from the pulpit, in the courtroom, and by the book. It is impossible to judge in any verifiable way the extent to which the exertions of Luther, his followers in the pastorate, princes, and magistrates affected women's (and men's) lives. We are left with generalizations that cannot be proved. The leaders of the Reformation sustained the old notion of the inferiority and domestic destiny of women. Through their use of the media, including the now ubiquitous sermon, they constructed a model of women and men that virtually every person encountered. By this means, the concept of the ideal mother and housekeeper gradually became available to every socioeconomic class.[16] It is probable that generations subjected to this indoctrination accepted the general outlines of the "good wife" and the "good husband."

Ideology and stereotype were broken up in the mortar and pestle of daily exigency. Because of this, Heide Wunder is justified in characterizing women's and men's relations in the early modern period as "partnership."[17] No matter what Luther taught, no matter what Katharina accepted, when the need arose Käthe took to the streets and marketplace, spoke out, doled out money to Martin, and ruled her household with as iron a fist as order demanded. Faced with crises of his own such as imperial diet or illness, Martin, the self-perceived lord of his family, tolerated in Käthe, and probably appreciated, the wielding of power. Prolonged necessity, whether collective as in the face of war or persecution, or uniquely individual, presented opportunities that may have stimulated thoughtful women to reassess their prescribed place in the universe. But in times of routine, people may fall back upon the generalities provided by their culture. Martin Luther renewed many venerable generalities and contributed them to a definition of women as weak and subordinate that helped to inform ideals of proper domestic relations

---

[16] H. Wunder, *He Is the Son, She Is the Moon: Women in Early Modern Germany*, trans. Thomas Dunlap (Cambridge, MA: Harvard University Press, 1998), p. 83. This is our answer to the question Wunder poses there about how this ideal spread.

[17] Ibid., *passim*.

down to the twentieth century. Yet he added the powerful leavening of love, and he left us his beneficent example.

We have been thinking about and working on this project for nearly eight years, and in the course of this have acquired many debts. We would like to thank Richard Fisher and Elizabeth Howard from Cambridge University Press, who encouraged us in this endeavor and were patient through our many delays. Special thanks go to our colleagues Michael Bruening, Martha Carlin, and Amanda Seligman, who provided assistance with the Latin translations. Susan Karant-Nunn wishes to note the inspiration she has taken from the memory of Heiko A. Oberman's devotion to scholarship, made concrete in the many books and articles that he left to his colleagues in late-medieval and Reformation studies, and adds that she is deeply grateful to Mrs. Toetie Oberman and Dr. Hester Oberman for the encouragement that they continue to extend. She also thanks Maria Luisa Betterton and Sandra Kimball for their daily assistance and high good humor, and Anne Jacobsen Schutte for holding her professionally aloft in the past two years. Merry Wiesner-Hanks would like to thank Scott Hendrix for his (perhaps unwitting) inspiration in getting this project started, and Kathy Miller-Dillon and Maria Carrizales of the Center for Women's Studies at the University of Wisconsin-Milwaukee for their efficiency and good will, which allowed it to get finished. Finally, the editors would like to thank each other for their forbearance, and are pleased to report that this joint project has only strengthened our twenty years of friendship. Our names are placed in alphabetical order.

CHAPTER 2

Eve and the nature of women

In his formal treatises, Luther revealed the very significant extent to which he retained and transmitted the traditional view that women by their nature were inferior to men. In particular, Luther's several commentaries on the first three chapters of Genesis demonstrate not only the Reformer's opinion that through their participation in the Fall women *became* subordinate to their husbands; Luther was convinced that from the moment of Creation, Eve *was* a lesser being than Adam. This was why, he explained, the devil first approached Eve; she was vulnerable to temptation. Compared to Adam, Eve had always been less rational and more emotional. Nevertheless, she was devoted to God and assisted Adam in carrying out the divine command that the pair and their progeny should subdue the earth and govern all other creatures. Before her seduction by Satan, she had had more leeway in her daily activities – could even be absent from Adam for a period in pursuit of her tasks. She was an excellent if a lesser being, like the moon in relation to Adam the sun; the moon, too, Luther said, was a most excellent body. This analogy, like that of woman as a house or a snail with her shell, is an ancient one and not original to either Luther or the Reformation.

Having succumbed to Satan, Eve's relation to her husband changed as part of the penalty imposed by God. Now she had to stay close to him and obey him in all things. Now they conceived their offspring in "evil lust" and became prey to the besetting ills of the flesh. Eve and all her female descendants, her "daughters," had to live with the consciousness, imprinted upon them by successive generations of preachers, of being primarily responsible for every affliction introduced into life upon the expulsion from Eden, including war, plague, and famine, and not just feminine subordination and bearing children in pain. However, Adam's responsibility was not far behind. As the more rational being, the one created fully in the divine image, and the one to whom God had personally forbidden the fruit of the tree of the knowledge of good and evil, he should never have consented to his wife's wayward act. When he did so, he knew what he was doing. Despite all that they deserved, God did not remove from the first couple and their children the ability, in faith, to attain salvation. The awareness of God's loving mercy along with their failure to deserve it, Luther thought, should sustain both woman and man in all that they had to endure on earth.

Again, Luther is hardly original in setting out these concepts. He fits squarely within a not very broad range of variations on the story of creation that were widely available in the late Middle Ages. Luther's view of women's nature is continuous with that of earlier thinkers and compatible with the opinions of many other sixteenth-century theologians.[1] Very few voices advocated a departure from these convictions; prominent among them was that of Heinrich Cornelius Agrippa von Nettesheim, who may have been entertaining male readers with a satire. Still, the misogynist aphorisms collected and published (along with sayings on many other topics) by Sebastian Franck were offensive to Luther.[2] The Wittenberg Reformer found many of them to be patently slanderous of women. If men took them seriously, they would never wish to marry. And as we know, Luther considered refraining from marriage – the celibate life – to be ruinous to men's and women's souls and destructive of society. Thus, he argued vociferously against Franck.

SERMONS

Sermons on Genesis, 1527, WA XXIV

[Pp. 76–81, quoting 2:18–20] "And the Lord God spoke: 'It is not good that man should be alone. I will make a helpmeet for him.' For as the Lord God had made out of the earth all sorts of animals on the land and all kinds of birds under the sky, He brought them to the man to see how he would name them. Exactly as the man would name all the living animals, so they should be called. And the man gave to each and every beast and bird under the heavens and animal of the field its name. But there was no one to help him."

Here Moses makes a repetition, and that is the summation: now that every living thing had been created, God brought them to Adam for him to name. But among them all Adam found no helper. And so much is

---

[1] For an introduction to views on either side of the debate, see Alcuin Blamires, *The Case for Women in Medieval Culture* (Oxford: Clarendon Press, 1997), and *idem*, ed., *Woman Defamed and Woman Defended: An Anthology of Medieval Texts* (Oxford: Clarendon Press, 1992). See Merry E. Wiesner, *Women and Gender in Early Modern Europe* (2nd edition; Cambridge: Cambridge University Press, 2000), chap. 1, "Ideas and Laws Regarding Women," pp. 13–47.

[2] Sebastian Franck, *Sämtliche Werke: Kritische Ausgabe mit Kommentar*, vol. XI, *Sprichwörter*, ed. Peter Klaus Knauer (Bern: Peter Lang, 1993).

said: God looked at Adam, that he alone was a man. But He had created all animals as female and male; He brought all the animals, female and male, to Adam, but his own female or companion he did not find among them. Our text reads "*Adiutorium simile ei*" [helper similar to himself]; but it ought to be called "*Coram eo*" [in his presence], that is, helper for the purpose of generation. There was no animal that would have joined itself to him. They went forward and let themselves be counted, as they still do, but none adhered to him as his companion...

"Then the Lord God let a deep sleep fall upon the man, and He went to sleep. And He took one of his ribs and closed the wound up with flesh; and out of the rib the Lord God built a woman, whom He had taken from the man, and brought her to him. The man spoke, 'That was once bone of my bone and flesh of my flesh. She will be called *wo-man* [*Mennin*] because she has been taken out of a man.'"

These words are not human words. For that reason, I wish that people did not treat them as though they were of little worth or mock them. God Himself speaks and acts, and for that reason it is a serious matter. Those who have made buffoonery out of it slander God. This means to say that God made Adam go to sleep. That is, when He works upon a person who is free of sin, He does so neatly, in such a way that the creature does not feel it. But He does not treat a sinner in this way – this one has to feel it, and it hurts. If Adam had awoken, it would have pained him too; but because he slept, he did not feel anything. When he wakes up, he sees her standing before him, an image that he has never before seen among the others. Now the Spirit was in him, as Christ explains in Matthew [Matt. 19:5], so that these are God's words that Adam speaks here. For that reason, one can conclude that at that time Adam was filled with God or that God spoke through Adam's mouth. Therefore, no one should mock this. And notice that as God made the woman out of the rib of the man, the text uses the word *to build* [*bawen*]: He builds a woman just as if she was supposed to be a house.

Now, that is the [basis for the] opinion, as Paul explains, that there is no greater union than between man and woman; and it would have stayed that way if Adam had remained without sin. Now this union has been spoiled, and there is seldom unity between spouses. That is why Moses says that Adam recognized that this creature was his image and likeness, for before there had been no animal that adhered to him as though it desired to help him to give birth in accordance with God's word, "Be fruitful and multiply." God implanted this in human beings, that there must be man and a woman, and without the other neither can bring forth fruit. And it was decided that the woman has been created for this purpose, in order to be a helpmeet to the man, not for reasons of lust or knavery, but so that the command may be carried out. Just as Adam could not have resisted being made a man, so he could not have prevented God from taking one of his ribs and creating a woman out of it. Likewise, it does not lie in her decision that she comes from the rib and not from somewhere else, nor that only the man can make her bear fruit.

But that has not helped; one has preached all over the world that virginity is to be praised. That is very well, good, and proper for whoever can maintain it, whom God specifically distinguishes with this ability. But God has the power to do just as He pleases. He could make a man a woman and the reverse. If we had not fallen, it would have happened that everyone had to produce young. The blessing had been pronounced so that this should take place without pain and without evil lust. But this has now been broken, and God has marked some with an inability to reproduce... If nature had not been overturned, we would all have had to raise children. How much more must we do it now that nature is ruined and lascivious. The healthy person is able to eat if he wants to, but a sick person has to be forced. One cannot prevent it, or if a person wants to prevent it, he makes it more offensive. Women are not created for any other purpose than to serve man and to be his assistant in producing children.

Now see how Adam gives her a name and calls her woman, because, he says, she has been taken from a man. In Hebrew the word is actually *ish*: a man among men, for among other animals the word used is *sohar*. From his own name he names her *isha*; she takes her name from and for him, and it remains [the practice] up until now that a woman is called after the man... So she has to take her name from him, and he gives it to her and maintains authority over her.

"Therefore, a man will leave his father and mother and cleave to his wife, and the two will become one flesh" [Gen. 2:24].

These words are not to be understood to mean that they only physically become one flesh and blood, but they pertain to everything that belongs to outward physical life. The written word *flesh* means everything that belongs to the flesh, that a person has to have: servants, children, money, fields, meadow, property, honor or poverty, shame, illness and health, and so forth – whatever may befall one in life. In other words, *flesh* means one's outward life in the flesh. It should transpire that everything belongs to both of them and that they accept everything together and that each one brings the other body, goods, honor, shame, poverty, illness, and whatever else there is...

"And they were both naked, Adam and his wife, and they were not ashamed" [Gen. 2:25].

We observe in all animals that they are not in a condition to sin. So it also was with human beings. But now that is past, as we shall hear, and we are forced to be shy and embarrassed. We have to endure shame until the Last Day, after which once again nobody will have to be ashamed in front of another, there will be so much joy in heaven . . .

The third chapter [of Genesis]

[Pp. 81–85] "And the serpent was more cunning than all other animals on the face of the earth that God the Lord had made, and it spoke to the woman, 'Did God say that you were not supposed to eat from all the trees in the garden?' The woman said to the serpent, 'We eat the fruit of the trees in the garden, but of the fruit of the tree in the middle of the garden God said, "Do not eat that. Do not touch it, so that you may not die." '

"Then the serpent said to the woman, 'You will not die, for God knows that on the day that you eat of it, your eyes will be opened and you will become like God and will know what good and evil are.' And the woman looked and saw that the tree was splendid to eat of and lovely to look at, that it would be a pleasant tree because it made one clever."

The first thing that Moses describes here is how the serpent talked with the woman. We cannot pass that by. We must, as I always say, allow the Scripture to remain in its simple, bare sense, just as the words are, and make no gloss. It is not proper for us to interpret God's word as we wish. We should not guide it but let it guide us and pay it the honor of being a better law than we can make it into. Thus, we must let it stand that this was a proper, natural serpent that the woman saw with her eyes. This is written so that the story is easy to understand. For if God had written that the devil spoke with her in person, this would not be suitable. Therefore, he had to speak through the serpent, and the scene is described as if the serpent itself has spoken. He [God] has sufficiently indicated, however, that the serpent was a natural one but that the devil dwelled within it. After all, He says that the serpent spoke with her, and speaking is given to no other animal than human beings. In that way, we are clearly given to understand that the devil was within the serpent and spoke with its tongue. Nobody should wonder at that, for the devil is a powerful spirit. God has not prevented him from going around with living things, just as we see today that he is the lord and prince of the world, who speaks not alone through animals but nowadays most of all through people.

For another thing, it is also a sign that he was an evil spirit when he spoke on such a high level about God's commands. For no animal is so clever that it knows what is or is not God's command. Thus, there must have been a degree of understanding here that was well above that of a natural serpent, indeed above that of a human. It must have been an angel; but because it deals with matters that are against God's command, it cannot be a good angel.

For another thing, Eve was a woman of the world, for she stands there, speaks with the serpent and is not afraid for herself, regarding it just as another animal. She was a master over everything, as we have heard, to whom God said, "Rule the fish in the sea and the birds under the heavens, and all animals that creep upon the earth." After that everything stood around her, and she was not to fear either poison or death, and there was nothing that could harm her.

But she was not aware that the devil was there. For Paul says, "Adam was not seduced but rather the woman, and she introduced sin." This is as much as to say that Eve was not as intelligent as Adam...that God spoke with Adam himself and ordered him to teach Eve. For that reason, he intends to say that Adam well knew and understood, but she was simpler and too weak for the crafty devil and was not aware of him. But Adam was well aware; he should and could have defended himself if he had wanted to. See here how the devil can disguise himself so that one does not recognize him; and how he undertakes every sort of temptation. We must be especially aware of this...

First of all he takes hold of a man where he is the weakest, namely through the feminine person, that is, Eve and not Adam. All his temptations are directed, and he tries to break in, where we are weak and not well in charge. Had he assailed Adam, he might well have received a different answer. He was afraid of that and thought, "I will first of all attack the female, and perhaps through her I will be able to make him fall." Here we see his true colors...

Secondly, see further how roguishly he attacks the woman, begins to argue against her: "Yes, and God is supposed to have said, 'You shall not eat of various trees in the garden.'" With these words he casts God's command to the wind and talks so flippantly about it as if he were saying, "Do you mean that God was such a fool as to forbid that?...He tricks the woman until she thinks, "Adam probably didn't understand it rightly."...

[Pp. 88–93] Now see what else happens. With Eve faltering and he [the serpent] resolved that it was not contrary to God, he had [already] won: faith was finished and strangled, and she had lost the word. The text says,

"And the woman sees, first of all, that the tree was fine to eat of"; secondly, "and lovely to look at"; thirdly, "that it was a pleasurable tree because it made one clever." These three fatal desires she had not had before; she has now fallen into evil desire and inclination, of which she was not possessed before. Whenever faith and the word of God are absent, it is unthinkable that one could resist evil desire and love. Inquisitiveness is present as well as vain, sinful, evil affection. Earlier, when she stood in faith and her heart was full of love for God, she did not notice that the tree was particularly desirable or that it especially made one clever. One tree was like another to her. But now there is a difference, and no other is as beautiful to her as that one. What God has ordained, she wants none of. What He has forbidden, that she wants, and she wishes to become clever.

"And she broke the fruit off and ate and gave some of it to her husband and he ate."

Now follows the deed. She would not have eaten if she had not already been dead. Her faith was already gone, and she was filled with sin and evil desire. That is the great pity, that she gives some to Adam and he eats it with her. For he would not have had to eat it. If he had remained constant, God might well have made him another wife. Adam, Paul says, was not seduced but rather the woman. But because he also transgresses, he makes the sin all the heavier and more gruesome. She was a fool, easy to lead astray, did not know any better. But he had God's word before him. He knew it well and should have punished her. But he stands there, looks on, and eats too, wantonly giving his consent to the devil's advice.

"And their eyes were opened."

Now follow the coarse sins. First of all, their eyes are opened, as the devil had said. They see and feel that they are naked. Now it became impossible to hold in check all their members or to restrain their evil desire. They regarded each other with evil lust and unchaste desires, for they were naked, which had been unknown to them before. They had fallen away and become disobedient to God. After this they practiced all the disobedience that was in their bodies, and they could not tame either their thoughts or their members. We have inherited this, and it remains in us: just as they were, so are all their children. Where there is neither faith nor Christians, there is no defense against evil lust and desire, nor can one control those members that are given to anger and unchastity: eyes, ears, tongue, and all other parts of the body.

Now Adam and Eve are damned along with all of their offspring and children. All without exception are mired in sin. We are all similar to our father and mother and bring the same disease and illness with us. The devil deals with us today in the same way: he leads us into the main temptation touching on faith. When he triumphs over the word and faith, he possesses everything. As we see, where priests and monks do not live in faith – as almost all of them do not – there are no more avaricious, unchaste, angry folk, and nobody who is so full of vice...

So the two see now that they are naked. They feel the shameful lust in their bodies and cannot help themselves. They go and make themselves an apron or a girdle braided out of leaves, which they wound around themselves and covered their bodies...

"And they heard the voice of the Lord God walking in the garden, for the day had grown cool; and in the trees of the garden, Adam hid himself with his wife from the countenance of the Lord God. And the Lord God called Adam and spoke to him: 'Where are you?' And he answered, 'I heard your voice in the garden and was afraid, for I am naked. That is why I hid myself.' And He [God] spoke, 'Who told you that you were naked? Have you eaten from the tree that I commanded you not to eat of?' And Adam spoke: 'The woman that you gave me, gave me of the tree, and I ate.' Then the Lord God spoke to the woman: 'Why have you done this?' The woman said, 'The serpent urged me, and I ate.'"

[Pp. 96–104]... Now God begins with him [Adam] and pushes him still deeper into hell, so that he is ruined. "Who told you," He asks, "that you were naked; weren't you already naked?" This question was so penetrating that he could not answer any further. The matter was closed, and he stood deep in hell, indeed damned by God. Then He renders judgment: "Because you perceive that you are naked and are afraid of me and flee, you must have undertaken something against me and been disobedient, so that you and I are at odds." But what does he [Adam] do? He goes on and avoids taking the blame himself, but pushes it off onto the woman, even onto God Himself, as if to say, "If you hadn't given me the woman, I would have remained pious." This is as much as saying, "If you had been sufficiently clever and pious, you would not have created the woman." What is that, other than to say, "You yourself have sinned"? This is how he answered the Divine Majesty...

Now she [Eve] is just as foolish as Adam and does not want to take the blame... "The serpent urged me," she says, as if to say, "Why did you create the serpent? If you were such a clever God and knew such things, couldn't you have prevented this?" This is abominable and horrible to hear. Now both of them are damned. But now comes comfort once again and God's word. Christ climbs down from heaven and helps out... "The Lord God spoke to the serpent: 'Because you have done this, you are accursed before all beasts and above all other animals of the field. All your life you will crawl upon your belly and eat dust. And I will establish enmity between you and the woman and between your seed and her seed. Her progeny will tread upon your head, and you will bite them on the heel.'"

This saying is well worth considering diligently because it contains the word of life, by which they came back to life. In it is said to them with plain, clear words: the woman shall bring forth offspring. As the Scripture uses it, *woman's seed* means a natural child borne by the woman, a child that derives its flesh and blood from the mother. He [God] wishes to say, "I will create a natural fruit, borne from the woman." What is not expressed is whether it will be a man or a little boy, but only that the mother will be able to say, "That is my child," and the child, "This is my mother." She herself is supposed to tread upon the serpent's head, which is to say that the damage that she caused, He [God] will suppress, walk upon, and crush. When Adam heard this, he came out of hell and was again consoled.

. . . "And to the woman He said, 'I will give you much pain when you are pregnant. You shall bear your children with sorrow; you shall humble [*tücken*] yourself before your husband, and he shall be your lord.'"

God continues and takes on the woman and punishes her too; it is a fine ordinance . . . He gives the woman her torment, but proceeds soberly and spares her, absolves her of spiritual misery, and lays the penalty upon her body as with Adam. He says to her, "I will give you much pain when you are pregnant," and after that, "You shall bear your children with sorrow," and thirdly, "You shall humble yourself before your husband, and he shall be your lord."

In these three passages you see nothing that does not affect the body. The soul is already saved and has become a child of God. For that reason, God turns eternal punishment into a temporal and physical one. He sets aside the rod of iron and uses instead the foxtail. This punishment falls upon all those who shall become the daughters of Eve. It is not said to her alone. It is said as though they should all become pregnant . . . He does not take away what He had established before, that they should be fruitful. That is God's word, and no one can change it. In addition to that, He commands her to humble herself before her husband. That means that she does not live according to her own free will. It would have been such that they [Adam and Eve] might have gone their separate ways, one here, the other somewhere else, though in moderation. But now the wife can undertake nothing without the husband. Wherever he is, she has to be with him, and humble herself before him. After this, God comes from the woman to Adam, imposes a penalty upon him too, and speaks.

"And to Adam He spoke: 'Because you have hearkened to the voice of your wife and eaten from the tree about which I commanded you "You shall not eat of it," cursed be the ground on your account. With trouble shall you nourish yourself from it all your life. It will produce thorns and thistles for you, and you shall eat the plants of the field. In the sweat of your brow you will eat your bread, until you return to the earth from which you came. For you are dust, and dust you shall become.'"

This is a gentle, gracious punishment. I am of the opinion that the text itself makes it so that the land is full of whores and knaves, for otherwise there would be many pious boys and girls who would enter into matrimony. But nobody who is not obligated to wants to do this, and everybody shies away from marriage because they might have grief with the bearing of children – that pertains to the woman – or the man because he has to provide for and nourish his wife and child, to which pertains effort and work. Nobody wants to bear this burden, but it must be borne. If you do not take a wife and eat your bread in the sweat of your brow, God will take His punishment from your body and lay it upon your soul. That is not a good exchange. He wants to be gracious to the soul and helpful, but He rightly wants to torment the body. On that account, where people stand in faith, they send themselves right in [to marriage] and bear this burden gladly – they take wives, labor, and let their lives be painful. It is not a fine thing in fleshly terms, but it is a good estate in spiritual ones. The whole world still cries out about what an evil thing marriage is. Who is to blame for that? God alone, because He did not say, "You should seat yourself upon a cushion, live in revelry, and have no misfortune."

And so I shall close: where one finds a marriage in which the wife has no misfortune with [bearing] children and in which the husband is not bitter, something is not right. If God gives you a rich wife or husband, so that you have [only] good days, without effort or work, then you are certainly absolved from the passage [in which God imposed punishment] and you are not in good shape. The world is so crazy and foolish, contrary to God, that it is of the opinion that one can be married and enter into this estate only to have good days and live well. But God wants exactly the opposite...

[P. 107] [God called Adam before His court, and then He called Eve.] Thereby, in my opinion, the Holy Spirit has shown that God orders the man to carry out the offices of governing, teaching, and preaching. For when Adam is called forward, it is nothing other than a sermon before the Law, by means of which he recognizes what he has done and what he owes to God. Preaching is entrusted to the man and not to the woman, as Paul also teaches, insofar as this has to do with Christian matters. Otherwise, it can occasionally happen that a woman gives better advice, as one reads in Scripture. But apart from that, the offices of leading, preaching, and teaching God's word are commanded to the man.

LECTURES

Lectures on Genesis, 1535, LW I
From *Luther's Works*, vol. I, edited by Jaroslav Pelikan, © 1968
Concordia Publishing Company. Used by permission of Concordia
Publishing House

[Pp. 66–69, Commenting on Genesis 1:26] Even this small part of the divine image we have lost, so much so that we do not even have insight into that fullness of joy and bliss which Adam derived from his contemplation of all the animal creatures. All our faculties today are leprous, indeed dull and utterly dead. Who can conceive of that part, as it were, of the divine nature, that Adam and Eve had insight into all the dispositions of all animals, into their characters and all their powers. What kind of a reign would it have been if they had not had this knowledge? Among the saints there is evident in this life some knowledge of God. Its source is the Word and the Holy Spirit. But the knowledge of nature – that we should know all the qualities of trees and herbs, and the dispositions of all the beasts – is utterly beyond repair in this life...

Eve had these mental gifts in the same degree as Adam, as Eve's utterance shows when she answered the serpent concerning the tree in the middle of Paradise. There it becomes clear enough that she knew to what end she had been created and pointed to the source from which she had this knowledge; for she said (Gen. 3:3): "The Lord said." Thus she not only heard this from Adam, but her very nature was pure and full of the knowledge of God to such a degree that by herself she knew the Word of God and understood it.

Of this knowledge we have feeble and almost completely obliterated remnants. The other animals, however, completely lack this knowledge...

In order not to give the impression that He was excluding the woman from all the glory of the future life, Moses includes each of the two sexes; for the woman appears to be a somewhat different being from the man, having different members and a much weaker nature. Although Eve was a most extraordinary creature – similar to Adam so far as the image of God is concerned, that is, in justice, wisdom, and happiness – she was nevertheless a woman. For as the sun is more excellent than the moon (although the moon, too, is a very excellent body), so the woman, although she was a most beautiful work of God, nevertheless was not the equal of the male in glory and prestige.

However, here Moses puts the two sexes together and says that God created male and female in order to indicate that Eve, too, was made by God as a partaker of the divine image and of the divine similitude, likewise of the rule over everything. Thus even today the woman is the partaker of the future life, just as Peter says that they are joint heirs of the same grace (1 Peter 3:7). In the household the wife is a partner in the management and has a common interest in the children and the property, and yet there is a great difference between the sexes. The male is like the sun in heaven, the female like the moon, the animals like the stars, over which sun and moon have dominion. In the first place, therefore, let us note from this passage that it was written that this sex may not be excluded from any glory of the human creature, although it is inferior to the male sex.

[P. 70] Lyra also relates a Jewish tale of which Plato, too, makes mention somewhere, that in the beginning man was created bisexual [androgynous] and later on, by divine power, was, as it were, split or cut apart, as the form of the back and of the spine seems to prove. Others have expanded these ideas with more obscene details. But the second chapter refutes these babblers. For if this is true, how can it be sure that God took one of the ribs of Adam and out of it built the woman? These are Talmudic tales, and yet they had to be mentioned so that we might see the malice of the devil, who suggests such absurd ideas to human beings.

This tale fits Aristotle's designation of woman as a "maimed man"; others declare that she is a monster. But let them themselves be monsters and sons of monsters – these men who make malicious statements and ridicule a creature of God in which God Himself took delight as in a most excellent work, moreover, one which we see created by a special counsel of God.

[Pp. 115–16] *The Lord God also said: It is not good that man is alone; I shall make him a help which should be before him.*

But Moses wanted to point out in a special way that the other part of humanity, the woman, was created by a unique counsel of God in order to show that this sex, too, is suited for the kind of life which Adam was expecting and that this sex was to be useful for procreation. Hence it follows that if the woman had not been deceived by the serpent and had not sinned, she would have been the equal of Adam in all respects. For the punishment, that she is now subjected to the man, was imposed on her after sin and because of sin, just as the other hardships and dangers were: travail, pain, and countless other vexations. Therefore Eve was not like the woman of today; her state was far better and more excellent, and she was in no respect inferior to Adam, whether you count the qualities of the body or those of the mind.

But here there is a question: When God says, "It is not good that man should be alone," of what good could He be speaking, since Adam was righteous and had no need of a woman as we have, whose flesh is leprous through sin?

My answer is that God is speaking of the common good or that of the species, not of personal good... Therefore "good" in this passage denotes the increase of the human race...

[Pp. 131–32] *And the Lord God built the rib which He had taken from Adam into a woman, and He brought her to Adam.*

Here Moses uses a new and unheard-of expression, not the verb "form" and "create," as above, but "build." This induced all the interpreters to suspect that there is some underlying mystery here. Lyra, in common with his Rabbi Solomon, believes that the reference is to the novel form of the woman's body. As the shape of buildings is wider in the lower part but narrower in the upper, so, he says, the bodies of women are thicker in their lower part but more drawn together in the upper, while men have broader shoulders and larger chests. But these are nonessential features of the body. Moreover, Scripture says of the entire body that it is a building, just as Christ calls the body a person's house.

Others look for an allegory and say that the woman is called a building because of an analogy to the church... A woman, especially a married one, is called a building, not for the sake of allegory but historically. Scripture employs this method of speech everywhere...

[P. 151] Satan's cleverness is perceived also in this, that he attacks the weak part of the human nature, Eve the woman, not Adam the man. Although both were created equally righteous, nevertheless Adam had some advantages over Eve. Just as in all the rest of nature the strength of the male surpasses that of the other sex, so also in the perfect nature the male somewhat excelled the female. Because Satan sees that Adam is the more excellent, he does not dare assail him; for he fears that his attempt may turn out to be useless. And I, too, believe that if he had tempted Adam first, the victory would have been Adam's. He would have crushed the serpent with his food and would have said: "Shut up! The Lord's command was different." Satan, therefore, directs his attack on Eve as the weaker part and puts her valor to the test, for he sees that she is so dependent on her husband that she thinks she cannot sin.

TABLE TALK

WA TR I, no. 12, pp. 5–6

The praise of women. The Holy Spirit praises women. Examples are Judith, Esther, Sarah, and among [other] peoples Lucretia, Artemisia are praised. Marriage cannot exist without women. To get married is a remedy for fornication; a woman is a pleasant companion in life. Women are accustomed to bearing and bringing up children, they administer the household, they are inclined to be merciful. They have been made by God to bear children, to delight men, to be merciful.

WA TR I, no. 55, p. 19

Men have broad chests and narrow hips; therefore they have wisdom. Women have narrow chests and broad hips. Women ought to be domestic; the creation reveals it, for they have broad backsides and hips, so that they should sit still.

WA TR I, no. 103, p. 40

God created male and female – the female for reproduction, the male for nourishing and defending. Already the world inverts these: women waste things for the sake of pleasure...

WA TR I, no. 445, p. 194

I consider Jerome to be a preserver of the faith in Christ, but the injury that he did to his own teaching – may God forgive him! I know well that he did me great harm. He rages at women and speaks about women who are absent [who are not present to defend themselves]. I would have given him a wife – [then] he would have written many things differently.

WA TR I, no. 1054, pp. 531–32

Women speak masterfully about housekeeping and with graciousness and loveliness of voice, so much so that they surpass Cicero, the most eloquent orator. And whatever they cannot accomplish by means of their eloquence they achieve by weeping. They are born to this eloquence, for they are by nature much more eloquent and qualified for this business than us men, who attain this [skill] through long experience, practice, and study. But when they talk about matters other than those pertaining to the household, they are not competent. Although they have words enough, they are lacking in substance, which they do not understand. For that reason, they speak foolishly, without order, and wildly, mixing things together without moderation. It appears from this that woman was created for housekeeping but man for keeping order, governing worldly affairs, fighting, and dealing with justice – [things that pertain to] administering and leading. [Cf. WA, TR II, no. 1979, p. 286.]

WA TR II, no. 1555, p. 130
There is no dress that suits a woman or maiden so badly as wanting to be clever.

WA TR II, no. 1975, p. 285
Doctor Martin Luther laughed at his Ketha, who wanted to be clever, and said, "God created man with a broad chest, not broad hips, so that in that part of him he can be wise; but that part out of which filth comes is small. In a woman, this is reversed. That is why she has much filth and little wisdom."

Again, he laughed at his Ketha on account of her chattering and talkativeness. He asked whether she had prayed the Our Father before she preached so many words. "But women," he said, "don't pray before they start to preach, for otherwise they would stop preaching and leave it alone; or, if God overheard them, He would forbid them to preach."

WA TR II, no. 2312b, p. 415
The greatest plague on earth is an evil, obstinate, strange wife. On that Solomon says, "Unrest is caused in a land by three things, and the fourth thing it cannot bear: a servant, when he becomes king; a fool, when he is overfed; a hostile woman when she is married; and a maid who becomes the heiress of her mistress." [Proverbs 30:21–23]

WA TR II, no. 2807b, pp. 3–4
Dr. Crotus is a slanderer of the feminine gender. Dr. Crotus is a heavy slanderer and derogator of priestly marriage and wrote in a book, "The most sacred bishop of Moguntinensis is disturbed by no annoyance more than by the fetid and putrid female pudenda." Luther became very angry and said, "Phooey to you, you godless, wicked man! Was not your mother a woman? Or did you grow and emerge alone out of balsam, contrary to nature and God's ordinance? You ought to think about your mother and sisters and not slander and insult that creature of God from which Christ himself was born. One could have borne it if he had found fault with and criticized the evil inclination of women, their improper gestures and bad practices; but to dishonor their nature and the creature [itself] is devilish.

How would it seem if I were to find fault with and despise the human face because the nose stands in the middle of our countenance, and the nose is nothing other than the latrine of the head and is located over the mouth; and nonetheless our Lord God must permit prayer and the entire service of God to come out of it [the mouth]?"

WA TR IV, no. 4081, pp. 121–22

An Englishman who was a very learned, pious man went with Dr. Martin to the table [but] did not understand the German language. He [Luther] said to him, "I will give you my wife as a teacher; she could teach you German very well, for she speaks very well and is so accomplished at it that she far surpasses me. Nevertheless, when women speak well it is not praiseworthy. It befits them to stammer and not to be able to speak well; that adorns them much better."

WA TR IV, no. 4090, p. 129

Fur and head coverings are women's most attractive and honorable and most genuine and most necessary adornment, just as men's most essential clothing is hose and doublet.

WA TR IV, no. 4434, p. 311

A woman is not to be trusted. It was said about women that no secret is to be entrusted to them. He [Luther] responded, "The ancient proverbs prohibit it. For what goes in through women's ears comes out again through their mouths. For that reason, a secret is to be entrusted only to a dead woman."

WA TR V, no. 5611, p. 276

A verse attributed to Luther:
> One ought to praise women
> Whether it is the truth or a lie,
> For many a man speaks [ill] of them
> And knows not what his mother did.

WA TR V, no. 6101, pp. 488–89

Her hair is a woman's best adornment. For that reason the maidens used to go around with long hair and tore it when one either triumphed or grieved and mourned. It is a spectacle to see and is a credit to the women, when they have torn their hair on the field [of battle].

WA TR VI, no. 6567, p. 67

The wives of the greatest lords, such as kings and princes, take part in no governance, but alone the husbands. For God said to the woman, "You shall be subject to your husband, etc." The husband has the governance in the house, unless he is . . . a fool, or unless out of love and to please his wife he lets her rule, as sometimes the lord follows the servant's advice. Otherwise and aside from that, the wife should put on a veil, just as a pious wife is duty-bound to help bear her husband's accident, illness, and misfortune on account of the evil flesh. The Law withholds from women wisdom and governance. St. Paul saw this in 1 Corinthians 7, when he says, "I charge you – but not I; rather the Lord," and in 1 Timothy 2: "I do not permit a woman to teach, etc."

CHAPTER 3

Mary

During its early centuries, Christianity did not stress the role of Mary, primarily because church leaders wanted to differentiate their religion from pagan religions with female goddesses. The first recorded prayer to the Virgin comes from the very late fourth century, and rituals and feasts in her honor grew slowly and steadily from that point. By the twelfth century, many churches dedicated to Mary began to be built, some of them on the sites of former Jewish parts of town when Jews were banned from various areas. Poetry and hymns were also written in her honor, special prayers to Mary became a focal point of penitential practice, and she became an increasingly important subject for paintings and statuary. Mary's peculiar status as virgin and mother allowed her to be honored as both pure and nurturing at the same time, and she came to be viewed as the exact opposite of Eve, creating a good woman/bad woman dichotomy that would become extremely strong in European culture. The effects of the cult of Mary on the actual status of women, or even on attitudes toward women, are ambiguous, however. Because Christianity taught that there was and would be only one Savior, Mary represented an unattainable ideal for all other women, for no other woman could hope to give birth to the Messiah. Yet Mary was also fully human and not divine, so that she set a standard for female behavior in a way that Jesus did not for men. Some of the men most devoted to Mary, such as the medieval mystic and church official Bernard of Clairvaux, were also the harshest in their condemnation of all other women. Nevertheless, Mary did provide a female focus for veneration, and though official theology always stressed her role as obedient helpmate, in popular worship she was often viewed as one member of the Trinity, one no less powerful than God or Jesus.

Many events of Mary's life are mentioned in the Gospels, such as the Annunciation (Luke 1:26–38, when the angel Gabriel informed her that she would give birth to God's Son), the Visitation (Luke 1:39–56, when she went to visit her relative Elizabeth, the mother of John the Baptist, and praised God in a series of statements that were later called the Magnificat), the birth of Jesus, and Mary's subsequent visit to the temple to be purified (Luke 2:22–38). All of these became official holidays during the Middle Ages, along with various events in Mary's life that are not mentioned in Biblical texts: her conception, birth, death, and ascension into heaven, generally termed the Assumption. Each of these was assigned a day on the calendar, and preachers developed sermons drawing lessons for Christians from Mary's words and actions and the words of others to her.

Luther preached many sermons for the feast days associated with Mary, and Protestant church ordinances retained some of these days as holidays, particularly those for which there was a Biblical basis such as the Annunciation. Those for which there were no Biblical references, such as Mary's conception, birth, and Assumption, were generally dropped as holidays by Protestants, and even some of the events that are mentioned in the Bible, such as the Visitation, were reduced to half-day holidays or dropped altogether in some areas. Luther stopped preaching special sermons on many of these days (his last sermon on Mary's birth was in 1522, for example), and, because holidays devoted to other saints were ended as well, the church calendar gradually came to revolve more fully around the life of Christ.

Though Luther criticizes devotion to Mary that overshadowed devotion to Christ, and has harsh words for those who emphasize her suffering or her virtues too extensively, he also praises her in his sermons and other works. She is a model of faith, obedience, and humility, whose fully human nature guarantees the humanity of Christ. Her response to the angel's message and her praise of God in the Magnificat show the power of faith over reason, and her poverty and lowly stature demonstrate God's power and human unworthiness. All Christians, male and female, are to learn from her example to trust completely in God and ascribe all their successes and triumphs to Him, not to their own actions or virtues.

Both Catholics and Protestants accepted the idea that Mary was simultaneously a virgin, wife, and mother, but they put different emphases on these three roles. Her motherhood took primacy for both groups, but pre-Reformation Catholic preachers and authors also focused on her virginity, while Luther and other Protestants regarded her being engaged to Joseph as an example of God's honoring marriage. Her actions and those of Jesus at the wedding of Cana also serve as signs of God's approval of marriage for Luther, while Christ's rebuke of his mother at this wedding was another example of God's authority taking precedence over that of any human, including one's parents.

The Reformation was not the first time that there were changes in emphasis in the veneration of Mary. From the fourth century onward, both texts and images depicted Mary in a number of different ways – as the powerful and regal Queen of Heaven sitting on a throne, as an enormous cloaked figure sheltering small humans under her arms, as the *theotokos*, the "God-bearer," with the adult Christ contained within her, as a loving mother holding the Christ child on her lap, as a peaceful woman reading in the sunlight, as a sorrowing older woman at the foot of the Cross, the *mater dolorosa*. Visual depictions of Mary in much of the Middle Ages showed her as a fully adult woman, sometimes with the infant or adult Christ, but often standing or sitting alone. During the fifteenth century, she gradually grew younger, softer, and more dependent, and Joseph appeared, first as an old and feeble man at the edge of the scene, but gradually becoming younger, stronger, and more central to the events. Mary's mother, Anne, and grandmother Emerentia (neither of whom is mentioned in the Bible, but in many of the traditions that developed about Mary), who had often been shown with Mary and Jesus, largely disappeared by the sixteenth century. Pictures of the Holy Family, both Protestant and Catholic, thus began to look more like the ideal human family envisioned by moralists and theologians: responsible and protective father, caring and loving mother, obedient and charming child. In Catholic areas, including Latin America, Joseph became the patron saint of fatherhood, a somewhat odd situation because Catholic teachings held (and Luther agreed) that Mary had no more children after Jesus, and, indeed, remained a virgin throughout her whole life.

Mary's virginity was important to Luther because it reinforced the purity of Christ and allowed Old Testament prophecies to be fulfilled. It was not to serve as a model to other women in the way that her status as mother and wife was, however, but was a necessary part of her unique role as the *theotokos*, the "Mother of God," a title that Luther accepted. Mary's position as the first preacher of the Incarnation – at the Visitation to Elizabeth – was also hers alone, and was not to be imitated by other women. In fact, what is striking in Luther's discussions of Mary is how rarely he uses her to say something specifically to or about women. Though occasionally, particularly in discussions of the Visitation, he holds up her chaste conduct as a lesson for women, more often he uses the Virgin as a model of faith for both female and male believers, an example of lowliness, humility, and modesty appropriate for both sexes.

MARY'S BIRTH

Sermon on the birth of Mary, 8 September 1522, WA X/3, pp. 312–31
Today we have the celebration of the birth of the Blessed Virgin Mary. For this we read the first book of Matthew, which contains the recitation of the ancestors of Jesus Christ and reads: "This is the book of the birth of Jesus Christ, who is a son of David, the son of Abraham, etc."

You know, my friends, that the honor accorded the Mother of God is set deep in people's hearts, yes, so deep that no one likes to hear anyone speak against this, but [they] make it stronger and more powerful. Now let it also happen that we honor her, because we read in Paul's words in Scripture that we are to honor others. For this reason honor is also due to her.

But it is right that she is honored correctly. When people are deeply engaged in this honoring, they honor her more than is proper, and from this two problems come: [first] an injury to Christ, for when human hearts are set more on her than on Christ himself, Christ is left at the back in the dark and is completely forgotten. Second, a serious injury to the common people, for when the Mother of God and the saints are served and honored so greatly, poor needy Christians are forgotten. I let it be that you believe strongly in her, honor and praise her greatly, but only in so far as you will not benefit from this and make a rule of this. So that no one will set his heart on her, Scripture says nothing about her birth. But now priests and monks have expanded the honoring of a woman and lifted Mary so high that they have made a goddess (like those of the pagans) out of a modest servant. In order to defend such things they must use lies and grab Scripture by the hair, forcing it into places where it does not belong. See, the Gospel that we read today concentrates on Christ's birth and not on Mary's; lies have arisen that are not to be tolerated.

I allow her to be honored, but also charge those who honor her not to make Scripture into lies. They also use the Epistles to refer to Mary, which actually concern only the eternal truth of Christ, who preceded the world and in whom all things are made. That such things are now interpreted as referring to the Mother of God is a lie and blasphemy to God. For this reason I wish that people would let things lie, if there is nothing in Scripture. Truly it is not good when they yank Scripture to where it does not belong. That is thus the first harm and injury, that through the deep honoring of the Mother of God the honoring and understanding of Christ is weakened. Because of Christ we are called "Christians," so we should depend on him alone and be his children and heirs. In this we are the same as the Mother of God; we are Mary's brothers and sisters. Otherwise there will be an injury to the holy blood of Jesus Christ, through which we are made clean from sin and given the benefits of heaven. In this we are just as holy as she is. She did receive great grace, but this did not happen because she earned it, but because of the mercy of God. We cannot all be the bodily Mother of God, but she is the same as us; she came to grace through the blood of Christ just as I did. So you can yourself measure how far the honor of the saints should go: namely, that it should not harm Christ. This will happen when we accept his blood and pain and set our hearts on this alone and not on any saints. Therefore honor the Mother of God in such a way that you do not stay with her, but come to God and set your heart on him alone and do not push Christ out of the middle. Know that we are all brothers and sisters, as he himself said: "I will tell of thy name to my brothers!" (Psalm 22:22).

The second harm that occurs because of the deep honoring of the Mother of God concerns poor needy Christians. People lift their eyes to heaven and yammer, forgetting about the saints that are here on earth. I do not forbid you to honor her, but I want to make clear whom we are instructed to honor. You are not asked to honor the saints who have been taken from this life, but those who are here; these are the living poor Christians, whom Paul writes about in Timothy, the saints who should be housed and whose feet should be washed...

We have attached ourselves to unnecessary things, have turned from the true judge to a creature and actually made that creature into a judge and jury or even a god. See what words we use for the Blessed Virgin Mary in the Salve Regina. Those who call her our life, our consolation, and our sweetness should actually be satisfied that she is a weak vessel. The whole world sings these prayers and rings large bells with them. It is the same with the Regina celi, which is not any better because it calls her the Queen of Heaven. Is it not a dishonor to Christ that something is attributed to a creature that properly belongs only to God?

Thus you should give up such bumbling words. I will gladly have her pray for me, but will not call her my consolation and my life; your prayers are just as good to me as hers. Why? If you believe that Christ lives in you just as much as he lives in her, you can help me as much as she can. Thus you should view the honoring of the saints as just the same as the honoring we are supposed to give each other. Everyone should honor each other as God's children. Guard yourselves against these two harms: do not obscure Christ, let him be our life and trust; honor Mary and the other saints by giving the living saints who are with us 100 gulden instead of giving this to the dead saints. You will not be damned, even if you do not honor Mary and the saints, or if you do not write any more about her. But if you neglect the living, then you will truly be damned...

See, now you honor the Mother of God [and believe] that she is a special child of God, gifted or graced more than other women; we call her our merciful lady. We wish to honor her because God honored her. But we should absolutely not make her into a goddess, as the priests and monks pretend we should. Though we should not have her as an intercessor, we want to have her as an intercessor along with the other saints. They have set Mary up above the choirs of angels next to her son, through which dishonor and damage is done to her dear child. That is such a major error that I think if she were to walk around on earth she would weep blood because of this dishonor, and the way fables have been turned into examples for her people. So let her receive the honor that is appropriate to her as a child of God, praise God in her, as she herself praised God in the Magnificat. And everyone should pay more attention to the saints that live here with us, and not run all over the place [to pilgrimage sites such as] Grimenthal, Oettingen, Einsiedel, Ach, etc., but run to his neighbor's house if they are needy, giving to them what you would have given there [for the saints]. That has been said regarding the honor of the dear saints.

Now we want to say something about the Gospel that speaks about the birth of Christ. Matthew begins his Gospel with a preface in which he gives his intentions, which are to write about the birth of Jesus Christ. He writes: "The book of the birth of Jesus Christ, who is a son of David, the son of Abraham," etc.

In this he counts thirty-seven generations from Abraham to Christ and divides these into three parts: ancestors, kings, and princes, and he says, "Abraham begat Isaac, Isaac begat Jacob," and he continues on until Joseph, when he changes his mouth or his pen and does not say "Joseph [begat] Christ" but "Jacob [begat] Joseph, the husband of Mary of whom Jesus was born."

First, we should notice that Matthew includes four women in the line of Christ who are almost infamous, namely Tamar, Rahab, Ruth, and Bathsheba, and he says "Judad begat Perez and Zerah by Tamar." We can read about this in Genesis 38. We can read about Rahab in Joshua 2 and 6, about Ruth in Ruth, and about Bathsheba in 2 Kings, twelfth chapter. He [Matthew] is silent about the four righteous women, Sarah, Rebecca, Leah, and Rachel. St. Jerome added a commentary about why this is so. It is because they are sinners; Christ was born from a great lineage, but this lineage also had whores and knaves, so that he could show what love he had for sinners. One is truly holy the closer one makes oneself to sinners. So is it

that he set himself right down in the middle of a line of sinners and was not
ashamed of this. Yes, he let them stay in his family line and be praised from
altars. If Christ had been a Pharisee, he would have run from this lineage
so fast that his shoes would have fallen off; they would have stunk so much
to him that he would have crinkled up his nose at them. This happened
so that Christ could show us how friendly he is to poor sinners, that they
could understand a little and say "Ah, Christ is such a man that he is not
ashamed of sinners, yes, he even includes them in his family tree." If the
Lord does this, we should not scorn anyone, for otherwise he would have
included the honorable women such as Sarah. If in past times someone
wanted to scorn these women, God would have said, "Let them alone.
I will give them an honor that the pious will not receive. See, they have
given birth to great patriarchs, they are in the lineage of Christ and are his
grandmothers, so that we must say 'My gracious lady Rahab, gracious lady
Ruth.'" This Ruth was a pagan from the line of Moab, but God gave her the
honor of being included in his lineage and the prophet Isaiah spoke about
her in the sixteenth chapter: "O Lord, send us your lamb, your ruler from
the city of the desert to the mount of Zion," because they wanted Petra to
be a pagan city. There He mixed pagan and Jewish blood and brought
them to each other. He did this so that we could see God's grace to sinners,
that we would follow Him and not be ashamed, but weave ourselves with
the sinners in order to help them. For that reason these women are listed
here...

THE ANNUNCIATION

Sermon on the day of the Annunciation, 1532, WA LII, pp. 625–27, 632–23
...We shall divide this sermon into three parts. The first is about the person
of the Virgin Mary, that she is from the house of David; the second is about
the angel's sermon, in which he teaches about the Lord Christ and his office;
the third is about the belief in the Virgin Mary.

The Evangelist discusses matters that concern the person of the Virgin
Mary only very briefly. He does not report about her social rank or position,
what she was doing when the angel appeared to her, or in what form
the angel appeared to her. Those who want to know something about
such matters should stay with plain and simple notions that fit with the
prophets and with the story that is told. There are many indications in
the Gospels that she did not have great wealth. So it is easy to assume
what type of situation and position a young woman like this would have

had: she probably was a servant in the house of a relative, and did general housework like any other young woman who was lowly, pious, and upright. It is certainly possible that she was doing such housework when the angel came to her and brought her this message. For one sees in many stories that angels come to people when they are going about their business and carrying out their normal occupations. The angel appeared to the shepherds in the fields, as they were watching their flocks. He appeared to Gideon as he was threshing grain. He appeared to Samson's mother as she sat in the field. Or perhaps the Virgin Mary, as a pious child, was alone in a corner praying for the salvation of Israel. Angels are also especially fond of appearing during prayers.

The Evangelist does not speak one word about the ancestors or the family of the Virgin. He does say, however, that Joseph, to whom she was engaged, was from the house of David. This seems not to matter to us. But it does matter that we know that the Virgin Mary is from the house of David. But the Evangelist regards it as unnecessary to tell us this because it has been said often enough previously by the prophets that Christ should come from the house of David and be called David's son ...

[Pp. 632–33] Luke writes further that the angel came to the young woman, greeted her and told her that she had a gracious God. "Hail," he said, "gracious one" or blessed one. "The Lord is with you, you who are highly praised among women." These are great and mighty words, which upset the pious child, so that she wondered what sort of a message this could possibly be. Whether she knew in the first moment that it was an angel that was speaking to her, we cannot know. The words of Luke almost make it sound as if she did not know him, for he says that she was not troubled by him, but by his speech and the greeting. It is an unusual greeting, so that afterwards she must have thought that this was also an unusual messenger, who so quickly said: "Oh Mary, you are blessed to have such a gracious God. No other woman on earth has been shown such grace by her God. You are the crown of them all, etc." Such words made the pious child blush and took her breath away with shock, for she did not know what they were about. Because of this the angel consoled her and told her what God had planned for her and why He would need her. He said: "Do not fear, Mary, you have found grace with God." Pay attention to this little phrase, for it not only served to console the maiden, but also to create horrible blasphemy afterwards among Christians led by the pope and his monks, which still continues among the papists. They make a God out of the Virgin Mary, give her all power over heaven and earth, as if she had this from herself. But even if the Virgin Mary is blessed over all women, so that no other woman had experienced such grace and honor, still the angel pulls her down with his words and makes her just like all the other saints. He says clearly that whatever she is is the result of grace and is not earned. There must always be a difference between those who give grace and those who receive grace. One should seek grace from those who give it and not from those who have enjoyed grace themselves. This was not done under the papacy, for there everyone ran to the Virgin Mary and sought and hoped for more grace and blessings than from the Lord Christ. This little phrase stands against such errors: "Mary, you have found grace with God." You should learn through this that you should hold her to be a person who has come to grace, and not someone who has grace to give out. Her child, our dear Lord Jesus, is supposed to do that, so that we seek grace from him and through him come to grace...

As the gentle maiden heard enough from the angel about what God wanted to do with her, she answered him and said: "Behold, I am the maid of the Lord, let it happen to me as you have said." This is a very fine answer, in which we can see not only great modesty but also strong belief and sincere love for all people. For first she says in all modesty and obedience: "I am the maid of the Lord." As if she wanted to say "Here I am; whatever my God and father in heaven wants to do with me, I am willing. And I am especially willing to do what you have just told me about." For she says: "Let it happen to me as you have said." These are words that she happily wishes from her whole heart, that it will be a good thing and that the blessed time is coming when the devil's head will be smashed and the poor miserable sinners will be helped. She wishes this from her heart and she is happy that God will use her for this, not because of her person or her honor, but because she knows that through this child she and the whole world full of sin and death will be helped. For she believes both that God will do through her the work that the angel has mentioned, and also that this child has an eternal empire, and will save her and the whole world from the realm of the devil and from death. And through such faith alone is she blessed and freed from sin, and not through the work of bringing the Son of God into the world. This was certainly a special grace and majesty, as she herself states in the Magnificat: "All children's children will call me blessed." But she is God's child and comes to eternal life only because she held her child to be what the angel had foretold him to be.

Just as she alone has glory in the fact that she is the Mother of God and brought the Son of God into the world, so we should believe with her that this child is holy and will have an eternal empire.

THE VISITATION AND THE MAGNIFICAT

Sermon on the Feast of the Visitation [2 July], 1523, WA XII, pp. 608–17
[Sermon on the Gospel of Luke 1, "Mary arose and went with haste into
the hills."] Luke presents a story here that is simple to consider, but still
contains a great deal. It is simple to consider because there is nothing more
to it than the service of Mary, that she arose and visited her cousin Elizabeth.
But when one looks at it correctly, it contains nothing but miracles and
works of love, which we will see.

Elizabeth did not yet know that she was pregnant, but when Mary came
to her, she realized that she was carrying a child. This is one [miracle] and
it is a major one; but it is still more astounding that she realized that Christ
lay in the body of the Virgin. She could not see this in her body, for Mary
was only a few days pregnant, but still she recognized this. She certainly
must have had acute vision. This shows the form and nature of Christian
belief, that we cannot understand anything about belief from our natures,
but the Holy Spirit does this alone and works in our hearts, as it did here
with Elizabeth. She perceived in her heart that Mary was the Mother of
God, and even if the whole world had said otherwise, she would have
stayed with this belief. See, this is how it must also be with us; everything
lies deep or is so hidden that reason cannot understand it, but belief sees
very clearly, which we will also see later in the Magnificat. You can see
here how strong Elizabeth's belief was; reason had blinded her completely,
and if she had assessed things according to reason, she would have said:
"Oh, she can't be carrying a child because she is too young." If she had not
come to the point that she believed Mary carried a child, she would not
afterwards have been able to come to the point at which she said "That is
God, my Lord." But belief sees. That is the nature of belief, which could be
called "evidence of things unseen"; one can see what one cannot see, hear
what one cannot hear. In sum, one can understand everything differently
when one understands what is needed. This is what will happen in dying
and other perils; we will naturally grope and look around, and when we
cannot grope or see how it is going anymore, we will fall on our backs and
have doubts. Then I must be so adept that I will say: "In the midst of
death I will find life. I might die, but I know my Lord is with me." As the
Psalmist said: "In peace will I both lie down and sleep; for you alone, O
Lord, make me dwell in safety" (Psalm 4:8). [I will say:] "You have given me
the confidence that I will find life. Thus I will lay myself down in peace."
That is why we sing in the hymn: "In the midst of life we are in death."
This will also happen in all other times of danger. When I have sinned and

my conscience is not at peace because of God's judgment and wrath, then I must say: "Righteousness lies beneath sin; peace and salvation lie beneath a bad conscience; goodness and mercy lie beneath the wrath of God." In sum, everything must be seen differently if it lets itself be seen in this way; that is the nature of belief.

Therefore it follows that Elizabeth is full of joy, a joy that has been poured completely through her. Thus nothing came out of her except praise and extolling, and she exclaimed: "Why is this granted to me, that the mother of my Lord comes to me . . . Blessed are you among women." See, these are the fruits of belief; one is capable in one's heart when one has belief. For this reason Elizabeth is an example for believers.

And now more about the Virgin. Luke says here that she arose and with modest steps went into the hills; in this he shows what a fine and honorable demeanor she had. This is as if he were to say that love had forced her to make this trip, and had also caused her to be dressed so well and to have such a proper demeanor while on the road that no one could take a bad example from her.

When she got there and greeted Elizabeth, heard the great praises and learned how she would be honored, she stood up, throwing everything away from herself, and said: "My soul magnifies the Lord and my spirit rejoices in God my Savior." See, the Virgin takes absolutely no merit for herself here, even though she would be the Mother of the Lord and was blessed among women, but stays in the middle and does not attach the merits to herself. It also says that she was prepared if this were to be taken away from her, and that she acted simply with a joyous heart toward God. For this reason she stood up and praised God and did not talk about [her own] merits; she said "Oh what a good and gracious God I have, my soul is consumed by Him; this and not my merits makes me rejoice." So must we attach ourselves to God, and not to His creatures or our merits, for this would be copulating with His creatures. See what a pure spirit the pious Virgin had, that she did not take this great honor and merit on herself. How could there be any honor greater than this, when a woman learns that she will be the Mother of God? But she did not praise herself, and would have been satisfied if it had been taken from her again right away. We poor people, however, get so worried when one or ten gulden are taken from us, or even when one penny is taken away. Oh what unclean spirits we are! We worry when our health or strength or similar things are taken away, but what does it matter? It is the unclean spirit that is in us; it sullies us and keeps us with the creatures rather than attaching itself right away to God's grace and mercy. But this is the true purity or virginity of Mary, that she stands on God alone and praises Him. This is as Christ says, "Blessed are the pure in heart."

We read further that she accepted the merit as a sign of God's blessing and love, and said "See, He has done great things for me." What a wonderful spirit is the one who recognizes God, for afterwards it can understand and need all of His creatures.

Then she lifted up her merits and through this praised all creatures; she portrayed for us what type of a man God is with great sweetness and said: "He has regarded the lowliness of His handmaiden." This does not refer to her modesty, but to her lowly, menial status. He has not lifted up a girl from the high nobility, such as Caiaphas's daughter, who went around with fancy clothes in the midst of servants, but a poor, lowly, low-status girl, of whom no one expected anything.

Now this is portrayed wonderfully for us; it is clearly shown what God's ways are here. He cannot overlook you, for no one is over Him; He cannot look to the side of you, for no one is like Him; therefore He only sees under you – the deeper and more lowly that you are, the more clearly God's eyes see you. For this reason Scripture praises "He who sits above the angels and considers the lowly." And another psalm says: "How admirable is our Lord God, who raises the poor..." (Psalm 113). See, it is important to note that those who want to climb above His head will not be seen by Him any more. Scripture always praises those who are like Mary here; He [God] cannot tolerate force or artifice or anything else with which one seeks to build oneself up; thus Mary says here: "He has regarded my lowliness."

Now I advise you, how should one praise her? Not with many "Hail Marys" and hymns, but in this way: see what a truly poor maiden she was, but God regarded her lowliness. She was completely naked and praised God, so why do we honor her? She wants to be praised because she has nothing, so why do we praise her as if she has everything? It would be the right way to praise the Mother of God and all the saints if we were to say: "Yes, that is certainly great grace, that God regarded the poor maiden so graciously and did so much, that He made her his mother." The same with St. Paul. Yes, what a great act of grace, that God made the bad boy Paul into His instrument. And the same is true with John the Baptist and all the saints. See, God is honored in His creatures; in this way He alone remains God and there is no idolatry.

Now, what purpose will this honoring have? Through this I will be consoled and strengthened, because I will say, "See, the Mother of God was completely empty and had nothing, but God did this for her. I hope that He will also show grace to this poor sinner." Great confidence that God will give His grace to me will grow in me because of this. So we should turn back, and honor the saints because they have shame in their hearts instead of honor, which could also bring us to ruin. Oh, wretched honor!

And further: see "what great things has He done for me," but what have you done for Him? Nothing. "Holy is His name": for He is the one who does good works, and for that reason the honor should go to Him alone.

Further: "And His mercy is on those who fear him." That is, those who remain terrified of His judgment and stay in the midst of fear will afterwards have the hope of His mercy; these two things go together. As deeply as the child was hidden from Elizabeth, just so deeply is the fact that one should expect good from God in the middle of fear hidden from reason; faith does this anyway, however.

Further: "He has scattered the proud in imagination in their hearts"; this is also a work of belief. For one sees that those who set themselves against the gospel let themselves be regarded as if they were strong and above everyone else. But in the midst of their haughtiness God strikes them to the ground, although it does not always happen right away; [sometimes] God lets them grow a little and lets them believe that the whole world thinks they are the ones with all the power. But this is worth nothing, because before God they are already knocked down; belief sees this easily.

And further: "He has filled the hungry with good things and left the rich empty." This He does as well, which we easily tell from looking at history. All of those who rise above soon fall down again; those who have the most break the soonest, for they do not trust in God, but in His goods and creatures, so they must fall. God cannot tolerate this, so they must be broken. But the hungry must have enough; if they do not have any bread, then the emperor should feed them, so that they will believe. Those who do not have bread will easily fall into doubt.

Further: "He has remembered mercy." This is the last good thing. "I carry the child that He has promised, and do not carry him for my needs alone, but for the house of Israel and the Seed of Abraham, that is, for all believers." She does this out of love for everyone. See what a fine song this is.

Those who want to can see the spiritual meaning. Mary stands for Christianity after the synagogue, and Elizabeth stands for the people under the Law in the synagogue. Elizabeth stayed home; that represents the people of the Law, who were very pious but were surrounded by many external laws. Mary, however, went over the mountains with decorum; this is Christians who go freely under the heavens and do not have to drag anything with them but are afterwards freely taken in. Not like false Christians. This is expressed in the saying: "Mary went there freely under the heavens, but afterwards she was truly modest and was taken in." Amen.

Commentary on the Magnificat [Luke 1:46–55], 1521, LW XXI, pp. 295–355
From *Luther's Works*, vol. XXI, edited by Jaroslav Pelikan, © 1968
Concordia Publishing Company. Used by permission of Concordia
Publishing House

[P. 299] When the holy virgin experienced what great things God was working in her despite her insignificance, lowliness, poverty, and inferiority, the Holy Spirit taught her this deep insight and wisdom, that God is the kind of Lord who does nothing but exalt those of low degree and put down the mighty from their thrones, in short, break what is whole and make whole what is broken...

[P. 301] The tender mother of Christ does the same here and teaches us, with her words and by the example of her experience, how to know, love, and praise God. For since she boasts, with heart leaping for joy and praising God, that He regarded her despite her low estate and nothing-ness, we must believe that she came of poor, despised, and lowly parents. Let us make it very plain for the sake of the simple. Doubtless there were in Jerusalem daughters of the chief priests and counselors who were rich, comely, youthful, cultured, and held in high renown by all of the people; even as it is today with the daughters of kings, princes, and men of wealth. The same was also true of many another city. Even in her own town of Nazareth she was not the daughter of one of the chief rulers, but a poor and plain citizen's daughter, whom none looked up to or esteemed. To her neighbors and their daughters she was but a simple maiden, tending the cattle and doing the housework, and doubtless esteemed no more than any poor maidservant today, who does as she is told around the house...

[P. 308] So little did she lay claim to anything, but left all of God's gifts freely in His hands, being herself no more than a cheerful guest chamber and willing hostess to so great a Guest. Therefore she also kept all these things forever. That is to magnify God alone, to count only Him great and lay claim to nothing. We see here how strong an incentive she had to fall into sin, so that it is no less a miracle that she refrained from pride and arrogance than that she received the gifts she did. Tell me, was hers not a wondrous soul? She finds herself the Mother of God, exalted above all mortals, and still remains so simple and so calm that she does not think of any poor serving maid as beneath her...

[P. 327] Mary also freely ascribes all to God's grace, not to her merit. For though she was without sin, yet that grace was far too great for her to deserve it in any way... As the wood had no merit or worthiness than that it was suited to be made into a cross and was appointed by God for that purpose, so her sole worthiness to become the Mother of God lay in her being fit and appointed for it; so that it might be pure grace and not a reward, that we might not take away from God's grace, worship, and honor by ascribing too great things to her...

[P. 329] She is not puffed up, does not vaunt herself or proclaim with a loud voice that she is to become the Mother of God. She seeks not any glory, but goes about her usual household duties, milking the cows, cooking the meals, washing pots and kettles, sweeping out the rooms, and performing the work of maidservant or housemother in lowly and despised tasks, as though she cared nothing for such great gifts and graces. She was esteemed among other women and her neighbors no more highly than before, nor desired to be, but remained a poor townswoman, one of the great multitude. Oh, how simple and pure a heart was hers, how strange a soul was this! What great things are hidden here under this lowly exterior!...

[P. 352] [T]his Seed of Abraham could not be born in the common course of nature, of a man and a woman, for such a birth is cursed and results in nothing but accursed seed...

[P. 353] [God] raises up seed for Abraham, the natural son of one of his daughters, a pure virgin, Mary, through the Holy Spirit and without her knowing a man. Here there was no natural conception with its curse, nor could it touch this seed; and yet it is the natural seed of Abraham, as truly as any of the other children of Abraham... This is Abraham's Seed, begotten by none of his sons, as the Jews always confidently expected, but born of this one daughter of his, Mary, alone.

Sermon on the Visitation, held according to the ordinances of Brandenburg
and Nuremberg on the day of Mary's ascension, 1532, WA LII,
pp. 681–88

[Pp. 681–83] The feast of the ascension of Mary is completely papist, that is, full of blasphemy and established without any grounding in Scripture. For that reason we have let it lapse in our churches and have used the day to preach about the story of how Mary went over the mountains to visit her relative Elizabeth and what happened there. In the first place there is no sign in Scripture of the feast of the ascension of Mary so that the papists themselves just use a saying from Jerome, who is supposed to have said:

"I do not know whether she ascended into heaven in her body or out of her body." And how is anyone supposed to know this when there is nothing in Scripture about it? The most annoying and dangerous thing about making this ascension into a feast is that people honor the Virgin Mary and call to her, as they sing in the response: "O you pure Mother of God, we ask that you, because you were taken up into heaven, be gracious to us and make us citizens in heaven."

But we Christians do not know of any ascension that we can enjoy except for that of our dear Lord Jesus Christ, who ascended into heaven and sits at the right hand of God, and intercedes for us. For that reason we can console ourselves in his Ascension and know that we will enjoy this, that we will also come to heaven and shall be heard here on earth by him in everything that we ask for in his name. For that reason it is a wonderful, exalted and comforting feast, the Ascension of Christ, that the Virgin Mary enjoyed just as we do. We, however, even if she has already gone to heaven, cannot enjoy her ascension, and should not for that reason call to her or take comfort in her intercession as the pope teaches and through this shames and dishonors the Ascension of our Lord Christ, because he wants to make the mother equal to the son in everything.

It is not only annoying in many cases, but also very laughable that the papists put up a big ostentatious display of plants on this day for no other reason than that they take a verse in Ecclesiasticus 22 [actually Ecclesiasticus 24:17ff.] to apply to the Virgin Mary and compare her to certain trees and roses. If children did this it would be rude enough to make such foolishness out of Scripture. But the pope, bishops, all the monks and priests do this and call us heretics because we have let such practices lapse and do not want to be fools with them. Everyone knows, however, what sorts of superstitions come from these displays of plants, how they are used for witchcraft and all types of superstitions. For that reason we have very good cause to do away with such a blasphemous and superstitious feast day . . . and our celebration is much different than the papists' celebration for we praise God and thank Him, as the dear Virgin praised and thanked Him.

It appears that Luke had a special fondness for this story, for he was so diligent with it and he portrayed the dear Virgin so well for us, and especially for the women folk, in a wreath that is bedecked with three lovely and beautiful roses. For he praises three special virtues, in which we should also apply ourselves: the first is faith, the second a very great modesty, and the third is fine and chaste conduct toward other people. Where such jewels can be found on women or virgins, they are far superior to all queens and empresses in their gold, precious jewels, pearls, velvet, and silk. Elizabeth talks about faith, for she says: "You are blessed, because you believe that what the Lord has said to you will be fulfilled." It is appropriate to praise Mary, not only for the faith common to all Christians that they will be saved, the belief that God will rescue them through His promised Seed from the curse and from sin and take them to grace and make them blessed, but also because of the faith that she has been given a special promise, that applies to her person alone, that she will bear Christ, the Son of God. She believes this promise and does not let herself be led astray, even though she could not know how this was to happen. Such faith was hers alone; in that we cannot be the same as her. Because faith must always be preceded by God's word, we would follow her example in this and also hold ourselves steadily to God's word. Women folk especially should better let themselves be found in church, at prayer, or at a sermon instead of at a dance, at the marketplace, or somewhere else. For it is certainly true that wherever one has the desire to hear God's word, hears it gladly and follows it gladly, there more virtues increase every day. On the other hand, where one does not hear it gladly, all sorts of sins will not be lacking. That is the first virtue.

The second virtue is [humility]: the young maiden has been honored greatly, for she will be God's mother, so that it would be appropriate for Elizabeth to follow her. But because God has ordained that one should honor older people, she followed the same teachings and did not become proud, but just like a pious child fell to the ground, bowed her heart, and abased herself. She traveled such a long way to visit her relative and troubled herself to help her in childbed. Elizabeth certainly noticed this and humbled herself in turn before the young maiden. "Why," she said, "is it granted to me that the Mother of the Lord comes to me?"

This is certainly a lovely jewel and great ornament on the dear Virgin, that she did not become proud because of the honor that she had, that she is God's mother and will bear the Son of God. It would not be a wonder (because women are certainly inclined to vanity) if she fell into vanity deeper than Lucifer with his angels...

[Pp. 686–88] The third virtue is that Luke says she went chastely, which means: be chaste and do not act out of forwardness or wantonness, as young servants go to dances and church festivals, run gossiping from house to house and chattering everywhere, letting their eyes rove here and there. These are not to be called modest young women, but slutty idlers. Maidens and women should stay in their houses and if they are on the streets go quickly to their place and not stand counting the tiles on the roof or the sparrows under the roof or hold little gossip sessions while they are on their way. The Virgin Mary did not act this way; she went quickly from the city, did not count the trees, did not stand or sit here or there, but thought about what she had to do and did it, letting other people also do what they had to do.

Luke wanted to report this clearly so that maids and women do not say: "Why should I always stay at home, like a nun in the convent, and not also go out walking; didn't the Virgin Mary do this? It was not a sin for her, so it is also not a sin for me." Yes, do this modestly, as she did it, and with fine and virginal deportment. For she did not go for pleasure, but she thought about helping her relative, because the angel had told her that she would have a son even though she was old. For that reason she went out of her house, even though she would have rather stayed home. If you do the same and do it modestly, with a chaste demeanor, in a way that is becoming to a maiden or woman, it will also not be sinful for you.

But in the same way that women do not follow the dear Virgin in modesty, but are haughty and proud, they also do not follow her in chastity, as is very clear to our eyes. There are very few among you women and maidens who let yourselves think that one could be happy and chaste at the same time. Clearly spoken, you are fresh and vulgar, immodest in your bearing, screaming and raging as if you were insane, which is seen as a good thing to be. But good behavior and happiness can and should go together, if one would only look at the example presented here. It is especially bad that young maidens are shameless in their words and actions, and swear as if they were mercenary soldiers. I will not repeat the shameful words and horrible, vulgar sayings that one hears and learns from the other. This comes from the fact that their mothers act like this in their houses and do not pay close attention to their morals when they are young. It is a clear and certain sign of our coming punishment when morals begin to fail among women, for children turn out like their mothers and maids learn it from their mistresses, until finally no decency nor honor remains among anyone. We see this, unfortunately, in our times and must therefore await the punishment we have earned.

This is the example that the fine Virgin Mary shows to us: she holds onto God's word with firm faith; she is proper and humble and brings us to shame with our stinking, loathsome vanity... These virtues are worthy to single out on a special feast day, especially with the young people, so that everyone will learn to be pious and God-fearing, and especially women learn to keep themselves in decency, respectability, and modesty.

THE INCARNATION AND THE BIRTH OF CHRIST

Sermon for Christmas, 1522, WA X, 1/1, pp. 66–68

Some people dispute about exactly how this birth happened, whether she was delivered of the child in the bed, in great joy, whether she was without all pain as this was happening. I do not reproach people for their devotion, but we should stay with the Gospel, which says "she bore him," and by the article of faith that we recite: "who is born of the Virgin Mary." There is no deceit here, but, as the words state, a true birth. We certainly know what birth is, and how it proceeds. It happens to her as it does to other women, with good spirits and with the actions of her limbs as is appropriate in a birth, so that she is his right and natural mother and he is her right and natural son. But her body did not allow the natural operations that pertain to birth, and she gave birth without sin, without shame, without pain, and without injury, just as she also conceived without sin. The curse of Eve does not apply to her, which says that "in pain shall you bring forth children," but otherwise it happened to her exactly as it does with any other woman giving birth. For grace did not promise anything, and did not hinder nature or the works of nature, but improved and helped them. In the same way she fed him naturally with milk from her breasts; without a doubt she did not give him any stranger's milk or feed him with any other body part than the breast. [Her breasts] were filled with milk by God without any uncleanness or injury.

Lectures on Genesis, 1544, LW III and IV
From *Luther's Works*, vols. III and IV, edited by Jaroslav Pelikan,
© 1968 Concordia Publishing Company. Used by permission
of Concordia Publishing House

[III, p. 134, commenting on Genesis 17:10–11, in which God commands circumcision for men as a sign of the covenant] The women have their own circumcision, which is burdensome and painful enough. Concerning it Moses says: "In pain you will give birth to your children." It is then that they are circumcised unto death. There is wrath in the word "pain," but there is mercy in the statement, "You will give birth."

Although the female sex, too, is condemned because of original sin, it is nevertheless not done away with for this reason; nor does it perish utterly. This burden was not imposed on Eve alone; it was imposed on all who give birth. Therefore believing matrons comforted themselves in their pains with the thought that even though these pains are a definite evidence of sin and of the wrath of God, it is nevertheless a sure sign of divine blessing that through birth the human race and the very church of God are being rebuilt...

[III, p. 136] Moreover, here the mystery of the incarnation of the Son of God is pointed out; for because of the Virgin Mary alone, from whom Christ was to be born, God spares the entire female sex, and only the males are required to be circumcised. There was to be a woman who would give birth without a man. Because of her God spares the entire sex, and with this seemingly foolish law He burdens only the males... In the other sex, on which circumcision is not imposed, there is a sign of grace. For it is pointed out that He who is to do away with circumcision and to deliver sin and death will be born of a woman.

[III, p. 206, commenting on Genesis 18:10, God telling Abraham He will give him a son] Physicians say that the fetus begins to live and stir in the fifth month after conception and that during the remaining five months it matures for birth. The same thing, says the Lord, will happen to Isaac. And thus He eliminates an unusual and miraculous birth, such as the effete Sarah could have had in mind.

In order that the normal course of nature might be preserved, the Virgin Mary carried Christ in this manner up to the tenth month; and during the entire time He, like other embryos, received nourishment from the drops of blood of His mother, who was sanctified by the Holy Spirit.

[IV, p. 161, commenting on Genesis 22:18, God's promise to Abraham, "by your Seed shall all the nations of the earth be blessed"] Accordingly, Mary did not conceive this Seed in the natural manner. She is not a mother like the mothers of all nations. She had to be a mother and give birth to a new man. But she was a pure mother and a virgin who conceived, not from a man or from an angel, whether good or bad, but from the Holy Spirit (Luke 1:35).

MARY'S PURIFICATION

Sermon on the Purification of the Virgin (Candlemas: 2 February), 1523, WA XII, pp. 421–22

[Luke 2:22–24] In this Gospel the humility of Mary and Jesus her son is demonstrated; they put themselves under the Law, although they were not required to do so. Moses wrote that a woman who had given birth to a son should wait forty days before her purification, and if it was a girl, [she should wait] just as long again, that is, eighty days. This same law did not apply to Mary, for he [Moses] says "when a woman has borne a child that

was conceived by a man"; with these words Moses excludes Mary from the
Law, for Jesus was conceived by the Holy Spirit, not from human seed.
Why else would Moses have thought it necessary to say "conceived by a
man," for everyone knows that women do not conceive by drinking a glass
of wine? Thus the Holy Spirit spoke to Moses well, so that he continued
after speaking of mothers and said "a woman who has conceived by a man."
But Mary and Jesus put themselves under the Law out of love, although
they did not need to, because they were not subject to the Law. So we
should do all of our good works out of freely given love for our neighbors
for their benefit, not because we are required to, but, like Mary, because we
do these things to honor God and love our neighbors. She will not use her
freedom here, but through this action strengthens the obedience of others,
who are subject to the Law because of their uncleanness. I do not know
if the second law that Moses gave, that every firstborn should be offered
to God, applies to Mary. I assume that it does apply to her, for He made
Christ her firstborn son, so that she became a mother and stayed a mother.
God gave this commandment in the Law, that every firstborn who opened
the body of his mother should be dedicated to Him in memory of the
fact that He had led the children to Israel out of Egypt. When a son was
born, one could redeem him from the priests for a quarter of a gulden. If
it was an ox or other animal, it remained the priests'. This law did apply
to Mary, for Christ is her firstborn, who was dedicated to God and is holy,
as the Bible says. Should someone say that because Christ did not break
his mother's body [this is probably a reference to Mary's hymen] (as the
Law says), he should not be counted in this number, you should answer "It
doesn't matter; he is counted among the firstborn even if he was born from
his mother without any type of injury to her, because he was a firstborn
and had a physical mother" ...

[P. 423] In all of this, God portrays for us what is true belief and love,
that we do not need these external things in order to follow the Law,
but follow it spiritually. We do not need to redeem children from priests,
nor does a woman have to lie so many weeks in bed before she can
be purified. Instead she should confess that she is a daughter of Adam
and has been made flesh, and if she does something small, she should
confess her sins and uncleanness and ask for mercy, so that she can become pure again. For daughters are a lesser good work, and sons a larger
and more powerful good work because they have less uncleanness. She
should confess: "Lord, I have done these things, the child is born; if you
wanted to judge it harshly, so you could. This living fruit is certainly
unclean. But, however impure it is, would you accept it anyway, for I

admit its uncleanness and ask for purification?" Such confession in the heart is the sacrifice and redemption of the first birth [i.e., the birth in Adam].

Sermon on the day of the Purification of Mary, 1526, WA XX, pp. 241–44
They expected a day of purification, which we call the six-weeks' day, because a woman stays inside [this long] after a birth. The commandment is in Leviticus, the twelfth chapter. There God through Moses ordered the Jews (for this and other laws of Moses do not pertain to us Christians or to the heathens) that when a woman became pregnant and gave birth to a boy, she would be unclean for forty days. She was thus put aside, set apart from other people, as the lepers are with us, for no one wants to be in their company. If she gave birth to a girl, she had to stay at home for eighty days, that is, twice forty days, and she was shunned and impure, and no one wanted to see her.

This was certainly a difficult commandment, and would not be tolerable or bearable to us if we followed it as strictly as they did. With us it is common that women stay or go out as they wish, and no one shuns them as strictly as the Jewish women were shunned. With the Jews it was damnable, and very repugnant. No one was allowed to eat, drink, sleep, or lie with the women, or sit next to them, and everything that they touched – whether a bed, chair, table, clothing, locks, drinking cups, food and drink – in sum, everything that they touched was polluted and cast off. This went on for six weeks if they bore a son, and if they bore a girl, twelve weeks. This commandment was serious for them and very strictly kept – our six weeks are only a shadow compared to their six weeks. This is the first commandment, that they had to spend six weeks inside, and were viewed as if they were a leprous and disgusting woman . . .

Christ is free from the Law

The Law speaks again and again about women who have children by men, saying that when the child has a bodily father and is born in the flesh it belongs under the Law, that it is impure with the mother for a certain time. But Christ does not belong under the Law and it also does not apply completely to Mary, for the text says clearly and plainly "a woman who has been impregnated" and with the word "impregnated" Mary was clearly not included, for she was not impregnated and had known no man, as she says herself in Luke 1, but she remained a virgin, as Isaiah said in chapter 9 [actually Isaiah 7:14], and, in contrast to the normal way with other women, she became pregnant by the Holy Spirit coming from heaven without any human seed. Thus this law applies only to women who become mothers through the flesh. She was a mother through the spirit. Moses and his whole Law therefore has no authority over this virgin and her son. For that reason it is wrong to say that they must follow it and lie imprisoned in it, for they are high above it . . .

THE WEDDING AT CANA

Sermon on marriage, 1525, WA XVII/I, p. 17

Some of the church fathers, such as Bonaventura, have asserted that the bridegroom at the wedding at Cana was John the Evangelist and the bride was Mary Magdalene. I do not agree with that, but believe, as the Greek teacher Nicephorus, who lived four hundred years ago at the time of the Byzantine Emperor Emanuel at Constantinople, wrote, that [the bridegroom] was Simon of Cana, the son of Lord Jesus Christ's mother's sister, Mary Jacobi.

It is easy to accept and believe that the bridegroom and bride must have been near to the Holy Mother Mary and her close relatives, because she was there herself. She helped to run things and concerned herself with what they were drinking at the wedding and that they needed wine.

For the Blessed Mother Mary is not so frivolous that she would mix with strangers or distant relatives for weddings or meals, but only if they were near relations. And the people here acted as if they were poor, simple peasant folk and near relations of Christ, as poor, simple relations take care to do.

Sermon on the Sunday after Epiphany, 1528, WA XXI, pp. 62–65

When Mary as a relative saw that wine was needed, she spoke to the Lord with good intentions, "They have no wine," as if to say that he could help them if he wanted to. But the Lord was stern toward her and spoke harshly to her: "Woman, what do I have to do with you?" or "What do we have to do with each other?" He does not honor her by calling her mother, but spoke sharply and crudely "woman," and then even more harshly "what do I have to do with you?" She believed and thought it certain that her words would count for something . . .

But you see here that Mary erred, though she came to the Lord in love and faith, believing that he would certainly do [what she asked]. There was love and there was a need that forced her to ask a favor for the poor people, so that they would not feel shame at this time of great honor. We should also do this, we should also believe that God will do what we ask in our fear, need, sorrow, and misery, but we should not set a means, time, or place for this, but firmly believe that it will happen when He wishes it and when His hour comes. The true Christian congregation and all believing people do not set a goal for God's help, but are certain that He will help and not remain apart.

This example is a good one to note against those who say that the Christian Church cannot err, that the Holy Father cannot err. Here you certainly see the opposite also in the holiest of people, in Mary the Mother of God, who certainly believed more firmly and strongly than any saint. But still she erred and because of her errors was rebuked sharply and roughly...

Christ did not exempt his mother, so how much less will he exempt the pope and all those who hang around him, who obscure or even suppress God's word with their human ordinances and laws.

With this, Christ also noticed that over the course of time more honor would be given to his mother than to himself, that is, that people would view her as an intercessor and mediator between God and us. He opposed this not only here, but even more harshly at other times, in order to show that it does not have to do with her, but with him. He is the one who should intercede between God and humans and not Mary or any other saint, no matter how holy that saint might be. If anyone else had said such a thing to Mary, he would certainly have been a heretic, but this was Christ himself. From this we can understand what a great error those people have made who have depended on her and her intercession and have sent the poor people to her.

If we proceed further in the Gospel, we see that the Lord made water into wine because of his own decision. He did not let his mother's intercession move him, but did this solely out of his own mercy and grace, just as he demands that we turn from her help and intercession to his help alone. For it is certain that before you die, you must remove all honor and trust in these things and place your trust and confidence in God alone, who will help you through Christ Jesus His Son, for he was made an intercessor and a means of grace. If you believe anything else, nothing in heaven nor earth can help you, that is certain.

Christ does not forbid us to make requests for others here, but says that trust and confidence must be placed in Christ alone. But until now people have pushed Christ out of the center and far into the background, have made his mother the intercessor and made Christ a stern and harsh judge. Paintings often portray Mary showing the Christ child her breast and coming to Christ for us. But he alone was the intercessor given by his father, as we see clearly in many places in Scripture.

WA TR IV, no. 4435, p. 311

And then Doctor Luther questioned the suspicions of Joseph about Mary, [saying]: "He would certainly have amazing thoughts about his bride, who as his fiancée with his permission had gone to the mountains; she was gone for a whole quarter year and returned pregnant. It would be the same as if she had gone to the oak [a pilgrimage site called "the oak" at Naunhof near Leipzig] in search of saintliness. And he certainly assumed adultery. This was a strong suspicion, for which Scripture cannot blame him. The angel thought to break off the dispute and to postpone the judgment. Dear God, how difficult are these things! And they are similar to legends, unless they are confirmed as great miracles."

Then he [Luther] questioned whether Mary knew [i.e., had sexual relations with] Joseph even after the birth of Christ, as Matthew calls him, "the firstborn son." He answered, "The church has left this alone and has not determined this. But nevertheless the same consequence is firmly demonstrated because she remained a virgin, but on the other hand she was viewed as the mother of the Son of God. She was not judged to be the mother of human sons and remained in that state."

WA TR V, no. 5839, p. 377

...Joseph died before the Passion, but for Mary, that is, for the church, this was never prophesied. Mary holds three stations [within herself], that is, she is a virgin, a wife, and eventually became a mother through the greatest injuries to her son.

WA TR V, no. 5977, p. 414

Respexit humilitatem ancillae suae [he has regarded the lowliness of his handmaiden (Luke 1:48)] How should we translate this into German? I know no better German than to say "the pitiful maiden," for she certainly was a pitiful maiden. *Stirps regia* (the royal lineage) was completely extirpated by Herod, so that there was no one left except these two; so the good maiden took [as her fiancé] a poor carpenter's journeyman. This is the reason she said, "Oh, I am a poor maiden, and how could I come to the honor, that I will become the mother of our Lord God?" And in the prophets the stem of Jesse was not a green root, but a rotten and withered one, though a green branch could still grow out of it.

WA TR V, no. 6320, p. 601

[Luther said:] "Marriage is a gift of God, which is why the devil is its enemy. Marriage is a beautiful, wonderful gift and order, confirmed with two types of love. One of these is natural and good, and the other is disorderly and evil. But the devil, who is an enemy and disturber of marriage, destroys not only the disorderly but also the natural love between spouses. For this reason people of old taught their children well, saying: 'Dear daughter, act toward your husband in such a way that he is happy when he sees the top of the house on his way home. And when the man lives with his wife and treats her so that she does not like to see him go away and is happy when he comes home, then everything is well.' "

He said further, "God did not change marriage when He ordained it, but preserved it; only in the conception and birth of His Son did He change it. The Turks believe that virgins can conceive and bear children, and are not astonished that Mary is both a mother and a virgin at the same time, for such things happen often. May such beliefs not enter my house!"

CHAPTER 4

Biblical women other than Eve and Mary

Both the Old and New Testaments abound with examples of individual women who play major roles in the history of the Jewish people, the life of Christ, and the first-century community of believers. Luther writes extensively and specifically about these women in his Biblical commentaries and lectures, speaks about them in sermons, mentions them in the table talk, and refers to them in his letters. He often uses the examples of Biblical women to make general points about God's commandments to female and male believers, and also as springboards for hostile comments about the papacy, Jews, or other individuals and groups he opposed.

As with his ideas on other subjects, Luther says so much about Biblical women that he sometimes contradicts himself. This emerges most clearly in his discussions of women's preaching or prophesying. When he is writing in opposition to Catholic notions of the priesthood, he uses the examples of women's prophesying in the Old and New Testaments as a sign that the office of the priesthood has been extended to all believers. When he is writing in opposition to those who took this statement literally and calls for an end to an ordained ministry, he terms women's preaching, like that of untrained men, as equal to that of children, fools, drunks, and the mute.

His strongest statements for and against women's preaching or other public religious actions emerge in the middle of polemics directed against those with whom he disagreed. In his more careful and balanced considerations, he generally asserts that though such actions are normally prohibited to women both by the words of Paul and by other restrictions imposed on women, such as God's words to Eve, in certain circumstances they are allowed or even praiseworthy. Four factors could justify a woman's preaching or leadership: she was called by God, often as a rebuke to men, and thus had a special gift; she was widowed or unmarried, so that the issue of wifely obedience did not apply to her; she was advised by men, or her authority was given to her by a man; no men were present, or no men who were qualified were present. The first factor was required for any instance of women's religious leadership to be judged acceptable, and the more of these factors that applied, the better. In his discussions, Luther did not break sharply with medieval commentators or his Protestant contemporaries, though he did offer a slightly wider understanding of the emergency situations in which women's speaking might be justified than did many of them.

Luther is largely positive in his evaluations of specific Old Testament women. He praises Sarah, for example, for her faith and rebukes her only slightly for laughing when God told her she would have a child. He does see this laughter as stemming from her doubts and disbelief, whereas Abraham's earlier laughter at the same news is a sign of his great joy and deep faith. This distinction is not made by Zwingli and Calvin, who view both the patriarch and matriarch as tainted by doubt. On the other hand, Luther is more generous than other Reformation theologians when discussing Sarah's telling Abraham to get rid of Hagar. All of them stress that Sarah has special instructions from God, but Luther also emphasizes that she did not really order him to expel Hagar, but rather begged him, so that she was still an obedient wife, and that she spoke to him in private, not in public, so she was not asserting a public role. Even this limited challenge to male authority was not to serve as a model for other women, however.

Luther also views Rebecca as having a special dispensation from God in her deception of Isaac. He states firmly that she and Jacob are sinners against both the rule of primogeniture and their duty to obey Isaac as their husband and father. As in his commentary on Sarah, he asserts that God has given Rebecca a higher command which allows her to go against earthly structures of authority; he also notes, in contrast to other commentators who make no mention of this, that Rebecca was advised by a male minister, Eber, so did not make this decision on her own. Tamar is a more difficult case, in that Genesis does not specifically describe a special sign from God justifying her actions, but Luther views both her honor and her desire for children as explanations for her incestuous relationship with her father-in-law, Judah. This relationship is clearly a sin, but explained also as a way in which God tested the patriarch and demonstrated that he, too, was a sinner.

Luther's lectures on Genesis include long discussions of Sarah, Hagar, Rebecca, and Tamar, which are excerpted here, and also somewhat shorter discussions of other prominent women, such as Rachel and Leah, Dinah, and Potiphar's wife. They also include excursuses on minor figures who merit only a verse or two in Genesis, including Lot's wife and Rebecca's old nurse Deborah, whom Jacob buries under an oak he calls the Oak of

Weeping after she dies. Almost all of these women serve to some degree as examples of positive female behavior for Luther: Leah, though "odious and hated," is an example of maternal affection, Lot's wife, of wifely obedience, and Deborah, of women's ability to provide consolation and grandmothers' special attachment to their grandchildren. Hagar is chastised for her pride and presumption, but ultimately praised for her faith and repentance. Dinah is criticized for her youthful curiosity and her rape is used as a warning to other young women, but Luther does not blame her for instigating the attack or note that she was guilty of sexual sin as most earlier medieval commentators had; she ends her life, in his commentary, taking care of the house of her widowed father. Potiphar's wife is alone in having no redeeming virtues, and her attempts at seducing Joseph are used as a springboard for a harsh denunciation of the power of unrequited love in women.

Though Luther discusses the women of Genesis and Deborah in the book of Judges as real historical figures, he does not view Judith, who kills the tyrant Holofernes and thus saves the Jewish people, as a real woman, but as a metaphor, a "theological poem." The book of Judith, which appears in the Apocrypha, is worthy of reading, in Luther's eyes, not for its historical details but for its eternal truths. Some of the stories about women in the New Testament serve the same function. Mary and Martha are real women, not metaphors, but the primary purpose of their story is to emphasize the importance of faith (Mary) as opposed to works (Martha). Luther explicitly rejects the most common medieval allegorical interpretation, in which Mary had stood for the contemplative life and Martha for the active life in the world. Anna the prophetess is also an actual figure, though her words and even her name have symbolic meaning.

Luther also discusses the meaning of the names of the women who came to the tomb on Easter Sunday, particularly that of Mary Magdalene, whom he sets forth in several contexts as an example of strong faith. He comments that the woman who washed Christ's feet with her tears at the banquet may have been Mary Magdalene as well, and that she and the woman who had been menstruating for twelve years are true examples of the power of faith to overcome social disapproval, self-doubt, and other obstacles. Their status as outcasts makes them particularly good demonstrations of God's desire to raise the lowly and pull down the powerful. This is, in fact, the most important function of all Biblical women, including, as we saw in the last chapter, the Virgin Mary: as the lowliest of the low, as "poor," "little," "simple," "odious," and most of all "weak" (nearly every discussion of a Biblical woman mentions women's weakness), their triumphs could always be attributed directly to the power of God and the faith He created in them. This lesson in humility was not simply for female hearers and readers, but perhaps even more for men, both Biblical and contemporary, whom Luther sees as more likely than women to attribute faith or success to their own abilities.

OLD TESTAMENT WOMEN

WOMEN'S PROPHESYING, PREACHING, AND OTHER ROLES

Sermon on Joel 2:28 "I will pour out my spirit on all flesh; your sons and your daughters shall prophecy," 1531, WA XXXIV

[P. 482] Joel says here "flesh"; this means all types of people without discrimination. The Holy Spirit will be poured out in heaven, and all will prophesy. Therefore the law of Leviticus about the priesthood is repealed and a new one is given, that reads: "Your sons," daughters, young men, old women. That means all types of flesh, that is, [all types of] people. I accept women, maidens, and will teach them all how they will prophesy. Servants will come into the [priestly] office, like Hannah, or maidservants. Therefore the description of the priesthood is no longer valid. Against this it is not possible for the Jews to respond that their priests must be correct and not deformed, as with Aaron, etc. But Peter was not from a priestly family, nor were the apostles nor was Christ. None of them took on a priestly office, and they were from other tribes. None of them was from the tribe of Levi or Aaron. But Joel says, all types of people are the same as bishops, priests, popes and cardinals. This is a powerful text that knocks priesthood onto its back. It is not valid to hold onto the office of the priesthood, because this was not endowed. And it will also be that priests will come out of all tribes. Today there are the sons of peasants; it is fit and proper that they have the gift of prophecy, about which we can use the phrase "is poured out." No one is discriminated against, neither city residents nor peasants. Therefore this text truly sets up a new priesthood, that does not depend so much on the person. The four daughters of Philip were prophetesses. A woman can do this. Not preach in public, but console people and teach. A woman can do this just as much as a man. There are certainly women and girls who are able to comfort others and teach true words, that is, who can explain Scripture and teach or console other people so that they will be well. This all counts as prophesying, not preaching. In the same way, a mother should teach her children and family, because she has been given the true words of the Holy Spirit and understands...

[P. 485] Scripture says that a woman is not a woman, a man is not a man. In Christ, Caiaphas the esteemed man is no better than a toll collector.

A Carthusian who has been forty years in his order is no better than a maid who carries grass for the cows.

"Infiltrating and clandestine preachers," 1532, LW XL
From *Luther's Works*, vol. XL, edited by Hartmut Lehmann, © 1967
Fortress Press. Used by permission of Augsburg Fortress Publishers

[P. 388] Undoubtedly some maintain that in 1 Cor. 14, St. Paul gave anyone liberty to preach in the congregation, even to bark against the established preacher... What a fine model I imagine that would be, for anyone to have the right to interrupt a preacher and begin to argue with him! Soon another would join in and tell the other two to hush up. Perchance a drunk from the tavern would come in and join the trio calling on the third to be silent. At last the women too would claim the right of "sitting by," telling the men to be silent [1 Cor. 14:34]. Then one woman silencing the other – oh what a beautiful holiday, auction, and carnival that would be! What pig sties could compare in goings-on with such churches?...

[Pp. 390–91] I am astonished that in their spiritual wisdom they have not learned to adduce examples of how women have prophesied and thereby attained rule over men, lands, and people. There was Deborah (Judg. 4[:1ff.]), who caused the death of King Jabin and Sisera and ruled Israel. There was the wise woman in Abel, in David's time of whom we read in 2 Sam. 20[:13ff.]). Long before, there was Sarah, who directed her husband and lord, Abraham, to cast out Ishmael and his mother, Hagar, and God commanded Abraham to obey her. Furthermore the widow Hannah (Luke 2[:36ff.]). and the Virgin Mary (Luke 1[:46ff.]). Here they might deck themselves out and find authority for women to preach in the churches. How much greater the reason for men to preach, where and when they please.

We shall for the present not be concerned about the right of these women of the Old Testament to teach and to rule. But surely they did not act as the infiltrators do, unauthorized, and out of superior piety and wisdom. For then God would not have confirmed their ministry and worked by miracles and great deeds. But in the New Testament the Holy Spirit, speaking through St. Paul, ordained that women should be silent in churches and assemblies, and said that this is the Lord's commandment. Yet he knew that previously Joel [2:28–29] had proclaimed that God would pour out His Spirit on His handmaidens. Furthermore the four daughters of Philip prophesied (Acts 21[:9]). But in the congregations or churches where there is a ministry women are to be silent and not preach [1 Tim. 2:12]. Otherwise they may pray, sing, praise, and say "Amen," and read at home, teach each other, exhort, comfort, and interpret the Scriptures as best they can.

In sum, Paul would not tolerate the wickedness and arrogance of someone interfering with the office of another. Each one should pay attention to his own commission and call, allowing another to discharge his office unmolested and in peace. As for the rest, he may be wise, teach, sing, read, interpret to his heart's content, in matters of his concern. If God wants to accomplish something over and beyond this order of offices and calling and raise up someone who is above the prophets, He will demonstrate with signs and deeds, just as He made the ass to speak and chastise his lord, the prophet Balaam [Num. 22:21ff.]). When God does not do so we are to remain obedient to the office and authority already ordained.

TABLE TALK

WA TR I, no. 12, pp. 5–6

In praise of women, and why they are created. The Holy Spirit praises women such as Judith, Esther, Sarah, etc.; among the pagans Lucretia and Artemisia are praised. Marriage cannot exist without women, nor can the world exist. Getting married is a remedy for whoredom, it puts a check on it to some degree. For flesh and blood remain impure through and through according to their nature, until shovels are doing their work above one [i.e., until one is dead]. A wife is a friendly, gracious, and pleasant companion in life. Women bear children and raise them, rule the house and distribute in an orderly fashion whatever a man earns and brings into the household, so that nothing is wasted or frittered away on unnecessary things, but that everyone receives what he needs. For this reason they are called "treasure of the house" by the Holy Spirit, because they should be the honor, jewels, and gems of the household. They are inclined toward mercy, for they are primarily created by God for this, that they should bear children, be compassionate, and bring joy and happiness to men.

SARAH

Lectures on Genesis, LW III and IV
From *Luther's Works*, vols. III and IV, edited by Jaroslav Pelikan,
© 1968 Concordia Publishing Company. Used by permission
of Concordia Publishing House

[111, pp. 200–201, commenting on Genesis 18:9–15, in which God visits Abraham and promises him that Sarah, his wife, will have a son; Sarah overhears this, and laughs.] Sarah seems to have had some doubt concerning the promise that was given above in chapter seventeen, namely, that she herself would be the mother of the Promised Seed. Therefore the Lord calls her in order that He, in person, may strengthen her in faith. For it is the perpetual work of God to instruct, enlighten, and strengthen weak hearts through His Spirit, not to condemn them or to cast them aside because of their weakness.

Accordingly, God asks where Sarah is, and Abraham gives the short answer: "She is in the tent." An indifferent heart reads this and pays no attention to it; but by means of these few words the Holy Spirit wanted to set before all women an example to imitate, so that, just as Abraham is presented everywhere as a rule, so to speak, of faith and good works, so Sarah might give instruction about the highest virtues of a saintly and praiseworthy housewife.

For the weakness and inborn levity of this sex is well known. Women are commonly in the habit of gadding and inquiring about everything with disgraceful curiosity. Or they stand idle at the door and look either for something to see or for fresh rumors. For this reason Proverbs (7:11) states about wicked women that they have "feet that do not tarry." This is due to their curiosity to see and hear things which nevertheless do not concern them at all. Therefore levity in morals as well as garrulousness and curiosity are censured in their sex.

In the case of Sarah, however, the opposite virtues are given praise in this passage, and this by means of Abraham's brief statement that she is in the tent. If she had been inquisitive after the fashion of other women, she would have rushed to the door, would have seen the guests, would have listened to their conversations, would have interrupted them, etc.; but she does none of these things. She busies herself with her own tasks, which the household demands, and is unconcerned about the other things.

Thus Paul prescribes (Titus 2:5) that a woman should be a domestic, so to speak, one who stays in her own home and looks after her own affairs. The heathen depicted Venus as standing on a tortoise; for just as a tortoise carried its house wherever it creeps, so a wife should be concerned with the affairs of her own home and not go too far away from it. This is demanded not only by the tasks peculiar to this sex but also by the requirements of the children and domestics, who need careful supervision.

Hence it is great praise for Sarah that on this occasion she tends to her own affairs and does not offend by being curious but, like a tortoise, remains in her little shell and does not take the time required to get a brief look at the guests she has and at what kind of guests they are.

This modesty and restraint surpass all the acts of worship and all the works of all the nuns, and these words, "Sarah is in the tent," should be inscribed on the veils of all matrons; for in this way they would be reminded of their duty to beware of inquisitiveness, gadding, and garrulousness, and to accustom themselves to managing the household with care. With this brief statement Moses has described all the virtues of a good housewife, one who gladly stays at home and takes care of the management of the household, in order that the things which her husband provides may be properly allotted and administered...

[III, p. 209] If the mistress of a household does these things, what fault will a reasonable husband find in her? But alas, few concern themselves with this; they are arrogant, proud, quarrelsome, abusive, rebellious, and puffed up by their supposed wisdom. Therefore they wish to be regarded as rulers, not as wives.

[III, p. 211] Surely the Holy Spirit depicts the saintly mistress Sarah with these colors to make it clear that even though she is married, she surpasses virgins in chastity. Therefore it is a great sin for the papists to inveigh against the marriages of the patriarchs, which are most honorable workshops not only of chastity but of all other virtues. These facts should be carefully noted in order to shatter the opinions of the fanatics...

[IV, p. 189, commenting on Genesis 23:1–2, the death of Sarah] One should consider how Abraham delivered a beautiful funeral address about Sarah. For in the Holy Scriptures no other matron is so distinguished. Her years, lives, conduct, and burial place are described. In the eyes of God, therefore, Sarah was an extraordinary jewel on whom extraordinary love was bestowed, and she is mentioned deservedly by Peter as an exemplar for all saintly wives. He says (1 Peter 3:6) that she called Abraham lord and that "you are her daughters." To all Christian matrons Peter holds her up as a mother.

Scripture has no comments even on the death of the other matriarchs, just as it makes no mention of how many years Eve lived and of where she died. All the other women it passes over and covers with silence, with the result that we have no knowledge of the death of Mary, the mother of Christ. Sarah alone has this glory, that the definite number of her years, the time of her death, and the place of burial are described. Therefore this is great praise and very sure proof that she was precious in the eyes of God.

HAGAR

Lectures on Genesis, LW IV
From *Luther's Works*, vol. IV, edited by Jaroslav Pelikan, © 1968
Concordia Publishing Company. Used by permission of Concordia
Publishing House

[P. 47, commenting on Genesis 21:14–18, in which Abraham expels Hagar
and Ishmael into the desert, and they nearly die] We know that it is a great
misery and a misfortune if an exile without a fixed abode wanders about
among strange people; but the misfortune which the circumstances in this
place reveal is greater. For Hagar is both a mother and a woman, and is alone
and in the desert at that, after being cast out so suddenly from a spacious
house. And now there is a lack of provisions, and her son is dying...

[Pp. 48–49] Here good Hagar is also in such a state of violent emotion,
and Moses indicates this by the word "to wander"; for her exceedingly great
sorrow prevents her from seeing anything. Despair makes her deaf, dumb,
blind, and thoughtless. Indeed, it simply kills her so far as her senses are
concerned...

[P. 58] Then she is enlightened with a new light of the Holy Spirit, and
from a slave woman she becomes a mother of the church, who later on
instructed her descendants and warned them by her own example not to
act proudly; for, as she said, she had been a lawful wife of Abraham, the
very saintly patriarch, and had borne his first-born son. But this physical
prerogative had been of no benefit to her. Indeed, this prestige had given
rise to her pride. But after she had been cast out on account of her pride
and had been humbled, she finally attained grace.

LOT'S WIFE

Lectures on Genesis, LW III
From *Luther's Works*, vol. III, edited by Jaroslav Pelikan, © 1968
Concordia Publishing Company. Used by permission of Concordia
Publishing House

[P. 298, commenting on Genesis 19:26, in which Lot's wife looks back at the
burning of Sodom, and is turned into a pillar of salt] Lot's wife, who goes
out with her husband, was undoubtedly a believing and saintly woman;
otherwise she would neither have followed her husband in so great a disaster,
nor would she have been seized by the angels and led out. Therefore let
us reject the Jewish legends, for they make nonsensical statements that she

was inhospitable and refused the angels salt to season their food, and that for this reason she was turned into a pillar of salt. The books of the Jews are full of such absurdities. Why do they not rather direct their attention to the account itself and carefully combine the circumstances, which prove clearly that this woman was not inhospitable but was godly and saintly, in whom faith was clearly discernible, since she follows her husband without hesitation and yet had this human experience that she looks back and perishes?

From the text it is clear that Lot's wife had entered the city of Zoar with her husband. Therefore – since women are rather weak by nature – she either forgot the command of the angels, or she thought there was no longer any danger after she had come into the city from the open country. But disobedience has its punishment, and she is changed into a pillar of salt...

[Pp. 299–300] Thus this account teaches us to remain steadfast, for he who wants to be a Christian must not change his purpose: he must not look for another way or another Gospel. In this one and only way there is salvation; if you enter upon another, you have perished and are like Lot's wife. But so far as Lot's wife is concerned, this example is instruction for us rather than a condemnation of the woman, who, I fully believe, was saintly and was saved; for one should have no other presupposition concerning God's mercy, especially since she has a splendid testimony of the life she previously led, inasmuch as the angels themselves bring her out and she follows her husband.

But you will say, "Why does she perish in this manner?" My answer is: She was overcome by human weakness and, contrary to the angels' command, she suffers a temporal punishment. Nevertheless, her soul is saved, as Paul says (1 Cor. 5:5) about the incestuous man. Therefore one must hold fast to this teaching – that the saintly woman is compelled to suffer this punishment – in order that it may reach all succeeding generations. Christ says (Luke 17:32): "Remember Lot's wife."

REBECCA

Lectures on Genesis, LW IV and V
From *Luther's works*, vols. IV and V, edited by Jaroslav Pelikan,
© 1968 Concordia Publishing Company. Used by permission
of Concordia Publishing House

[IV, pp. 269–71, commenting on Genesis 24, where Abraham's servant, whom Abraham has sent to find Isaac a wife, first sees Rebecca] Holy

Scripture also praises Rebecca's beauty, for beauty is something good created by God and should by no means be despised. A little drop of external
pleasure is granted to the flesh, since our nature has either been so corrupted
or so created that we have a greater fondness for women who are beautiful, especially for those who are respectable, well-mannered, and endowed
with fine talents, those who show some promise that they will make good
housewives. Such women are very excellent gifts of God...

[IV, p. 271] Rebecca's manners and upbringing are also depicted when
Moses relates that she went out to the spring and carried a jar to draw
water. From this it is evident that she was not a lazy virgin accustomed
to leisure and luxury. No, her mother taught her and accustomed her
to the usual works of the household, no matter how mean or irksome
they were. She used her as a servant or handmaid. For this reason she
sent her to fetch water. Rebecca herself serves her mother in sincerity and
obedience. She concerns herself with nothing else than the performance
of her duty in those things which the mother of the house commands.
And she was destined to be the mother of prophets, or patriarchs, and of
Christ!...

[V, p. 110, commenting on Genesis 27, the story of Rebecca and her
son Jacob tricking Isaac into giving Jacob his blessing rather than Jacob's
older brother Esau] But now a very weighty and almost unsolvable problem
presents itself. Did Rebecca and her son Jacob have the right to lie, to deceive
the very saintly patriarch who was a blind old man, in such an important
matter, and to deprive brother Esau of the blessing and primogeniture?
For, in the first place, they sin against the Law and the rule. In the second
place, they sin against the prophecy, which Isaac did not understand in
the way she interpreted it. In the third place, they sin against the wish
and authority of the father. Besides, Rebecca appropriates to herself the
regal and priestly vestments and brings Jacob, who has been adorned with
these, to his father, who had never thought of appointing him as his heir.
This is great rashness and boldness coupled with extraordinary deception
and very great harm, for this lie is not playful or obliging but is decidedly
harmful. The primogeniture, you see, is a matter which people quarrel
about in the church and which brings with it eternal as well as temporal
life. Consequently, it is a great crime of which you would never consider
anyone, even the most worthless person, capable, much less such saintly
people as Rebecca and Jacob...

[V, pp. 113–14] Accordingly, since Jacob and Rebecca, as a result of the
prophecy and of Esau's evil fruits and morals, were sure that the primogeniture belonged to Jacob, they were in duty bound to disregard the law

and rule and to follow the exception by which God transferred the primogeniture from Esau to Jacob. Therefore Rebecca gave thought to how she
might be able to deceive her husband Isaac, her son Esau, and all who were
in the house; for now she is not obeying the rule or the law. No, she is
obeying God who transfers and dispenses contrary to the rule. Therefore
she did not sin...

[v, p. 120] Although Rebecca acted rashly, yet on account of her outstanding faith she had divine providence as her guide, so that although
father Isaac heard Jacob's voice, he, filled as he was with confidence and un-
concern, was deceived in spite of this... many things happen in the lives of
the saints in order that we may see how God governs His saints, turns their
foolishness and rashness into the greatest wisdom, and grants to their plan
which at first seemed very stupid, very beautiful results. Saintly people act
unwisely often enough, just as here Rebecca errs shamefully in her thinking.
Yet she forces her way through because she believes.

LEAH AND RACHEL

Lectures on Genesis, LW V
From *Luther's Works*, vol. V, edited by Jaroslav Pelikan, © 1968
Concordia Publishing Company. Used by permission of Concordia
Publishing House

[Pp. 314–15, commenting on Genesis 29 and 30, which relate the story of
Leah, the wife Jacob was forced to marry by her father, Laban, and Rachel,
the wife Jacob loved] Jacob has possession of his wife, for whom he has had
such a great desire. In addition, he has Leah, whom he did not love or care
about. Rachel understands this, and she has the keys and the management
of the whole household. She is always close to Jacob and is the dear girl.
But the whole house and the neighborhood attend to the lady of the house,
and they know that Leah is despised and neglected even by Jacob. For his
fondness for her springs from mercy, not from marital ardor and the love
of a bridegroom. It is only the giving of alms. Therefore wretched Leah sits
sadly in her tent with her maid and spends her time spinning and weeping.
For the rest of the household, and especially Rachel, despises her because she
has been scorned by her husband, who prefers Rachel and is desperately
in love with Rachel alone. She is not beautiful, not pleasing. No, she is
odious and hated. There the poor girl sits; no one pays any attention to
her. Rachel gives herself airs before her; she does not deign to look at her.
"I am the lady of the house," she thought, "Leah is a slave." These are truly

carnal things in the saintly fathers and mothers, like the things that usually happen in our houses...

[P. 317, commenting on Leah's giving birth to her first son Reuben] The fruitfulness and childbearing of women has always been regarded as an outstanding blessing even among the heathen, and for this reason women were held in honor. In Rome men were forbidden to wear gold, but women were permitted to do so. Therefore Leah is now a great lady, for she is fruitful and gives birth before her sister does, who, as all wished and hoped, would give birth first. But when Rachel heard this, she was undoubtedly impelled to envy and hate her sister, and the whole household was also amazed at this wonderful change. But God did it. He has regard for what is lowly and cast off...

[P. 331, commenting on Rachel's cry to Jacob that she must have children or die] Rachel is set forth as an example of very beautiful and motherly affection and chastity. The only thing she seeks is offspring from her flesh. Likewise Leah. They [the papists] hear that these people [Leah and Rachel] give utterance to nothing else than "The Lord has given; the Lord has blessed."... All their conversations are about God, about His blessings and works yet the papists regard all these things as sins, and they consider the saintly matrons as unworthy of having examples set forth in the church.

What better and more useful thing can be taught in the church than the example of a godly mother of a household who prays, sighs, cries out, gives thanks, rules the house, performs the function of sex, and desires offspring with the greatest chastity, gratitude, and godliness? What more should she do? But the pope, the cardinals, and the bishops should not see this, for they are not worthy. The Holy Spirit allowed them to walk in wonderful and superheavenly things and to admire their chastity, which is worthy of brothels. But they should by no means see these things. In the meantime He governs the saintly women in such a way that He gives evidence that they are His creation and that He wants to rule them not only according to the spirit but also according to the flesh, in order that they may call upon and adore God, give thanks for their offspring, be obedient to their husband, etc...

[P. 351] Leah wishes to please her husband with her fertility, which is a most praiseworthy virtue in a wife who desires to dwell with her husband and not to follow a stranger, yes, to be anxious to please this husband alone, to have the favor of him alone, but especially such a great man, to whom the Savior of the world was promised. Therefore these are truly and most especially manifestations of marital love full of godliness, chastity, and obedience, not of lust, as the Roman sow and many of the fathers and monks have interpreted it...

[P. 355] The saintly women desire nothing else than the natural fruit of their bodies. For by nature woman has been created for the purpose of bearing children. Therefore she has breasts; she has arms for the purpose of nourishing, cherishing, and carrying her offspring. It was the intention of the Creator that women should bear children and that men should beget them – with the exception of those men whom God Himself has excepted...

[P. 362] Rachel herself points out sufficiently what her cross and trial was. For she says: "He has gathered up my reproach." For five or six years in succession she bore reproach and disgrace on account of her sterility, and in her own judgment and in the judgment of others she was regarded as the most wretched of women. For she saw that her sister was fruitful; she saw that the maidservants, her sister's and her own, and all other women bore children and for this reason were praised, loved, and held in honor. "But I alone," she thought, "am regarded as rejected and cursed. The Lord, however, has seen all this manifold and burdensome reproach and disgrace which I have borne, and He has gathered it up and removed it from me. Now I am the wife and mother of the house"...

Elizabeth, the mother of John the Baptist, also gives thanks in nearly the same words when she says (Luke 1:25): "Thus the Lord has done to me in the days when He looked on men, to take away my reproach among men"...

DINAH

Lectures on Genesis, LW VI
From *Luther's Works*, vol. VI, edited by Jaroslav Pelikan, © 1968
Concordia Publishing Company. Used by permission of Concordia
Publishing House

[Pp. 192–93, commenting on Genesis 34:1–2, in which Dinah, the daughter of Jacob and Leah, went out to see the girls of the region in which she was living, and was raped by Shechem, the son of the prince] Dinah wanted to see the daughters of this region, how they were decked out and adorned and how beautiful they were. The text seems to indicate the same, namely, that she was curious, since, indeed, she went out without the permission of her father and mother, on her own without a companion. She is too secure and confident, for she was still a child and did not fear any danger to her modesty. It seems, then, that she sinned out of curiosity, because she went out to the daughters of the land and their associates without consulting her parents. By nature girls find pleasure in the society of other maidens of equal age in their neighborhood. Meanwhile, the brothers are away from home in the field. Leah is at home with her little daughter Dinah, who goes out without consulting her mother. Accordingly, it is an example which should be carefully noted and inculcated in girls. They should not form the habit of strolling about and looking out of the window (cf. 2 Sam. 6:16) and lounging around the door, but should stay at home and never go anywhere without the permission of their parents or without companions. For the devil is laying snares against the modesty of this sex, which by nature is weak, irresponsible, and foolish and hence exposed to the snares of Satan.

TAMAR

Lectures on Genesis, LW VII

From *Luther's Works*, vol. VII, edited by Jaroslav Pelikan, © 1968
Concordia Publishing Company. Used by permission of Concordia
Publishing House

[P. 17, commenting on Genesis 38:6–30, in which Judah marries Tamar to two of his sons in succession and God kills both of them. He then neglects to do so with his third son, so Tamar eventually feels dishonored, dresses as a prostitute, and goes to Judah. He does not recognize her and has sex with her, and she becomes pregnant by him with twins. Judah orders her killed, but she proves the twins are his and takes back her honorable widow's clothing.] The name of the wife was Tamar. It is not certain whose daughter she was. We take for granted that she was a Canaanite woman, just as the wife of Judah was. But it is necessary to mention her, and this chapter is written for her sake alone; for she is a mother of the Savior, God's Son, for whose sake all holy Scripture had been given, in order that He might become known and be celebrated. From this Tamar, then, the Messiah was descended, even though through an incestuous defilement...

[P. 22] Tamar was an unhappy woman, and it appears in general that this sex was decidedly servile and degraded among that people and was forced to seek a livelihood by its own labor, by spinning and weaving. Thus Tamar seems to have supported herself with difficulty and in a wretched manner, by weaving and washing. And we heard above (Gen. 31) that Laban was made wealthy through the labors of his daughters Rachel and

Leah... [pp. 27–28] Tamar rages, and not without cause. Although she acts foolishly, she feels more indignation than lust in her heart. For she thinks: "Behold, I have been despised and rejected without any cause, and I shall have to bear this perpetual reproach. That I was a wife according to the law but was rejected by my father-in-law without any guilt or crime on my part. Thus I shall be deprived of the fruit of my womb, and no hope of another marriage is left; but I, deserted and scorned, shall be compelled to spend my whole life in perpetual and extraordinary sorrow." Therefore she goes as far as she can. And thus it is certain that she resorts to extreme measures to see whether she can deceive Judah... The law gives her courage, although reverence for this blood relationship should have deterred her. For this is incest. But because of indignation and because she is unable to bear that reproach and abuse, she has the audacity to perpetuate a disgraceful crime altogether unbecoming to her...

[P. 45] But what the duty of the saintly matrons Sarah, Rebecca, Leah, Rachel, and Tamar was is clear from the histories of the patriarchs. They were the wives of shepherds. Therefore they administered the household and took care of the stock. They milked cows and goats; they collected wool, milk, cheese, butter, and suchlike... They were excellent matrons. They were not spoiled by ease and luxury but were industrious and diligent in their household duty.

POTIPHAR'S WIFE

Lectures on Genesis, LW VII
From *Luther's Works*, vol. VII, edited by Jaroslav Pelikan, © 1968
Concordia Publishing Company. Used by permission of Concordia
Publishing House

[P. 79, commenting on Genesis 39:6–15, in which the wife of Potiphar, an Egyptian official, attempts to seduce Joseph, who is a slave in their house] She did not cease urging her wicked and impious demand, no matter how much Joseph tried to dissuade her and to deter her from her disgraceful love. Thus he preaches earnestly and in a saintly manner for the purpose of turning her from the raging of lust...

[Pp. 87–88] Joseph flees and leaves his garment in the woman's hand. From this it is apparent that she held him in her grasp with all her strength and tried to bend him to her will not only with her lips, embrace, and kisses but even wanted to keep him there by force, and that she threatened that if he did not obey her, she would arouse all the neighbors by her shouts, with the result that they would punish him severely for plotting against her chastity.

This, to be sure, was a very fierce battle against the very wicked and shameless harlot. For she sees that all her strongest arguments, plots, opportunities, wishes, and thoughts, and all her plans, are in vain. Therefore she despairs of subduing his inflexible heart of iron; and her love is changed into madness, as usually happens. When women accomplish nothing with their blandishments and charms, they are driven to madness, so that they want those whose love they are not permitted to enjoy to be destroyed.

JUDITH

Foreword to the book of Judith, WA Bibel XX, pp. 5–7

Some people think that this is not a history, but a beautiful spiritual poem, written by a holy and reverent man who wanted to paint and portray the successes and victories of the entire Jewish people against all of their enemies, which God miraculously gave to them at all times. Just like Solomon, in his song, also writes and sings about a bride, but is not talking about a person or a story, but about the whole people of Israel. And as St. John, in the Book of Revelation, and Daniel, speak of animals and paint pictures, in which they are not talking about specific people, but about the whole Christian Church or the kingdom. And Christ our Lord himself speaks in a roundabout way with metaphors and stories in the Gospels, and compares heaven to ten virgins, or a merchant and pearls, a woman baking, a mustard seed, or fishers and nets, or shepherds and sheep, etc.

This opinion pleases me almost completely, and I think that the poet intentionally and energetically made errors in terms of the chronology and the names to warn the reader that he is to regard and understand it as a spiritual and holy poem.

The names also fit with this interpretation. For Judith means Judea, that is, the Jewish people; she is a chaste and pious widow, just as God's people are also widows who have been left behind, but are chaste and pious. They stay pure and holy in the word of God and in correct belief, live devoutly, and pray. Holofernes means a general or governor of the heathens, a heathen, godless, or unchristian lord or prince, who was always an enemy to the Jewish people. Bethulia (a city that is also not otherwise known) means a virgin, in order to show that at that time the pious and believing Jews were pure as virgins, without any idolatry or unbelief.

WA TR I, no. 444, pp. 193–94
I consider Judith to be a poem. Judith is Judea; Holofernes and Nebu-
chadnezzar are all kings; Hosea is a prince and Bethulia is the virgin Israel,
and this is its meaning: that the people of God will defeat the devil and all
things. Thus Judith is a theological poem.

NEW TESTAMENT WOMEN

WOMEN'S ROLE

On the councils and the church, 1539, LW XLI
From *Luther's Works*, vol. XLI, edited by Hartmut Lehmann, © 1967
Fortress Press. Used by permission of Augsburg Fortress Publishers

[Pp. 154–55] The church is recognized externally by the fact that it con-
secrates or calls ministers, or has offices that it is to administer... The
people as a whole cannot do these things, but must entrust them or have
them entrusted to one person. Otherwise, what would happen if everyone wanted to speak and administer, and no one wanted to give way to the
other? It must be entrusted to one person, and he alone should be allowed to
preach, to baptize, to absolve, and to administer the sacraments. The others
should be content with this arrangement and agree to it. Wherever you see
this done, be assured that God's people, the holy Christian people, are
present.

It is, however, true that the Holy Spirit has excepted women, children,
and incompetent people from this function, but chooses (except in emer-
gencies) only competent males to fill this office, as one reads here and there
in the epistles of St. Paul that a bishop must be pious, able to teach, and the
husband of one wife – and in 1 Corinthians 14[:34] he says, "The women
should keep silence in the churches." In summary, it must be a competent
and chosen man. Children, women, and other persons are not qualified for
this office, even though they are able to hear God's word, to receive baptism,
the sacrament, absolutions, and are also true, holy Christians, as St. Peter
says [1 Pet. 3:7]. Even nature and God's creation makes this distinction,
implying that women (much less children or fools) cannot and shall not
occupy positions of sovereignty, as experience also suggests and as Moses
says in Genesis 3[:16], "You shall be subject to man." The gospel, however,

does not abrogate this natural law, but confirms it as the ordinance and creation of God.

ANNA THE PROPHETESS

Sermon on the gospel for the Sunday after Christmas,
Luke 2[:33–40], 1521, LW LII
From *Luther's Works*, vol. LII, edited by Hans J. Hillerbrand, © 1974
Fortress Press. Used by permission of Augsburg Fortress Publishers

[Pp. 123–24] In the first place Luke says that she was a prophetess, without a doubt a saintly, pious prophetess. Assuredly the Holy Spirit was in her, and so she was good and justified without any work; her subsequent works were also good and justified. You see that St. Luke does not wish to say that she became pious and a prophetess through works, but that she was, first of all, a pious prophetess and that good works came into being through her. Why do you want to destroy her example and the Gospel and turn them upside down, reading first and solely about works, when Luke writes first of the character and not of works.

In the second place Luke praises her as a widow who performed works suitable to her widowhood and stayed with her station in life. But thereby Luke does not cite these works as if they alone were the right kind of good works and divine service, rejecting all others. St. Paul, 1 Timothy 5[:3–6], describes a widow's life as follows: "Those widows you shall honor who are widows indeed. For if there is a widow who has children and grandchildren, she shall first learn to manage her household in a Christian manner and to do good in turn to her parents; that is pleasing to God and good. The one, however, who is a widow indeed and alone, she places her hope in God and continues in prayer day and night. The one, however, who lives in pleasure is dead while she is still living."

From this you see that Anna must have been a lone widow, without children and parents to take care of – otherwise she would not have served God, but the devil, by never leaving the church and neglecting to manage her household in a God-pleasing manner. Luke indicates this when he writes that she had been a widow until her eighty-fourth year. Everyone can easily calculate that her parents must have been dead and her children provided for, so that she, being an old mother, was taken care of by them and that there was henceforth nothing more for her to do except pray, and to fast, and to forego all carnal desires. Luke does not say that she had lived all of her eighty-four years in this manner, but that she began to live thus at the time when Christ was born and brought into the temple, when, children and parents having been taken care of, she became very lonesome.

And so it is a rather dangerous thing, if one looks only at the works and not at the person or station or calling. It is most unpleasing to God for somebody to give up the duties of his calling or station and to want to take up the works of the saints. Hence if a married woman should want to follow Anna and forsake her husband and children, house and parents, in order to go on a pilgrimage, to pray, to fast, to go to church, she would only tempt God. To confound the matrimonial estate, and that of widowhood, to leave one's own calling and to attach oneself to alien undertakings, surely amounts to walking on one's ears, to veiling one's feet, to putting a shoe on one's head, and to turning everything upside down. Good works must be performed, and one should pray and fast to the extent that the work of one's calling and station are not neglected or impeded. Serving God is not tied to one or two works, nor is it confined to one or two callings, but it is distributed over all works and all callings. Anna's work and that of lonely widows is nothing but fasting and praying, and St. Luke agrees with St. Paul. The work of a married woman is not continuous praying and fasting, but the godly administration of children and the household, and the taking care of parents, as St. Paul says [1 Tim. 5:4]...

[Pp. 140–41] This saintly woman was also shown that she was worthy of great honor in that she received the grace to recognize in this poor child the true Savior. Undoubtedly, there were priests present who received similar offerings from Mary and Joseph and yet did not recognize the child, and who, perhaps, considered the words of Simeon and Anna as old wives' tales. There must have been a special illumination of the Spirit in her, and she must have been regarded as a great saint in the eyes of God, that He gave her the light in preference to all other people.

TABLE TALK

WA TR V, no. 5840, p. 377

Aged Anna. (Luke 2:36) Old Anna made the testimony of her prophecy known to the listeners in the synagogue. She was old at the time of Christ's birth, but Mary was young, for she refers to the new church. Anna means "God's grace and compassion." She knew nothing except to praise the God of her husband. We are all God's little chicks, that is, we have nothing more to do than praise God's grace. [Anna was] a daughter of Phanuel. Phanuel means the face of God, and it is what Jacob named the place where he wrestled with the angel (Genesis 32:30). However, the face of God signifies the recognition of God. She [Anna] was from the lineage that had been created by the recognition of God, the lineage of Asser (salvation in marriage, under the law in outward behavior). For just as a wife is under duress in marriage, so are the Jews under the law. Romans 7: the Law is, etc. She had been a widow for more than eighty-four years, that is, twelve times longer than she had been a wife. That is, life after the Law – which is the belief in Jesus Christ - is twelve times or rather uncountably longer than the Law. This is why we get twelve apostles but only one preacher of the Law, Moses. Her days of being a virgin were not counted, for the unfruitful life before the Law and before grace is nothing; for this reason virginity was despised in the Law. The temple is Scripture; she let herself be found there. Not like the Jews, who build new temples outside the gates, in the mountains and the fields, even though Moses had forbidden them to do this in Deuteronomy 5 and 12, or like us, who tear down our temples and want to shove the Bible behind the bench.

MARY AND MARTHA

Sermon on the day of Mary's Ascension, 1523 (Luke 10:38–41),
WA XII, pp. 651–54

We can dismiss what has been said until now about the active and the contemplative life. Even if it comes from Augustine or others, I would cover up their words and let them be unknown. For we know no life on earth except for one of faith and charity. Truly, the contemplative life has been established, but you must be called to this by God. The word of God obliges us first to listen and believe, and then next to love. Those who do this, walk well. Those who do not, go to the devil...

We are discussing this Gospel and other Gospels. Mary hears the word, Martha wants Mary to stop listening to the word, and Christ makes a judgment. I make a distinction between faith and works. This is the difference between heaven and earth. Faith is higher than life, and all people's works are transitory things; there is nothing except the word of God and faith. The word remains eternally, and is steadfast against the devil, death, and hell. The word of God is a "strength of God" which alone allows us to be justified and freed from sin, death, and hell without all works or before we have done them. It is thus not said that we should "do works and become godly." We see Mary here doing nothing except sitting still. But the word alone allows her to become godly. If it was different, he would have said, "Mary, go and do something here or there." But he wants to let her stay. Not only stay, but also get nothing done. He does not reject Martha's works, but he says "You worry, and that is also the right portion, but you want to force Mary away from the word." As it were, he said: "Martha, understand this – first there is the pure word and faith hangs on this. My word is eternal, your works will pass by in an instant"...

Martha did badly in this; she should no longer be troubled, but let Mary listen to the word and not fault her. It is in our nature, however, not to be satisfied with faith, but to require works as well. We should be active, but we should not worry. The word is for me, works are for my neighbor. Works do not make you godly, but they make you useful. This story should be helpful for those who serve the belly or are gluttons. Martha has been like a cook, she wants to care for people's bellies. Although it is good to feed those who appreciate it, yet he wants this appreciation to remain small, and regards more highly those whose bellies are hungry for the spirit. Christ forgets about eating with his preaching. And if Christ said: "Do not worry about what you will eat." "First try to obtain the kingdom of God." If he orders this, Mary pleases him. This is what Luke means here.

Two realms are necessary in the world; one cannot force a Christian life to be ruled by Law... The house is the kingdom of Israel, the people who are under the Law. Martha is the pious Jews, who have made all supporting laws, and have drawn up rules. Christ lets these remain, but meanwhile he sets up another realm and preaches the word. It is the spirit that is within Christianity, and not works, as is often thought. But they voluntarily follow this [the spirit] with that which pleases God. They do not have to be restricted to certain times or days. Such people want to have Christ, they cling only to his word...

The word must be free to go, which does not mean that we place it under the secular power and let it be forced by laws. In this house God keeps one of His own, that is to say, Mary. Here He obliges us to be the same. But I do not want this to be forced, but done freely and willingly, only done because I want to be helpful to you. If it is possible to be in convents or monasteries, good, be there. Anything that we do, we should do freely. Those who do not want to do it willingly, leave. If today one does not have the desire, return [from there] tomorrow. A Christian will not be bound; if he is willing, he will do it freely without force. Christ rules in the world in this way, and does not make Christians as we commonly do, putting them all in positions that are not free, in monasteries or convents. Just as he says "Martha, you are being forced, and you suffer from this." Mary stays quiet and yet she does works, with a willing heart, by choice. We see the same thing in many people. If the Gospel is proclaimed, they become rough people, if the Law [is preached] then they become intolerable to the heart of God. If the Gospel [is preached], they become intolerable to the heart of the world.

WOMAN WITH THE ISSUE OF BLOOD

Sermon on the 24th Sunday after Trinity, 1533 (Matthew 9), WA XXII, pp. 394–97

[The first and third parts of this sermon concern the raising of the centurion's daughter; the second concerns the woman with the issue of blood, Matthew 9:20–22: And behold, a woman who had suffered from a hemorrhage for twelve years came up behind him and touched the fringe of his garment; for she said to herself, "If only I touch his garment, I shall be made well." Jesus turned, and seeing her he said, "Take heart daughter; your faith has made you well." And instantly the woman was made well.]

The second example of belief is not to be praised any less. This is the poor woman who had a flow of blood for twelve years, through which she must certainly have lost all the strength in her body and also come to have doubts about any human help or encouragement. She also came to Christ as soon as she heard about him and could come to him, with certain undoubting trust that he could help her in her need and the full confidence that he was so pious and kind that he would help her and not let her go away. Of this she was so certain and secure that her heart no longer had any worries or concerns, although she had many reasons to do so and no doubt had many strong feelings nudging her into doubt, as we will hear. But she was only worried about how she might reach the Lord Christ, and she thought, "Oh, if I could only touch the hem of his garment." With this [thought] she realized for certain what the consequences would be, for she said, "I would become healthy." But then she did not know how she would reach him, because she saw that the crowd of people around this man was very large, and as a poor sick woman she could not break through this crowd. There was also the law that she was not supposed to be among people. But her belief drove her on, and she did not run away, but made her way through the people until she reached him from behind and touched his garment.

Here you can see how her faith was able to overcome two great obstacles. First, [she believed] that he was so powerful he would know that she had the faith that she would certainly be helped if only she touched his garment. She knew it was not necessary to come before him, explain her complaints and make the request that he should take pity on her and help her with many words, nor [was it necessary] that others would have to ask for her, but only that she got to him and touched him. If only that could happen, she would certainly be helped. She did not doubt, either in his power or in his will. She did not think it necessary to talk with him, but she was so sure of his help that she knew she would not fail if she only touched the outermost part of him...

And see what faith in this person Christ is and does. It creates a heart that holds him to be the Lord and Savior, God's Son, through whom God is revealed and His grace is promised to us, through whom He hears and helps us for his sake. This is true, spiritual inward service to God; the heart approaches Christ and calls to him, even if it does not speak a word. It gives him honor, believes him to be the savior who knows and hears the heart's secret wishes, and shows his help and strength, even if he does not outwardly indicate this, as we think, feel, and fumble around.

The other masterpiece of her belief is that she can overcome her own unworthiness and throw down the huge stone that presses her heart and makes her so hesitant that she would not let herself come into Christ's view the way other people did. That is the judgment of the Law in her case, through which she was an unclean woman, and was forbidden the company of other people. For Moses says in the fifteenth chapter of the third book [Leviticus 15:19–30] that women will be unclean as long as they have their flow of blood [i.e., are menstruating]. All that they have around and on them is also unclean, and those who touch them, or touch what they have touched, will also be unclean, etc.

This was not a minor trouble; not only because of her illness and loathsome uncleanness, but because she saw and experienced God's punishment because of this laid on her in front of all people: she must be separated from the community of God's people, and this for twelve whole years. She had tried everything with every doctor and nothing had helped, but it became steadily worse. She had to think that God had punished her in particular for her sins and did not want to help her. She must have doubted all human advice and contemplated that she would die of this plague and punishment.

Because of this there must have been some conflict [in her mind] as her faith sought to obtain what she wanted in Christ. She must have thought: "See, I am an unclean woman, punished by God, which everyone knows. If I come to this man, everyone, including him, will justly damn me because I come before his eyes so unashamedly and presumptuously. I would thus be more likely to merit anger and the harsh punishment of God from him than grace. I must admit that it would be proper if he were to push me away from him with anger." These conflicts are also evident (as the text says) in the fact that as she saw that she had been seen, she was terrified and trembled. Even after she had been helped, she worried that he would be angry with her because she had not been ashamed to come near him and secretly steal help from him.

Her faith pulled her through all this; she believed completely in the good and gracious heart of this Christ, and this drove her through her doubts, so that she appeared before God unashamed...

WOMEN AT THE TOMB

Sermons from the Year 1529, WA XXIX, pp. 272–73

You see that the Resurrection remained such a secret, that no one knew about it until it was announced by the angels, and afterwards by the weak women... What were the pious women and the dear disciples lacking, that in the empty tomb they concluded that Christ had been there, but did not understand the Resurrection of Christ without this being proclaimed in words? It is therefore the word that is the chariot of the knowledge of God. Those who seek without the word will find an empty grave but will not recognize Christ... The angels said: "Why do you seek the living among the dead?" The Gospel is preached here, which says, do not seek Christ among the dead, Christ is higher than all the dead. You will not find him among the dead. Pope Gregory said that the women seeking Christ with perfumes and ointments discovered this – that you will not find him with good works, but with the word and preaching and hearing, not with doing. The women sought him with expensive ointment, but the angel said "do not seek him" and punished their seeking. What else did he do? He announced the Resurrection. The words indicate this, that he is not with the dead, but resurrected. This is the preaching of the Gospel, that Christ is not reached with good works, but with listening to words. The works of the women are indeed good, but they are lost. And also the announcement, "He is not here." This is not spoken for the rabble, but for Christians, though scholars in the schools and kings do not comprehend. A Christian understands, for this applies to him; he will therefore want to proclaim it. And these were women. See, it must happen [like this], that the proclamation of the Resurrection of Christ was from angels and women, and that men were not the first. No man heard this, but only women. Examine the proclamation, namely that of the angels, and next the words. Both of them are strong enough and powerful, and we are certain of the words. But the disciples, to whom the poor, simple, shocked women brought the words – what absurdly foolish men, that this treasure should be preached [first] to the weakest vessel [i.e., women]! In this there is nothing wrong with Christianity, just with the disciples. They are too weak for such strong teaching. The women remain disciples and the disciples remain women! Hearing these words from women certainly makes them [especially] fragile. But the poor women were not put down because of their weakness; they saw Christ, and understood him to be resurrected, and they understood through these words [his] power over Satan, death, and sin. Mary Magdalene: Mary means the star of the sea. Magdalene means a good strong castle, a tower. The names of these women indicate their illustriousness. It is a poor Mary, a little drop. But she is also a Magdalene, a very strong tower in the name of the Lord. Thus there is the greatest strength in the greatest weakness. Satan can lick up the little drop with his hot tongue, but it is not possible for him to conquer the strong tower. And also "Jacobi": "one who takes shelter"; Salome, "a peaceful one"; all these names allude to their affections and influence...

No matter what type of works you seek to enter heaven with, he throws them on a heap. The justification of the fool Mary Magdalene, who came to the grave with her container thinking Jesus was dead and not living, but saw that the stone had been rolled away, is just the same. The good intentions of the women cover over their foolishness. But all the deeds of the women were forgotten when they got the words of the angel. For this their names are enough: "Tower," "She who tramples," "Peacemaker"; the preeminence of these words leaves behind the empty tomb. I am also still a weak disciple of these teachings; I also depend on the container and the salve and the grave, and do not have confidence in or cling to the words, just as the women first were affected; the Lord sustains us.

MARY MAGDALENE

Sermons from the Year 1529, WA XXIX, pp. 276, 277
Certain doctors hold and put forward this sound doctrine... in such a way that there can be no doubt or uneasiness about their word. The teachers are not lacking but rather the pupils. For indeed on account of the weakness of their faith, they are unable to bring themselves to hold these things... Trembling women, who are the neighbors of full fear and death and because of that are not strong enough to comprehend or grasp this doctrine, are those by whom it must be accepted. It is a great comfort, expressed to us in these little women by the word, since they are the form and figure of all who desire to cling to the word. Their faith is so weak that it should not be possible for them to believe it. They are all dejected, weak, scorned, and wretched, so that we might know that not the righteous, not the powerful,

not the strong, but the troubled sinners, the dejected and scorned adhere to the word of God before the world. And this itself has been represented in the name of this little woman, Mary Magdalene. For Mary means "a drop of the sea" in Hebrew, and Magdalene means "fortress." Therefore, she is like a certain drop that is scattered and thrown down by the wind; yet she is none the less the most secure fortress and firmest fortification, which no one can conquer. Solomon speaks of this idea in Proverbs, "The name of the Lord is the strongest tower; the righteous man runs to it and is saved." And this holds true for all the pious and faithful. In appearance they are barely the smallest drop of water, but they are actually the strongest and most invincible rocks.

Mary says, "What shall we do? We will effect nothing"... Scripture says that man is of greater courage and stronger body than woman, [but] the most splendid preaching of the angel is revealed to the weakest vessel... You see in those women the great, excellent, unconquerable strength which they hold from the word since they stand against all the insults of the devil. For, by themselves, women are absurd [and] foolish. Thus it is appropriate, and packed into them is a combination of weakness, strength, wealth, [and] poverty because those who take up the Gospel are Magdalene, weak, and nevertheless the word which they hear goes through death [and] sin. By this, the Evangelist wanted to indicate that the Gospel brings this immense treasure for us, even if we are weak, provided that we do not fight against it. Mary means a star of the sea, Magdalene a good, firm, strong castle. Therefore, John calls her alone by name.

Sermon on the day of Mary Magdalene, 1544 (Luke 7:36–50),
WA LII, pp. 664–70, 673

This is a wonderful story, that should rightfully be preached on a special day every year in the church, for it highlights two of the most important points of Christian belief, that is, what correct penance is, and how one comes to the forgiveness of sins. Those who see this story with just their fleshly eyes and judge it by its outward appearance, however, will not only not see anything special here, but also have the grounds, just as the Pharisees do here, to become angry and let the whole matter become offensive. For it is considered very bad, when a woman runs into a strange house and shoves her way past honorable, respectable people who are sitting at the dinner table. For that reason the Pharisee became angry with the woman here, and indeed became so angry that though he had earlier regarded Christ as a prophet, he thought now that he was not much of a prophet. For if he were a prophet, he would certainly have pushed this woman of ill fame away and not tolerated her at a party in a strange house with such fine and honorable people.

But those who understand this story correctly and who want to know this woman correctly do not look only at her external actions, but they look in her heart, where they will get a much different idea about her intentions. But how can we look in her heart? Is she not totally silent? If she said something, one could probably understand enough from her words so that one knew what she had in mind, but this is an action with no words. But look carefully at her actions, for these are not voiceless actions, but they speak and show very well what type of heart this poor woman had, for she followed after the Lord, laid herself at his feet and cried bitterly. Is it not true that this is a sign that she is certainly not wanton, but is deeply troubled in her heart? Such bitter crying does not come from a happy heart. Sadness, grief, care, fear, terror and deep worries are the real fountain out of which such heart's water pours. Her bitter tears are the first way that we can know her.

She does not say why her heart is so troubled, but Lord Christ understands this very well and says this clearly in plain terms twice. First he says to Simon, "Her sins, which are many, are forgiven." And after that he says to her, "Your sins are forgiven." That is the reason that she does not stay at home, but goes out among the people; she knows that she will find Christ. She does not question or judge or discuss with other people what she wants; the only thing that matters is that she comes to Christ and can hear his grace-filled words: "Your sins are forgiven."

This is the first thing that was required in the woman toward Christ; she was not secure or self-righteous like the Pharisees, but recognized her sins and desired from her heart to be free from them. She said this not with words, but her crying showed this, as Christ himself understood and explained.

The second point is that she did not know how to approach Christ in an agreeable way or uncover and show the love that she felt for him. She lay down at his feet, which she wet with her tears, dried with her hair, kissed, and anointed with expensive ointment. This is a sign that the Lord Christ was not a stranger to her. This was the other virtue that pleased the Lord Christ very much, so that he did not want the poor woman to be criticized or punished by his host...

The Evangelist does not give a name to this poor woman, but it is very possible that this was Mary Magdalene, for in the following chapter the Evangelist mentions that the Lord drove seven demons out of her and that she followed the Lord wherever he was preaching. Whatever her name is, it is true that she was a poor sinner and had let the devil lead her into whoredom, adultery, and other sins, and it is not necessary to tell you what harm such sins do to the soul, body, and spirit, for one sees this before one's eyes every day. She had fallen into such troubles and perhaps stayed there for many years, but then our Lord Christ began to do miracles and preach, and this poor woman also came to hear him preach, and her heart was so troubled that she looked inside herself and said to herself: "You wretched person, how have you proven yourself that you are living contrary to God's commandments, have given in to immorality and have pulled others also into danger to their bodies and souls? If God's judgment came now, what would your villainy reduce you to? Instead of shameful joy and debauchery there would be eternal pain and damnation. Oh God, be gracious, forgive me my sins, do not damn me, I will repent and leave my villainy and improve my life!"

That is true penance, that one does not continue in sin, but thinks it over, lets it be, and finally follows another life . . .

It is natural to love and hold dear those who are friendly toward you and can be advantageous to you, and to be hostile to those who are your enemies or have done you harm. For that reason Simon answers, "The one who was forgiven more" when asked who would love more. He who does not believe that God has forgiven all sins and lifted the punishment for sin – eternal death – might say that he loves God with his mouth, but it is impossible that this is truly in his heart. For that reason the Lord makes a distinction here between the poor sinful woman and the holy Pharisee, his host: "Those for whom much is forgiven" (he says) "love much." The Lord demonstrates this with the comparison of the two debtors, and then he says, "This poor woman has loved much." She showed this with her actions, for she had wet his feet with her tears, dried them with her hair, kissed them with her mouth, and anointed them with precious ointment. He spoke to his host again: "You did not love me, for you did not do what this poor woman has done for me." What conclusions can we draw from this syllogism? Nothing other than what the Lord himself concludes very succinctly and exactly: "I say to you, those for whom many sins are forgiven, love greatly. Your sins and those of your colleagues are not forgiven, but you sit in the middle of them up to your eyes, and you will die and be destroyed in them. For I can feel no special love from you toward me, a love which would certainly be there if you recognized yourselves as sinners and believed that you would be free of your sins through me."

The papists use these words to answer our teachings about faith, and say that because Christ says "much is forgiven in her because she loved much" forgiveness of sins comes through her love, rather than through faith. But this is not the meaning, for the point is right there, that love is a result of faith: "Those to whom much is given" (says the Lord) "love much." Therefore, those who have had their sins forgiven and believe, love. If this has not happened, there is no love...

WA TR V, no. 6100, p. 488

As Doctor Luther's wife smeared his legs [with salve] to help his lameness, he said: "Though you are smearing salve on me, at one time women were smeared. For the word 'woman [*uxor*]' in Latin comes from smearing, from applying unguents or ointments. For the heathens saw that marriage had much unpleasantness and many obstacles and dangers, and against such bad luck they smeared ointment on the doorposts of new brides.

"When women accept the teaching of the Gospel, they are much stronger and more ardent in their beliefs than men, and they hold to these much more firmly and solidly. We see this in the dear Anastasia, and Mary Magdalene was more valiant than Peter."

CHAPTER 5

Marriage and the family

Martin Luther became a family man, and he wanted everyone else to be situated similarly. He saw one of his primary targets as the celibate life of the Catholic clergy and nuns. He rhetorically took aim at it over and over again, across the span of his career. Celibacy could lead to no good, he reiterated, but only to fornication and social disorder. He attacked Catholic vows on two primary grounds, both Biblical. First, God had ordained marriage as His first estate when He created Eve out of Adam's rib and brought her to him; this presentation constituted the first wedding. Second, in order to ensure the propagation of the human race, He had – one must assume after the Fall – implanted in Adam and Eve, and in their progeny down through the ages, an irresistible sexual desire that found no other release than through sexual acts. The only such acts that accorded with God's plan for reproduction were potentially generative ones between wife and husband. All others He condemned.

The perpetuation of the species and the channeling of the sex drive were primary reasons for marriage, but others were close behind. Wives and husbands shared the burden of work, their proper spheres complementing each other. The Reformer was adamant concerning men's proper activities in the public arena and women's adherence to the home. The husband went out to engage in whatever activities enabled him to earn his and his dependants' livelihood, and the wife frugally disposed of whatever he brought in. Technically, the husband was as much in charge of the household as he was of the workshop or market-stall, yet he could delegate the domestic administration to his wife. Marriage was connected not just to two individuals but to the place where they dwelled and to their personal economy.

Marriage was also meant to be an intimate, emotion-laden, rewarding bond. Nothing, Luther wrote, was as sweet as "bridal love," the intense feeling that bride and groom bore exclusively for one another. This bridal love provided a foundation that could sustain a married couple through the tribulations that ineluctably came, whether from illness, children's crying and mischief, or poverty. Throughout such trials, husband and wife "cleaved to" and comforted one another.

Luther well knew that such ideal marriages were rare. Even after the founding of marriage courts in major cities, cases were brought to his attention. He found these consultations aggravating because they cut into the time that he could otherwise have used for writing or praying. His participation in parish visitations and his preaching duties in Wittenberg brought him in contact with the sometimes harsh realities of concrete marriages.

Luther did not go as far as political thinkers did in drawing a parallel between the microcosm of the family headed by the father, the territory presided over by the prince, and the universal macrocosm governed by God. Nonetheless, he advocated marriage, and the family life that ordinarily followed it, as a godly and salubrious norm. His own marriage, because it was widely publicized, provided a vivid example to his followers. It demonstrated that clergymen, too, could be wed, sexually active within the nuptial bond, fathers, *and pious*. A married standard for the adult laity had always obtained, but the Luthers lived out, in addition, the mutual respect that Martin Luther promoted. Reciprocal love between the spouses did not mean equality, and Luther did not believe in this. The wife was and had to be the husband's helpmeet and subordinate.

SERMONS

A sermon on the estate of marriage, 1519, WA II, pp. 166–71

The first point: when God had created Adam and brought all the animals before him, among which Adam did not find any that was like him and a suitable companion for purposes of marriage, God spoke: "It is not good that man should be alone. I will make him a helper who will be close to him." He cast a deep sleep upon Adam and took out one of his ribs and closed the flesh again. Out of the rib that He had taken from Adam, He built a woman and brought her to Adam. Then Adam spoke: "That is bone of my bone and flesh of my flesh. She shall be called 'wo-man', for she has been taken from her husband." On that account a man will leave his father and mother and cling to his wife, and the two shall be one flesh.

This all is God's word, in which is described where husband and wife come from, how they are brought together, and for what purpose a woman is created, and what kind of love ought to exist in married life.

The second point: unless God Himself has given a wife or a husband, things will turn out as they may. For here it is shown that Adam found no marriage partner; but as soon as God had created Eve and brought her to him, he felt a proper spousal love for her and recognized her as his wedded wife. Therefore, one ought to teach those who want to commit themselves to the marital estate that with appropriate seriousness they should pray to God for a marriage partner. For even the wise man [Jesus Syrach = Ecclesiasticus] says that parents may provide their children with acreage and house, but a wife is given by God alone, in accordance with each person's worthiness, just as Eve was given to Adam by God alone. And even though frivolous young people out of excessive carnal lust deal fraudulently in this matter, it is nevertheless a great matter in God's eyes. Not for nothing did the Almighty God, with great consideration and thought, establish His marital estate for human beings above all the animals. To the other animals He says simply, "Be fruitful and multiply!" It is not written that He brought the female to the male; for that reason no marriage exists. But for Adam, and out of Adam's body, He creates his own particular wife, brings and gives her to him, and Adam consents and accepts her; that is then a marriage.

Thirdly, a wife is created for the man to be a companionate helper in all things, and especially for the production of children. And this still remains – except that after the Fall it has been mixed with evil lust. And now the desire of the husband for his wife and the reverse is not pure. For not only companionship and offspring are sought – for which it [marriage] was founded – but very much also the evil lust.

Fourthly, He distinguishes love such that the love of husband and wife is, or should be, the greatest and purest love of all loves. For He says that a man shall leave his father and mother and cleave to his wife, and the wife to him, as we see before us every day. There are three kinds of love: false, natural, and marital. False love seeks for its own sake money, property, honor, and women outside of marriage, and it is contrary to God's commandment. Natural love is between father and child, brother and sister, relatives and in-laws, and similarly. But married love is above all these. It is a bridal love, which burns like fire and seeks nothing more than its spouse, who says, "I desire nothing that is yours, neither gold nor silver, neither this nor that; I desire you yourself, and I would have all or nothing." All other forms of love seek something other than simply the one who is loved. Only this kind wants the entire beloved for itself. And if Adam had not fallen, a bride and groom would have been the loveliest thing. But now love is not pure, for even though one spouse desires the other, each one also seeks to satisfy its lust with the other, and this falsifies their love. As a result the marital condition itself is no longer pure and without sin. Carnal temptation has become so great and raging that the married estate is for evermore as a hospital is to the sick, so that they [spouses] do not fall into [even] greater sin. For before Adam fell, it was easy to maintain virginity and chastity, which is now rarely possible and only with God's particular grace. For that reason neither Christ nor the apostles wanted to command abstinence. Instead they advised and turned over to every person [the duty of] self-examination. If one is unable to be continent, he should marry; if one is able with God's grace, then abstinence is better.

The doctors [of the church] have found three good things and uses in the marital estate, by means of which sinful desire (with which it [marriage] is permeated) may be compensated for and not damning.

First of all, that it is a sacrament. [In 1519, Luther had not yet abandoned the sacramental nature of marriage.]...

Secondly, that it is a union in faith. That is the basis and the entire existence of marriage, that one gives oneself to the other and promises to be faithful and to allow no other person to intervene. Because each one binds himself to the other and gives himself into captivity, such that all other carnal outlets are closed off and each one is satisfied with one sleeping companion, God therefore regards the flesh as subdued, so that lust does not rage crosswise through the city. He graciously allows that this same desire, within the fidelity of marriage – even more than is needed for reproduction – is somewhat permissible, on the condition that one seriously tries to moderate that desire and does not make a manure-heap and a sow-bath out of it...

Thirdly, in order to produce offspring, for that is the end and chief duty of marriage. But it is not enough that a child is born...for heathens also bring forth children. A person has to raise children to the service, praise, and honor of God and seek nothing else out of it, which unfortunately seldom happens. People look for heirs or pleasure in their children – the service of God remains only when it can. One also finds people who enter into marriage and become fathers or mothers before they themselves can pray or know what God's commandments are.

But married people ought to know that they could do no better and useful work – either for God, Christianity, the whole world, themselves, and their children – than to raise their children well...That is their straightest road to heaven...

Oh, truly, the marital estate is a noble, great, blessed estate when it is rightly lived! Oh, truly, the married estate is a miserable, horrifying, dangerous estate when it is not rightly practiced! And whoever considers these matters could well forgo the longings of the flesh and perhaps just as well take on himself the virginal [celibate] as the married condition. Young people value this little, follow only their desires; but God will regard it as important and follow the proper way...

Sermon no. 59 (2 November 1522), WA X/3

[Here Luther is explaining the metaphor of Christ's love for his church as like the love of groom and bride; pp. 415–16] Now we want to see a little of what is symbolized in the wedding. First of all, the wedding is a union of the divine nature with the human nature, like the love that Christ bears us. That is shown here by means of the image of the wedding. For there are many kinds of love, but none is as fiery and hot as the bridal love that a bride has for her groom; again, the love is not looking for pleasure or presents, not wealth nor golden rings, but rather looks at him alone. Even if he were to give her everything there was, she would disregard it all and say, "I want to have you alone." And if he had absolutely nothing, she still would pay no attention to that but would want him anyway. That is the proper bridal love. Where one seeks pleasure, that is whore's love, which seeks not him [the groom] but the purse, and this love does not last long. God demonstrated His love for us by means of Christ, in that for our sake He had him become flesh and join with human nature, so that we could sense and recognize his friendly inclination toward us. Just as a bride loves the groom, so does Christ love us and we him, if we believe and are a true bride. Even if he were to give us heaven, the wisdom of all the prophets, all the saints, the holiness of all the angels, we hold it as naught if he gives himself to us. The bride lets nothing else satisfy her and is insatiable, but desires only the groom himself, as she says in the song: "My beloved is mine and I am his" [Song of Songs 2:16]. "He is mine and I am his." The bride cannot rest until she has the groom himself. This is how Christ is toward me: he wants me alone and nothing else. And if I were to give him everything I could, still it would be nothing to him. He would regard it as nothing even if I were to put on every monk's cap. He would not see it. He wants me. For outward things, outer virtues are simply serving-maids; he wants the lady herself. He wants me to say from the bottom of my heart, "I am yours." Now, the announcement [of the nuptials] and the betrothal take place by means of faith, that I freely trust that he is mine. For when I have him, what more could I want? What do we give him? A sour bride? An ugly, wrinkled old hag? But he is eternal wisdom, eternal truth, eternal light, and, what's more, a handsome youth. He gives me his entire self. He does not cut off a piece of himself and give only it to me, but instead the whole fountain of eternal wisdom, and not a little bowlful. So now that I am his and he mine, I possess eternal life, righteousness, and all that he has. Because of this I am justified, blessed, such that nothing that opposes me – sin, hell, or devil – is able to hurt me...

[P. 419] Now the wedding gown is Christ; we put him on through faith, as the apostle says, "Put on the Lord Jesus Christ." After that the gown gives off a gleam – that is, faith in Christ produces fruit, and that is the love that is effected by means of faith in Christ...

Sermons on Genesis, 1523/24, WA XIV

[Pp. 127–28] Woman is *isha*; *ish* is a man among men, *isha* a little man, and of itself means not a woman because it is made of the substance of a man. From this it comes, and still is, that the woman is named for the man, just as a tankard made of wood is called a wooden tankard, a tailor['s wife] a tailoress, a shoemaker['s wife] a shoester, a doctor['s wife] a doctoress. Today husbands are called "she-men" [*Syeman*]. This is the devil and death...

"And the two shall be one flesh," etc. One flesh – would that they were also of one spirit! It would be better if they were one of spirit... Scripture takes the flesh to mean external matters. Thus, one flesh [comprehends] one home, one family, field, conversation, education of the children, money, and all things in common, etc. Everything that belongs to the flesh – fields, meadows, children, house, honor, poverty – in sum, whatever may happen to the flesh the wife shall accept. The young woman goes to the bridegroom with her body and possessions, and the groom in return, except that the man should be the master...

[P. 141] "And you will be under the power of the man," etc. That is, you will not live in accordance with your own will as you properly did before the Fall; you shall no longer follow your own will. It was possible before the Fall to be with the man or not. Now she ought to remain with her husband. She must accompany him wherever he wants to go. Now we see that the woman is not able to be without the man. Wherever the man dwells the woman has to dwell too; the wife follows her husband wherever he may go. And beyond this, she is obligated to submit to the man; authority pertains to the husband in all the matters of this life. Women shall have grief and misery. Indeed, stupid women try not to submit to their husbands, but they are not able to govern cities and territories, etc. In short, wives have their part, are mildly punished if only they have faith. [Luther takes up the theme again that Eve's punishment could have been much worse.]...

[P. 144]... It may happen that women sometimes give advice, for we read this in Holy Scripture, but it is rare...

Sermon on the second Sunday after Epiphany, WA XV,
Predigten des Jahres 1524

[P. 419] A woman does not have a better friend than her husband; this fidelity does not exist in other conditions [relationships] . . .

[P. 420] Faith believes that the Lord will nourish you; charity endures all things, etc. 1 Peter 3 [giving honor unto] the wife [as unto the weaker] vessel, etc. He had a poor opinion of women: the body of woman is not strong, she does not bear arms, etc. In the ordinary course of things, their spirit is still weaker. This means, if the Lord joins to one [a man] either someone wild or mild, the wife is a half-child. Therefore, the man who marries a wife should know that he cares for a child. Some impetuous husbands want everything to be ready at home. If the wife has not always accomplished this, be indulgent with her. Scripture anticipates this second good, which they [other writers] are ignorant of and even condemn. This kind of person has written in many places, condemning this condition. Where you find such a wife, etc. Indeed, this one is a foolish animal; recognize her weakness. Paul [says], "Love your wives." Charity, which is able to bear [all things], as it says in [1] Corinthians 13. Where there is no bearing and tolerating, there is no occasion of charity. It is imaginary that one loves because of esteem and thanks; in truth, one loves when one is tolerated and loves one's enemy. If you ought to love your wife, the Lord will give you occasion for loving her. If she does not always proceed rightly, endure her infirmity. A woman remains eternally woman. If you acknowledge this, you will have opportunities to exercise faith and charity. For her part, the wife should have the qualities of fearing, venerating, and obeying the husband; he should love and rule her with reason. Nevertheless, sometimes you will find a husband who is not so disposed, and then the fuss between them begins immediately. So you yourself are flesh and blood; nevertheless, in a certain respect the man is the stronger.

A sermon on marriage, 15 January 1525, WA XVII/1

[This was the Sunday when all preachers were to talk about marriage, usually using the wedding at Cana as their text; p. 14]. The fourth honor is that God has laid a serious command upon marriage, just like a gardener who, having a lovely herb or rose garden that he loves and does not want anyone to climb in and break anything off or do damage to it, builds a fence around it. God does just this with the Sixth Commandment: "You shall not commit adultery." For marriage is His most beloved herb or rose garden, in which the most beautiful little roses and carnations grow, and these are the dear children of humans, who are created in the image of

God. They come out and are born so that the human race is maintained. So God bids one to keep marriage in the fear of God, in modesty and honor, and not to commit adultery. For whoever commits adultery God will punish horribly in body and soul and cast out of His kingdom...

[P. 24] Men should govern their wives not with great cudgels, flails, or drawn knives, but rather with friendly words and gestures and with all gentleness so that they do not become shy...and take fright such that they afterward do not know what to do. Thus, men should rule their wives with reason and not unreason, and honor the feminine sex as the weakest vessel and also as coheirs of the grace of life...

[Pp. 26–27] "Women, be subject to your husbands as to the Lord, for the husband is the head of the wife" [Eph. 5:22–23]. Again to the Colossians in the third chapter [3:18]. Because of this, the wife has not been created out of the head, so that she shall not rule over her husband, but be subject and obedient to him.

For that reason the wife wears a headdress, that is, the veil on her head, as St. Paul writes in 1. Corinthians in the second chapter, that she is not free but under obedience to her husband.

The wife veils herself with a fine, soft veil, spun and sewn out of pretty, soft flax or linen; and she does not wind a coarse bunch of woven fabric or a dirty cloth around her head or mouth. Why does she do this? So that she speaks fine, lovely, friendly words to her husband and not coarse, filthy, scolding words, as the bad wives do who carry a sword in their mouths and afterward get beaten to the edge of town [*auf die Scheide*]. Therefore, the wife should have the manner of a grapevine, as it says in the 128th Psalm, for this lets itself be bent and directed with a little band of straw, as the vintner desires. Just so should wives let themselves be guided and taught by their husbands, so that the great and coarse blows and strokes are not used. As pious, obedient wives are accustomed to saying, unbeaten is the best.

That is now part two, what the wife should do in marriage, namely, that she should be subordinate and obedient to her husband and not undertake or do anything without his consent.

Sermons on Genesis, chapter one, 1527, WA XXIV, pp. 52–57
There would be much to say here about the marital estate, and it would be good if the person who dealt with it was well experienced. Nonetheless, we want to say something about it, and in my opinion I will not go much astray because the Scripture will not lie to us. First of all, we have heard how God divides humans into two parts. From that we conclude that just

as others of God's works do not lie within human power, so too [we do not decide] whether a person is a man or a woman... The sun cannot say, "I want to be the moon," and, conversely, the moon cannot change itself into the sun; but each has to stay as it was created by God. A man has to stay as he is and cannot be a woman, and, the other way around, a woman has to stay a woman, as she has been made. It does not stand within their power to alter such things.

Secondly, God said to humans after they were created, "Be fruitful and multiply!" This utterance is a clap of thunder against the pope's law and liberates all priests [*Pfaffen*], monks, and nuns to get married. For just as the sun must shine and cannot restrain itself – for this [its radiance] is implanted in its nature through God's word and command – so it is also implanted in the nature of human beings, whether they are boys or girls, to be fruitful. That God exempts some, such as the handicapped and incapacitated, and some lofty spirits – this is among other miraculous signs. But the nature of people in general is that it does not lie within their power either to resist or to comply; rather, it [nature] must take its course and have its way. For that reason, it does not lie within my will to swear to such a thing, for it is impossible for us to keep this [promise]. No vow against this [nature] is of any value; for it is already decided: no one can resist an act that God has created. How would it be if the sun took an oath not to shine? It would be the same as if you vowed not to be fruitful nor to raise or bear children. Whether you swear or not, you can be nothing other than what God has made you. Whether you want to or not, you must do what accords with your nature – or go in other directions, out of which great misery follows that is not to be named...

But now God has broken into His creation in such a way that some people are incapable [of reproduction]; He gives them a special, high grace so that they can live without it. The person who is freed by such grace should thank God and live accordingly. He to whom it is not given should commit himself to ordinary married life. If he does not do it, he will make things more abominable than we see that they are in the world, which is full of prostitution and fornication...

Sermon on the second Sunday after Epiphany, 19 January 1528,
WA XXVII, pp. 27–28

[Again, this is a sermon given on the day, the second Sunday after Epiphany, that was reserved for preaching on marriage.] We have said that nuptials are ordained by God. We add [that they are] for the instruction of weak consciences. There one eats and is festive, and people dress up, dance, and sing. When I was young, it was preached that people should not dance or [wear] red shoes, etc. Our teaching has it that no one should do anything that is against his conscience, but should do everything [that derives] from faith. Therefore, when a wedding is to be held, we ought to do in these matters what does not give us a bad conscience. It is not a sin that a person is jolly in eating and drinking. People who were happy are not condemned. Christ drinks wine and serves wine. Some preached that this was not necessary and some that it was. On that account, [I say] that when one lives well, a good conscience is possible, in honor of the groom and the bride, [and] of the wedding and marriage – unless someone eats and drinks like a sow, who is called a sow-mouth [*seumal*] ... Weddings are not to be condemned on account of those people who get drunk; they are incapable of celebrating without sin.

In Scripture [it says that] the voice of the groom and the bride will be taken away [Revelation 18:23]. This voice? If someone is singing? When someone is piping and drumming, this is the voice of these [bride and groom]. When we hear it, we know that a joyous event is at hand. The prophets show this, and you can use it. If one pipes and drums well, it does honor to the wedding. Dancing in and of itself is not a sin; let the wedding proceed properly. At that time, it was not thought that one pleased God when he celebrated his nuptials ... And nothing was preached about rejoicing being prohibited, etc. The voice of the spouse was praised in Scripture. John says of Christ, "who has a bride"; he hears her voice, that is, the drumming and piping. The Gospel is her pipe and drum. People dance because they rejoice and they praise. Those who are present and lend their help honor the wedding – insofar as no overindulgence occurs. If you disregard the warning of the master, of the mistress, of the parent, you sin, not on account of dancing but because of your disobedience.

Sermon given at the wedding of Sigmund von Lindenau in Merseburg,
4 August 1545, WA XLIX, pp. 797–805

[The second sermon of Dr. Martin Luther on the text, Hebrews 13, "All people are to keep marriage in honor and the marriage bed unspotted." In Merseburg at the wedding of the Honorable Lord Sigmund von Lindenau, Deacon of the Chapter of Merseburg, 4 August 1545 ...

[P. 798] Therefore, all of us must ever say and confess that we have not made and created ourselves; nor can we do it, just as our parents could not do it. Who then can? The almighty, eternal God, Creator of all things, who first created and ordained little men and little women for marriage – He also created us. For I must freely confess and state that I am created a man, another person a woman, by God; I must acknowledge that I was born and created not a stone or clod but a human being, a woman or a man. No one in the whole world, from the first to the last, can say otherwise. Still the people rave and rage – especially the papists without moderation – against this splendid creation of God, as though it should not be so but should stand within the pope's power to create human beings. But it must not be, for he would create no women nor let them exist in the entire world. And what would be the result of that? The human race would go out of existence. For this much is certain: nobody is born without a mother; whatever is born comes forth from the mother and has made itself as little as Adam did, but is created by God. So must all people also be made by God in the body of their mother, be maintained there, and afterward with God's help be born into the world...

[Pp. 799–803] "Marriage shall be held in honor by all, and the marriage bed unspotted," etc.

They should rejoice and console themselves that they are married, for here one can say: I thank God that I have been created a man; or a woman; I thank God that I have been created a woman, and that we have been placed by God in the holy estate of matrimony in order to raise children in accord with His blessing and will. That is a great glory that married people have. For that reason, no one should hate or condemn the estate and ordinance of God, as the pope does with his following; rather, they should hold it high and treat it with love and appreciation.

... It is sufficient for us to know that God sees us together with His only Son our Lord Jesus Christ, who sits at the right hand of God and is Lord of all, as He ordained the wedded estate, set us in it, and presides over it until the Last Day. Because I believe and am certain of that, I am happy and comforted and live with a good conscience and a joyful mood in the holy order of marriage. For God says to the man: "You are my man," and to the woman: "You are my little woman"; and because I know that God speaks like this to me, so I also know that all the angels say likewise [and] love and regard me. I also know that the sun and moon and all the stars look at me and serve me with their light and their effects...

Marriage shall be kept honorably by all, and the marriage bed unspotted: All married people should adhere to this.

St. Augustine writes in one place about married people, that even if one of them were somewhat fragile, etc., he should not fear the sudden and unforeseen day of the Lord. Even if the day of the Lord were to come precisely in that house when husband and wife were sleeping together [having intercourse], they should not be afraid or frightened on that account. And why not? For this reason: that even if the Lord comes in that hour, He finds them in the ordinance and estate in which God has placed them and for which He has ordained them.

And so much the more does it follow from that that no emperor's, pope's, or bishop's mandate should stand in my way or hinder me. Let me be content that I have a gracious God whom this ordinance pleases, who watches after me and blesses and protects me. Who made them so bold and authorized them to rip apart such a splendid foundation of God?

Therefore, it is worth nothing that you swore with your vow or oath to remain chaste when you do not have the power to keep it. If you have sworn this, you have sworn it to the devil and are not obligated it keep it, for it is opposed to God. Furthermore, this practice of swearing is not of longstanding. In the times of St. Augustine and St. Ambrose, people did not know anything about this oath or vow. Rather, each person was free to decide whether to remain single or to marry, as long as he desired. Binding people and vowing to remain abstinent and unwed is new, an invention and device of the devil and of the disagreeable monks, the profaners of God's ordinance and of holy matrimony...

Those people who raise children with one another outside marriage are parents, to be sure, but they have no honor. For that reason it says, "The marriage bed shall be pure," that is, it should be neither a whore's nor an adulterer's bed. But here you have an objection: how can the marriage bed be pure? Is there not also much impurity in marriage? It is true that there is not much purity there. If you want to see impurity, consider also the young women's and young men's condition; there not everything is pure either. For while they eat and drink, they cannot be pure: they have to purge themselves and pick and blow their noses and whatever more uncleanness there is [Luther is alluding to masturbation.]...Why do you only look at the impurity that exists in marriage? If you want to talk about the kind of purity and chastity that the angels have, you will find it nowhere, neither in marriage nor out of it in the unmarried condition. Purity does not exist; even children are not pure...St. Paul does not speak about impurity, for all people are stained and impure. He speaks about a sort of purity that ought to exist in marriage – that married people should not be whores or adulterers and adulteresses. Whatever else happens in marriage, God covers heaven over so that that may take place which pertains to the raising of children. God says yes to that, for this is His ordinance, etc. "This impurity," says God, "I do not want to see." Here parents, fathers and mothers, are pardoned. God does not count this as impurity on account of original sin.

He will not hold it or count it as sin. Instead, God makes above this act a "kingdom of heaven" [*Himmelbett*, the German name for a four-poster bed with canopy, the marriage bed] and cover over everything that is impure, for the sake of His ordinance and Creation, etc. . . .

TREATISES ON MARRIAGE

The Estate of Marriage, 1522, LW XLV, pp. 17–49
From *Luther's Works*, vol. XLV, edited by Walther Brandt, © 1962
Fortress Press. Used by permission of Augsburg Fortress Publishers

[P. 17] How I dread preaching on the estate of marriage! I am reluctant to do it because I am afraid if I once get really involved in the subject it will make a lot of work for me and for others. The shameful confusion wrought by the accursed papal law has occasioned so much distress, and the lax authority of both the spiritual and the temporal swords has given rise to so many dreadful abuses and false situations, that I would much prefer neither to look into the matter nor to hear of it. But timidity is no help in an emergency; I must proceed. I must try to instruct poor bewildered consciences and take up the matter boldly . . .

Part One

[Pp. 18–19] In the second place, after God had made man and woman He blessed them and said to them, "Be fruitful and multiply." From this passage we may be assured that man and woman should and must come together in order to multiply. Now this [ordinance] is just as inflexible as the first, and no more to be despised and made fun of than the other, since God gives it His blessing and does something over and above the act of creation. Hence, as it is not within my power not to be a man, so it is not my prerogative to be without a woman. Again, as it is not in your power not to be a woman, so it is not your prerogative to be without a man. For it is not a matter of free choice or decision but a natural and necessary thing, that whatever is a man must have a woman and whatever is a woman must have a man.

For this word which God speaks, "Be fruitful and multiply" . . . is more than a command, namely, a divine ordinance which it is not our prerogative to hinder or ignore. Rather, it is just as necessary as the fact that I am a man, and more necessary than sleeping and waking, eating and drinking, and emptying the bowels and bladder. It is a nature and disposition just as innate as the organs involved in it. Therefore, just as God does not command anyone to be a man or a woman but creates them the way they have to be, so He does not command them to multiply but creates them so that they have to multiply. And wherever men try to resist this, it remains irresistible nonetheless and goes its way through fornication, adultery, and secret sins, for this is a matter of nature and not of choice.

From this you can now see the extent of the validity of all cloister vows. No vow of any youth or maiden is valid before God, except that of a person in one of the three categories which God alone has Himself excepted [eunuchs from birth, manmade eunuchs, self-made eunuchs for the sake of the kingdom of heaven]. Therefore, priests, monks, and nuns are duty-bound to forsake their vows whenever they find that God's ordinance to produce seed and to multiply is powerful and strong within them. They have no power by any authority, law, command, or vow to hinder this which God has created within them. If they do hinder it, however, you may be sure that they will not remain pure but inevitably besmirch themselves with secret sins or fornication. For they are simply incapable of resisting the word and ordinance of God within them. Matters will take their course as God has ordained...

[Pp. 21–22] Beyond these three categories, however, the devil working through men has been smarter than God, and found more people whom he has withdrawn from the divine and natural ordinance, namely, those who are enmeshed in a spiderweb of human commands and vows and are then locked up behind a mass of iron bolts and bars. This is a fourth way of resisting nature so that, contrary to God's implanted ordinance and disposition, it does not produce seed and multiply – as if it were within our power and discretion to possess virginity as we do shoes and clothing! If men are really able to resist God's word and creation with iron bars and bolts, I should hope that we would also set up iron bars so thick and massive that women would turn into men or people into sticks and stones. It is the devil who thus perpetrates his monkey-tricks on the poor creature, and so gives vent to his wrath.

In the fourth place, let us now consider which persons may enter into marriage with one another, so that you may see it is not my pleasure or desire that a marriage be broken and husband and wife separated. The pope in his canon law has thought up eighteen distinct reasons for preventing or dissolving a marriage, nearly all of which I reject and condemn... In order to expose their folly we will take a look at all eighteen of them in turn.

The first impediment is blood relationship... [ML refutes Catholic rules.]

[P. 23] The second impediment is affinity or relationship through marriage...

[P. 24] The third impediment is spiritual relationship. If I sponsor a girl at baptism or confirmation, then neither I nor my son may marry her, or her mother, or her sister – unless an appropriate and substantial sum of money is forthcoming! This is nothing but pure farce and foolishness, concocted for the sake of money and to befuddle consciences...

[P. 25] The fourth impediment is legal kinship; that is, when an unrelated child is adopted as son or daughter it may not later marry a child born of its adoptive parents, that is, one who is by law its own brother or sister. This is another worthless human invention. Therefore, if you so desire, go ahead and marry anyway. In the sight of God this adopted person is neither your mother nor your sister, since there is no blood relationship...

The fifth impediment is unbelief; that is, I may not marry a Turk, a Jew, or a heretic. I marvel that the blasphemous tyrants are not in their hearts ashamed to place themselves in such direct contradiction to the clear text of Paul in 1 Corinthians 7, where he says, "If a heathen wife or husband consents to live with a Christian spouse, the Christian should not get a divorce." And St. Peter, in 1 Peter 3, says that Christian wives should behave so well that they thereby convert their non-Christian husbands; as did Monica, the mother of St. Augustine...

The sixth impediment is crime...

[Pp. 26–37]... No sin or crime is an impediment to marriage...

The seventh impediment they call public decorum, respectability. For example, if my fiancée should die before we consummate the marriage, I may not marry any relative of hers up to the fourth degree, since the pope thinks and obviously dreams that it is decent and respectable for me to refrain from so doing – unless I put up the money, in which case the impediment of public decorum vanishes. Now you have heard a moment ago that after my wife's death I may marry her sister or any of her relatives except for her mother and her daughter. You stick to this, and let the fools go their way.

The eighth impediment is a solemn vow, for example where someone has taken the vow of chastity, either in or out of the cloister. Here I offer this advice: if you would like to take a wise vow, then vow not to bite off your own nose; you can keep that vow...

The ninth impediment is error, as if I had been wed to Catherine but Barbara lay down with me, as happened to Jacob with Leah and Rachel. One may have such a marriage dissolved and take the other to wife.

The tenth impediment is condition of servitude. When I marry one who is supposed to be free and it turns out later that she is a serf, this marriage too is null and void. However, I hold that if there were Christian love, the husband could easily adjust both of these impediments so that no great distress would be occasioned. Furthermore, such cases never occur today, or only rarely, and both might well be combined in one category: error.

The eleventh impediment is holy orders, namely, that the tonsure and sacred oil are so potent that they devour marriage and unsex a man. For this reason a subdeacon, a deacon, and a priest have to forego marriage, although St. Paul commanded that they may and should be married, 2 Timothy 3, Titus 1. But I have elsewhere written so much about this that there is no need to repeat it here...

The twelfth impediment is coercion, that is, when I have to take Greta to be my wife and am coerced into it either by parents or by governmental authority. That is to be sure no marriage in the sight of God. However, such a person should not admit the coercion and leave the country on account of it, thus betraying the girl or making a fool of her, for you are not excused by the fact that you were coerced into it. You should not allow yourself to be coerced into injuring your neighbor but should yield your life rather than act contrary to love. You would not want anybody to injure you, whether he was acting under coercion or not. For this reason I could not declare safe in the sight of God a man who leaves his wife for such a cause.

The thirteenth impediment is betrothal, that is, if I am engaged to one girl but then take another to wife. This is a widespread and common practice in which many different solutions have also been attempted...

The fourteenth impediment is the one touched on already, when a husband or wife is unfit for marriage. Among these eighteen impediments this one is the only sound reason for dissolving a marriage.

There are still four more impediments, such as episcopal prohibition, restricted times, custom, and defective eyesight and hearing. It is needless to discuss them here. It is a dirty rotten business that a bishop should forbid me a wife or specify the times when I may marry, or that a blind and dumb person should not be allowed to enter into wedlock. So much then for this foolishness at present in the first part.

Part Two

In the second part, we shall consider which persons may be divorced. I know of three grounds for divorce. The first, which has just been mentioned and was discussed above, is the situation in which the husband or wife is not equipped for marriage because of bodily or natural deficiencies of any sort. Of this enough has already been said.

The second ground is adultery. The popes have kept silent about this; therefore we must hear Christ, Matthew 19...

Here you see that in the case of adultery Christ permits the divorce of husband and wife, so that the innocent person may remarry. For in saying that he commits adultery who marries another after divorcing his wife, "except for unchastity," Christ is making it quite clear that he who divorces his wife on account of unchastity and then marries another does not commit adultery...

Now in the law of Moses God established two types of governments; He gave two types of commandments. Some are spiritual, teaching righteousness in the sight of God, such as love and obedience; people who obeyed these commandments did not thrust away their wives and never made use of certificates of divorce, but tolerated and endured their wives' conduct. Others are worldly, however, drawn up for the sake of those who do not live up to the spiritual commandments, in order to place a limit upon their misbehavior and prevent them from doing worse and acting wholly on the basis of their own maliciousness. Accordingly, he commanded them, if they could not endure their wives, that they should not put them to death or harm them too severely, but rather dismiss them with a certificate of divorce. This law, therefore, does not apply to Christians, who are supposed to live in the spiritual government. In the case of some who live with their wives in an un-Christian fashion, however, it would still be a good thing to permit them to use this law, just so they are no longer regarded as Christians, which after all they really are not.

Thus it is that on the grounds of adultery one person may leave the other, as Solomon also says in Proverbs 18... We have an example of this in Joseph too. In Matthew 1 the gospel writer praises him as just because he did not put his wife to shame when he found that she was with child, but was minded to divorce her quietly. By this we are told plainly enough that it is praiseworthy to divorce an adulterous wife. If the adultery is clandestine, of course, the husband has the right to follow either of two courses. First, he may rebuke his wife privately and in a brotherly fashion, and keep her if she will mend her ways. Second, he may divorce her, as Joseph wished to do. The same principle applies in the case of a wife with an adulterous husband. These two types of discipline are both Christian and laudable.

But a public divorce, whereby one [the innocent party] is enabled to remarry, must take place through the investigation and decision of the civil authority so that the adultery may be manifest to all – or, if the civil authority refuses to act, with the knowledge of the congregation, again in order that it may not be left to each one to allege anything he pleases as a ground for divorce.

You may ask: What is to become of the other [the guilty party] if he too is perhaps unable to lead a chaste life? Answer: It was for this reason that God commanded in the law [Deut. 22:22–24] that adulterers be stoned, that they might not have to face this question. The temporal sword and government should therefore still put adulterers to death, for whoever commits adultery has in fact himself already departed [*gescheyden*] and is considered as one dead. Therefore, the other [the innocent party] may remarry just as though his spouse had died, if it is his intention to insist on his rights and not show mercy to the guilty party. Where the government is negligent and lax, however, and fails to inflict the death penalty, the adulterer may betake himself to a far country and there remarry if he is unable to remain continent. But it would be better to put him to death, lest a bad example be set...

The third case for divorce is that in which one of the parties deprives and avoids the other, refusing to fulfil the conjugal duty or to live with the other person. For example, one finds many a stubborn wife like that who will not give in, and who cares not a whit whether her husband falls into the sin of unchastity ten times over. Here it is time for the husband to say, "If you will not, another will; the maid will come if the wife will not." [This was a well known proverb and not of Luther's invention.] Only first the husband should admonish and warn his wife two or three times, and let the situation be known to others so that her stubbornness becomes a matter of common knowledge and is rebuked before the congregation. If she still refuses, get rid of her; take an Esther and let Vashti go, as King Ahasuerus did.

Here you should be guided by the words of St. Paul, 1 Corinthians 7, "The husband does not rule over his own body, but the wife does; likewise the wife does not rule over her own body, but the husband does. Do not deprive each other, except by agreement," etc...

In addition to these three grounds for divorce there is one more which would justify the sundering of husband and wife, but only in such a way that they must both refrain from remarrying or else become reconciled. This is the case where husband and wife cannot get along together for some reason other than the matter of the conjugal duty. St. Paul speaks of this in 1 Corinthians 7, "Not I but the Lord gives charge to the married that the wife should not separate from her husband. But if she does, let her remain single, or else be reconciled to her husband. Likewise, the husband should not divorce his wife." Solomon complains much in the Proverbs about such wives, and says he has found a woman more bitter than death [Ecclesiastes 7:26]. One may also find a rude, brutal, and unbearable husband...

What about the situation where one's wife is an invalid and has therefore become incapable of fulfilling the conjugal duty? May he not take another to wife? By no means. Let him serve the Lord in the person of the invalid and await His good pleasure. Consider that in this invalid God has provided your household with a healing balm by which you are to gain heaven. Blessed and twice blessed are you when you recognize such a gift of grace and therefore serve your invalid wife for God's sake.

But you may say: I am unable to remain continent. That is a lie. If you will earnestly serve your invalid wife, recognize that God has placed this burden upon you, and give thanks to Him, then you may leave matters in His care. He will surely grant you grace, that you will not have to bear more than you are able. He is far too faithful to deprive you of your wife through illness without at the same time subduing your carnal desire, if you will but faithfully serve your invalid wife.

Part Three

In the third part, in order that we may say something about the estate of marriage which will be conducive toward the soul's salvation, we shall now consider how to live a Christian and godly life in that estate. I will pass over in silence the matter of the conjugal duty, the granting and the withholding of it, since some filth-preachers have been shameless enough in this matter to rouse our disgust. Some of them designate special times for this, and exclude holy nights and women who are pregnant. I will leave this as St. Paul left it when he said in 1 Corinthians 7, "It is better to marry than to burn"; and again, "To avoid immorality, each man should have his own wife, and each woman her own husband." Although Christian married folk should not permit themselves to be governed by their bodies in the passion of lust, as Paul writes to the Thessalonians [1 Thess. 4:5], nevertheless each one must examine himself so that by his abstention he does not expose himself to the danger of fornication and other sins. Neither should he pay any attention to holy days or work days, or other physical considerations.

What we would speak most of is the fact that the estate of marriage has universally fallen into such awful disrepute. There are many pagan books which treat of nothing but the depravity of womankind and the unhappiness of the estate of marriage, such that some have thought that even if Wisdom itself were a woman one should not marry...I imagine that if women were to write books they would say exactly the same thing about men. What they have failed to set down in writing, however, they express with their grumbling and complaining whenever they get together.

Since God had to suffer such disdain of His work from the pagans, He therefore also gave them their reward, of which Paul writes in Romans 1, and allowed them to fall into immorality and a stream of uncleanness until they henceforth carnally abused not women but boys and dumb beasts. Even their women carnally abused themselves and each other. Because they blasphemed the work of God, He gave them up to a base mind, of which the books of the pagans are full, most shamelessly crammed full...

[Pp. 39–41] Now observe that when that clever harlot, our natural reason ... takes a look at married life, she turns up her nose and says, "Alas, must I rock the baby, wash its diapers, make its bed, smell its stench, stay up nights with it, take care of it when it cries, heal its rashes and sores, and on top of that care for my wife, provide for her, labor at my trade, take care of this and take care of that, do this and do that, endure this and endure that, and whatever else of bitterness and drudgery married life involves? What, should I make such a prisoner of myself? O you poor, wretched fellow, have you taken a wife? Fie, fie upon such wretchedness and bitterness! It is better to remain free and lead a peaceful, carefree life; I will become a priest or a nun and compel my children to do likewise."

What then does Christian faith say to this? It opens its eyes, looks upon all these insignificant, distasteful, and despised duties in the Spirit, and is aware that they are all adorned with divine approval as with the costliest gold and jewels. It says, "O God, because I am certain that thou hast created me as a man and hast from my body begotten this child, I also know for a certainty that it meets with thy perfect pleasure. I confess to thee that I am not worthy to rock the little babe or wash its diapers, or to be entrusted with the care of the child and its mother. How is it that I, without any merit, have come to this distinction of being certain that I am serving thy creature and thy most precious will? O how gladly will I do so, though the duties should be even more insignificant and despised. Neither frost nor heat, neither drudgery nor labor, will distress or dissuade me, for I am certain that it is thus pleasing in thy sight"...

Now you tell me, when a father goes ahead and washes diapers or performs some other mean task for his child, and someone ridicules him as an effeminate fool – though that father is acting in the spirit just described and in Christian faith – my dear fellow, you tell me, which of the two is most keenly ridiculing the other? God, with all His angels and creatures, is smiling – not because that father is washing diapers, but because he is

doing so in Christian faith. Those who sneer at him and see only the task
but not the faith are ridiculing God with all His creatures, as the biggest
fool on earth. Indeed, they are only ridiculing themselves; with all their
cleverness they are nothing but devil's fools.

St. Cyprian, that great and admirable man and holy martyr, wrote that
one should kiss the newborn infant, even before it is baptized, to honor the
hands of God, caught in the very act (of creation). What do you suppose he
would have said about a baptized infant? There was a true Christian, who
correctly recognized and regarded God's work and creature. Therefore, I
say that all nuns and monks who lack faith, and who trust in their own
chastity and in their order, are not worthy of rocking a baptized child or
preparing its pap, even if it were the child of a harlot. This is because their
order and manner of life has no word of God as its warrant. They cannot
boast that what they do is pleasing in God's sight, as can the woman in
childbirth, even if her child is born out of wedlock...

[Pp. 45–47] Physicians are not amiss when they say: If this natural function [the sex drive] is forcibly restrained, it necessarily strikes into the flesh
and blood and becomes a poison, whence the body becomes unhealthy,
enervated, sweaty, and foul-smelling. That which should have issued in
fruitfulness and propagation has to be absorbed within the body itself.
Unless there is terrific hunger or immense labor or the supreme grace, the
body cannot take it; it necessarily becomes unhealthy and sickly. Hence, we
see how weak and sickly barren women are. Those who are fruitful, however, are healthier, cleaner, and happier. And even if they bear themselves
weary – or ultimately bear themselves out – that does not hurt. Let them
bear themselves out. This is the purpose for which they exist. It is better to
have a brief life with good health than a long life in ill health.

But the greatest good in married life, that which makes all suffering
and labor worth while, is that God grants offspring and commands that
they be brought up to worship and serve Him. In all the world this is
the noblest and most precious work, because to God there can be nothing
dearer than the salvation of souls. Now since we are all duty bound to suffer
death, if need be, that we might bring a single soul to God, you can see
how rich the estate of marriage is in good works. God has entrusted to its
bosom souls begotten of its own body, on whom it can lavish all manner
of Christian works. Most certainly father and mother are apostles, bishops,
and priests to their children, for it is they who make them acquainted
with the gospel. In short, there is no greater or nobler authority on earth
than that of parents over their children, for this authority is both spiritual
and temporal. Whoever teaches the gospel to another is truly his apostle

and bishop. Mitre and staff and great estates indeed produce idols, but teaching the gospel produces apostles and bishops. See therefore how good and great is God's work and ordinance!

Finally, we have before us one big, strong objection to answer. Yes, they say, it would be a fine thing to be married, but how will I support myself? I have nothing; take a wife and live on that, etc. Undoubtedly, this is the greatest obstacle to marriage; it is this above all which prevents and breaks up marriage and is the chief excuse for fornication. What shall I say to this objection? It shows lack of faith and doubt of God's goodness and truth. It is therefore no wonder that where faith is lacking, nothing but fornication and all manner of misfortune follow. They are lacking in this, that they want to be sure first of their material resources, where they are to get their food, drink, and clothing. Yes, they want to pull their head out of the noose of Genesis 3, "In the sweat of your face you shall eat bread." They want to be lazy, greedy rascals who do not need to work. Therefore, they will get married only if they can get wives who are rich, beautiful, pious, kind – indeed, wait, we will have a picture of them drawn for you...

[P. 49] With all this extolling of married life, however, I have not meant to ascribe to nature a condition of sinlessness. On the contrary, I say that flesh and blood, corrupted through Adam, is conceived and born in sin, as Psalm 51 says. Intercourse is never without sin; but God excuses it by His grace because the estate of marriage is His work, and He preserves in and through the sin all that good which He has implanted and blessed in marriage.

On Marriage Matters, 1530, LW XLVI, pp. 265–320
From *Luther's Works*, vol. XLVI, edited by Robert C. Schultz, © 1967
Fortress Press. Used by permission of Augsburg Fortress Publishers

[Pp. 265–70] To the worthy gentlemen, Messrs. N. and N. [any pastors], pastors and preachers at N. [any parish], my dear brothers in Christ.

Grace and peace in Christ, our Lord and Savior. You are not the only ones, my dear sirs, who are having a great deal of trouble with marriage matters; others are having the same experience. I myself am greatly plagued by them; I put up a stiff resistance, calling and crying out that these things should be left to the temporal authorities... God grant that they may do this, rightly or wrongly, for we are supposed to be servants of Christ, that is, we are to deal with the gospel and conscience, which gives us more than enough to do against the devil, the world, and the flesh.

No one can deny that marriage is an external, worldly matter, like clothing and food, house and property, subject to temporal authority, as the many imperial laws enacted on the subject prove. Neither do I find any example in the New Testament where Christ or the apostles concerned themselves with such matters, except where they touched upon consciences... And what use would it be if we Christians set up a lot of laws and decisions, as long as the world is not subject to us and we have no authority over it?

Therefore, I simply do not wish to become involved in such matters at all and beg everyone not to bother me with them. If you do not have sovereigns, then you have officials. If they do not render just decisions, what concern is it of mine? They are responsible, they have undertaken the office...

Now the whole world knows (praise God) what effort and zeal I have already expended and how hard I am still toiling to see that the two authorities or realms, the temporal and the spiritual, are kept distinct and separate from each other and that each is specifically instructed and restricted to its own task...

But since you persist so strongly in asking instruction of me, not only for yourselves and your office, but also for your rulers who desire advice from you in these matters, and ask me what I for my part would do if I were asked for advice... I will not withhold my opinion from you. Yet I give it with this condition... that I want to do this not as a judge, official, or regent, but by way of advice, such as I would in good conscience give as a special service to my good friends...

I define a secret engagement as one which takes place without the knowledge and consent of those who are in authority and have the right and power to establish a marriage, such as father, mother, and whoever may act in their stead. Even if a thousand witnesses were present at a secret betrothal and it nonetheless took place without the knowledge and consent of the parents, the whole thousand should be reckoned as acting in the darkness and not in the light, as only one voice, and as assisting treacherously in this beginning without the presence of orderly public authority...

Who would approve my action if after I had reared my daughter with so much expense and effort, care and danger, zeal and toil, and had risked my whole life with body and goods for so many years, she should receive no better care than if she were a cow of mine that had strayed into the forest where any wolf might devour it? Should my child be standing there, unprotected, so that any young rascal who is unknown to me and may even have been my enemy would have free access to steal her from me secretly and take her away without my knowledge and consent?... Now this rascal is not only taking my money and property, but also my child whom I have reared with great effort, and in addition he gets my money and property along with my daughter. So I am forced to reward him, and for all the wrong he has committed against me I must let him be my heir to the property I have acquired with great toil and effort. This is rewarding evil with honor...

[Pp. 273–74] Likewise they have carried on pure tomfoolery with verbs in the present and future tense; they have broken up many a marriage which was valid according to their law and made binding those that were not valid. The words, "I will have you as a wife," or, "I will take you, I will have you," "you shall be mine," and the like, they have generally called future verbs and pretended that the man should say, "*accipio te in uxorem*," "I take you to be my wife," and the wife should likewise say, "I take you to be my husband." They have not seen or noticed that this is not the custom in speaking German when one is speaking in the present, for in German one says in the present, "I will have you," "*ego volo te habere*"; this is present tense, not future. Thus, no German is speaking of a future betrothal when he says, "I will have you" or "take you," for one does not say, "I am going to have you," as they juggle with *accipiam te*. On the other hand, *accipio te* really means in German, "I will take you" or "have you" and is understood to be present, that the man now is saying "yes" in these words and giving his consent to the bargain...

[P. 278] But suppose you ask, "Now I know how and when God joins a man and a woman together, but how do I know when God puts them asunder?" My reply is this: First, by death, as Paul in Romans 7 cites God's word and says, "If the husband dies, the wife is discharged from the law concerning her husband." Second, when one party commits adultery, for God's commandment judges and punishes adultery with death [Deut. 22:22]; therefore an adulterer is already divorced from his spouse by God Himself and by His word...

[P. 282] But what is one to do if the secret engagement is not merely an engagement, but is followed by a secret lying together?...

[P. 284] Marriage which is open, public, and based on God and honor is to maintain its integrity and right against the stolen, treacherous, disobedient marriage hidden in corners, so that henceforth girls and women will beware of lying with a man in secret and not believe the fine words of the seducer so easily and thoughtlessly. For they believe in the words of a man, and so they fare according to the Scripture, "Whoever trusts in men will surely be mistaken," and again, "He who trusts in men will surely come to grief." The woman who is openly betrothed, however, stands and trusts in God, for she has God's word and testimony which one must believe, but the one who is secretly betrothed has no word of God, no witness, but only the fine words and promise of her seducer, who is human and alone, and therefore she deserves to be deceived...

[Pp. 293–94] A woman who has lost her honor is quite worthless because we do not regard the fruit of the womb as highly as the Jews. Yet this lying together in secret in anticipation of betrothal cannot be reckoned as whoredom, for it takes place in the name and with the intention of marriage, which spirit, intention, or name whoredom does not have. Therefore there is a great difference between whoredom and lying together in secret with the intention of betrothed marriage...

Loose fellows are wandering around and running through the land from one place to the other, and wherever one of them sees a wench that takes his fancy he starts getting hot and right away he tries to see how he can get her, goes ahead and gets engaged again, and thus wants to forget and abandon the first engagement that he entered into elsewhere with another woman. And what is worse, they go ahead and have their wedding – some even get married in several places and so carry on a great and shameful scandal in the name and under the appearance of marriage.

This is where the pastors should be careful to warn their people and point out this danger, namely, that no citizen or peasant should give his child in marriage to a strange fellow or man, and that the authorities, too, should not permit such a marriage. The pastor should not publish the banns, marry, or bestow his blessing upon any of these people, but if they are strangers, men or women, they should be required to furnish adequate testimonials of their character, both written and oral, so that one may be certain what kind of people they are, whether they are single or married, honest or dishonest, as do some craftsmen who demand letters of recommendation from their fellow craftsmen...

I know a village not far from here – I will not mention the name of the region (I do not want to mention it for the sake of its reputation) – where, when our gospel came, we found thirty-two couples living together out of wedlock, where either the husband or the wife was a fugitive. I did not think that there were many more than thirty-two houses or inhabitants in the place. The good bishops, officials, and authorities had so managed and looked after things that in this hiding place there were gathered together all those who had been driven out of or had run away from other places. But now, praise God, the gospel has swept away this scandal so cleanly that no open adultery, whoredom, or illicit cohabitation is any longer tolerated anywhere...

[P. 301] If someone comes to you and reports that your bride or wife is not chaste and boasts how he has seen and heard it and is sure of all this, etc., then take him at his word and say, "Will you stick to your word and openly state and testify to this in court (if I accuse her)?" If he refuses to do this and pretends that he wants to warn you secretly in a friendly and confidential way, then you may firmly believe and have no doubt that the devil himself has sent him to you, and that he is lying like a rascal and a fool, even if it were your father, mother, brother, or sister. Mark this too: he wants to warn you and advise you in secret, after it happened. Why did he not do it before? And since he refuses to testify publicly so that you could get free of her, his poisonous warning and counsel is equivalent to this: he sees you caught fast and does not want to help you get free by testifying publicly, but wants to embitter your heart in secret and cause eternal hatred and unrest in you against your bride. In this way you see that he is lying when he says that he wants to warn you and is doing it in your best interests. This is a devil's trick, as I have said.

So then, tell him that he should in God's name keep his mouth shut, which he has opened in the name of the devil, or you will take him to court where he must either prove his statement or be punished as a vile and vicious slanderer...If one were to believe such treacherous tongues, however, nothing, not even God and justice, would remain, either in heaven or on earth. But if you want to believe him, your reward will be that you will never have any peace in your marriage or betrothal. If you believe this you will be doing just what the devil wants, for he is an enemy of marriage and an unclean spirit of whoredom, so he does not want a man to marry, or fills the marriage with unrest when a man does take a wife...

[P. 302] I personally know of four or five fine maidens who enjoyed the reputation of being honorable and virtuous and did not have a single flaw of character, but as soon as they became engaged, the devil's tongue came to the bridegrooms or their good comrades. One had seen and heard this, the other that, and it all had to be true, true, true, although it was twice foully invented and three times a lie. So I finally had to make this proverb for myself: Surely no good child ever becomes a married woman without first becoming a whore. I saw that although they were pious and pure as far as their bodies were concerned, these stinkmouths had to make them out to be whores.

The poor women have nothing more precious or noble than their honor, and this the devil must by no means let them retain...

[Pp. 307–9] What if a child has already been forced into marriage? Shall this be and remain a marriage? Answer: Yes, it is a marriage and shall remain one, for although she was forced into it, she still consented to this coercion by her action, accepted it, and followed it, so that her husband has publicly acquired conjugal rights over her, which no one can now take from him. When she feels that she is being coerced, she should do something about it in time, resist, and not accept it, call upon some good friends, and if that were of no avail she should appeal to the authorities or complain to the pastor or give public, verbal testimony that she did not want to do it, and thus cry out openly against the compulsion...

If the girl remains silent during her public betrothal, however, and leaves these means untried, then she is to keep the promise she has made and afterward keep silent and not complain or pretend that she was forced. One is not to believe her if she does complain...

However, if a case could be found where a child was closely guarded and could not gain access to these means and was betrothed without her cooperation through intermediaries who married her off by force, and she could afterward furnish witnesses that she had not given her consent, I would pronounce her free, even after the consummation...

Further, one also finds people so crude that they simply will not give their daughters in marriage, even when the child is willing. To that extent there is a marriage which would be honorable and beneficial to her, but the father puffs up his belly like a crude peasant and even wants to use the gospel to justify his caprice and contend that the child must be obedient to him. He is unwilling, however, because he can use her at home instead of a maid and is seeking to use his child for his own advantage. This is not forcing into marriage, but away from it; and yet they have no conscience about such unpaternal malice, just as if they were doing right by it... I would rather advise their children and tell them to get engaged without the consent of such fathers. For paternal power is not given to the fathers by God for their caprice or to do harm to their children, but to further and help them. And anyone who uses paternal power in any other way or to the disadvantage of his children forfeits it thereby and is not to be considered a father, but an enemy and destroyer of his own children.

It is my advice, then, that if the father or father's deputy refuses to give a child in marriage, and if good friends, the pastor, or the authorities recognize that the marriage is honorable and advantageous for the child and that the child's parents or their deputies are seeking their own advantage or caprice, then the authorities shall adopt the child in the father's stead, as they do with abandoned children and orphans, and compel the father...

[Pp. 312–13] In addition there is another case, namely, when one spouse runs away from the other, etc. May this one in turn marry still another? Here my answer is this: Where it happens that one spouse knowingly and deliberately leaves the other, such as merchants or those required to go to war, or for any other reason of necessity, and both of them agree to this – here the other partner shall wait and not marry again until there is certain and trustworthy evidence that the spouse is dead, even if the pope in his decretals decrees and permits more than I do. Inasmuch as the wife consents to this journey of her husband and enters into this risk, she is to adhere to it, especially if it takes place for the sake of goods, as may happen with merchants...

But if he is such a villain – and I have found many in my time – who takes a wife and stays with her for a while, spends a lot of money and lives well, then runs away without her knowledge and consent, secretly and treacherously, leaves her pregnant or with children, sends her nothing, writes her nothing, offers her nothing, pursues his villainy, and then returns in one, two, three, four, five, or six years and relies on her having to take him back when he comes, and on the city and house being open to him, then it would be high time and necessary for the authorities to issue a stern decree and take severe measures. And if a villain were to undertake such an action or trick, he should be forbidden to enter the country, and if he were even caught, he should be given his deserts as befits a villain. Such a villain shows his contempt for matrimony and the laws of the city.

ADVICE BOOK TO PASTORS

A Book of Advice and Consolation for the Simple Pastor, 1529,
WA XXX/3, pp. 74–80

Every land has its own customs, according to the common saying. In keeping with this, because weddings and marriage are the business of the world, it is not proper for us clergymen or servants of the church to arrange or govern them. On the contrary, let each city and land follow its own usage and custom, however they go. Some lead the bride to church twice, once in the evening and once in the morning. Some do it only once. Some announce the banns from the chancel two or three weeks in advance. All this and related matters I leave to the lords and council to establish and do as they wish. It is no business of mine.

If somebody desires us to [pronounce the nuptial] blessing outside the church or inside, to pray over them or to marry them, we are obligated to do it. For that reason I have wanted to set out these words and this pattern for those who do not know anything better, in case some of them wish to use them and are in agreement with us…

Because until now one has staged such huge ostentation in the blessing [when they took final vows] of monks and nuns (even though their estate and manner of living is ungodly and the sheer invention of human beings, which has no grounding in Scripture), how much more should we honor, pray [for], and adorn this godly estate and bless it in many splendid ways? For even though it is a secular condition, it nonetheless has God's word as its basis and has not, like the estate of monks and nuns, been invented or founded by people. For that reason it is a hundred times more proper that it should be spiritually respected rather than the cloisterlings' condition, which should properly be regarded as the most worldly and most carnal because it was invented and endowed from flesh and blood and entirely out of worldly sense and reason.

Also, so that young people learn to respect [marriage] and keep it in honor as a godly work and commandment and not so insultingly and foolishly laugh, mock, and treat it with similar foolishness as one has been accustomed to doing until now, just as though it was a joke or children's game to get married or hold a wedding.

Those who first established the practice of leading bride and groom to church have surely thought of it as no joke but treated it with great seriousness. There is no doubt that they wished thereby to obtain the blessing of God and the prayers of the congregation and not to create something laughable or a heathen monkey-business.

The work of itself shows this, for whoever requests the prayer and blessing of the pastor or the bishop demonstrates well (even if he does not precisely say this in so many words) that he commits himself into danger and distress, and what great need of the divine blessing and communal prayer he has in the estate that he has in mind. One well sees every day what misfortune the devil prepares for marriage in the form of adultery, infidelity, discord, and every sort of misery.

So we want to deal in this manner with groom and bride (in case they desire and request it).

First of all to announce the banns from the chancel, with such words:

Hans N. and Greta N., in accordance with the divine ordinance, wish to enter upon the estate of marriage. They desire the community to pray for them, that they may undertake this in God's name and fare well.

And if anyone has any objection, he should state it in a timely fashion or afterward be silent. May God give them His blessing, Amen.

To marry a couple outside the church with words such as these:

Hans, do you want to have Greta as your wedded wife? Let him say: "Yes."

Greta, do you want to have Hans as your wedded husband? Let her say: "Yes."

Here have them give the wedding rings to each other, and join their right hands and say: "What God has joined together, let no man put asunder."

Thereafter let him say before all who are gathered there:

"Because Hans N. and Greta N. desire to be joined in marriage and have confessed this openly here before God and the world, and have joined hands and exchanged wedding rings, I declare that they are married, in the name of the Father and the Son and the Holy Spirit, Amen."

Before the altar let him read God's word over the groom and bride, Genesis, the second chapter:

And the Lord God spoke: "It is not good that man should be alone; I will make him a helper who will be close to him." Then the Lord God made a deep sleep fall upon the man and he went to sleep; and He took one of his ribs and closed up the place with flesh. And the Lord God built a woman out of the rib that He had taken from the man and brought her to him. Then the man spoke: "That would be bone of my bone and flesh of my flesh; she will be called 'little man' because she was taken from the man." For this reason a man will leave his father and his mother and cleave to his wife, and the two will be one flesh.

After this let him turn to them both and address them in this manner:

"Because you both have committed yourselves to marriage in God's name, so hear first of all the commandment of God concerning this estate. St. Paul says, 'You husbands, love your wives just as Christ has loved the church [*gemeine*] and has given himself for her, so that he might save her; and he has purified her through the water-bath of the word so that he may present her to himself as a splendid church [*gemeine*], without any flaw or wrinkle or the like, but holy and blameless.' So should husbands love their wives like their own bodies. Whoever loves his wife loves himself. For no one has ever hated his own flesh; rather, he nourishes and cares for it, just as the Lord does his church [*gemeine*].

"Wives are subject to their husbands as to the Lord, for the husband is the wife's head, just as Christ is the head of the church [*gemeine*]; and he is the savior of his body. Just as the church [*gemeine*] is subject to Christ, so also are wives subject to their husbands in all things.

"Second, hear about the cross that God has laid upon this estate. Thus God spoke to the woman: 'I will give you much trouble when you become pregnant. You will bear your children in sorrow, and you shall bow yourself before your husband, and he shall be your lord.'

"And to the man God said: 'Because you have obeyed the voice of your wife and eaten of the tree that I forbade you, saying, "You shall not eat of it!", cursed will be your field on your account; with worry you shall nourish yourself from it all your life, and it will bear thorns and thistles for you; you shall eat herbs of the field. In the sweat of your brow shall you eat your bread, until you return to the earth from which you were taken. For you are the earth and you shall become earth.'

"Thirdly, this is your consolation, that you know and believe that your estate is pleasing and blessed to God. For it is written, 'God created man in His own image, in the image of God created He him. He created a little man and a little woman. And God blessed them and spoke to them: "Be fruitful and multiply and fill the earth, and bring them among you, and have dominion over the fish in the sea and the birds in the sky and over all animals that crawl upon the earth. And God saw everything that He had made and saw that it was very good." ' Solomon also writes about this: 'He who takes a wife gets a good thing and will obtain favor from the Lord.' "

Here he extends his hands over them and prays as follows:

Lord God who has created man and woman and ordained them for marriage, and has blessed them with offspring, and who has symbolized it [marriage] by the Sacrament of your dear Son, Jesus Christ, and the church, his bride, we ask your boundless goodness not to let this your Creation, ordinance, and blessing be disturbed or spoiled, but rather graciously to preserve it in us, through Jesus Christ our Lord, Amen.

OTHER WORKS

To the councilmen of all cities in Germany that they establish and maintain Christian schools, 1524, LW XLV, pp. 347–78
From *Luther's Works*, vol. XLV, edited by Walther Brandt, © 1962
Fortress Press. Used by permission of Augsburg Fortress Publishers

[P. 368] Now if (as we have assumed) there were no souls, and there were no need at all of schools and languages for the sake of the Scriptures and of God, this one consideration alone would be sufficient to justify the establishment everywhere of the very best schools for both boys and girls, namely, that in order to maintain its temporal estate outwardly the world must have good and capable men and women, men able to rule well over land and people, women able to manage the household and train children and servants aright. Now such men must come from our boys, and such women from our girls. Therefore, it is a matter of properly educating and training our boys and girls to that end...

[P. 370] My idea is to have the boys attend such a school for one or two hours during the day, and spend the remainder of the time working at home, learning a trade, or doing whatever is expected of them. In this way, study and work will go hand-in-hand while the boys are young and able to do both. Otherwise, they spend at least ten times as much time anyway with their pea shooters, ballplaying, racing, and tussling.

In like manner, a girl can surely find time enough to attend school for an hour a day, and still take care of her duties at home. She spends much more time than that anyway in sleeping, dancing, and playing.

Lectures on Genesis, LW I
From *Luther's Works*, vol. I, edited by Jaroslav Pelikan, © 1968
Concordia Publishing Company. Used by permission
of Concordia Publishing House

[Pp. 117–18] What appears in the Latin text as "like unto himself" is in Hebrew "which should be about him." With this expression the text also makes a difference between the human female and the females of all the remaining animals, which are not always about their mates: the woman was so created that she should everywhere and always be about her husband. Thus imperial law also calls the life of married people an inseparable relationship. The female of the brutes has a desire for the male only once in the whole year. But after she has become pregnant, she returns to her home and takes care of herself. For her young born at another time she has no concern, and she does not always live with her mate.

But among men the nature of marriage is different. There the wife so binds herself to a man that she will be about him and will live together with him as one flesh. If Adam had persisted in the state of innocence, this intimate relationship of husband and wife would have been most delightful. The very work of procreation also would have been most sacred and would have been held in esteem. There would not have been that shame stemming from sin which there is now, when parents are compelled to hide in darkness to do this. No less respectability would have attached to cohabitation than there is to sleeping, eating, or drinking with one's wife.

Therefore was this fall not a terrible thing?... Although this activity, like the other wretched remnants of the first state, continues in nature until now, how horribly marred it has become! In honor husband and wife are joined in public before the congregation; but when they are alone, they come together with a feeling of the utmost shame.

Today you find many people who do not want to have children. Moreover, this callousness and inhuman attitude, which is worse than barbarous, is met with chiefly among the nobility and princes, who often refrain from marriage for this one single reason, that they might have no offspring. It is even more disgraceful that you find princes who allow themselves to be forced not to marry, for fear that the members of their house would increase beyond a definite limit. Surely such men deserve that their memory be blotted out from the land of the living.

[Pp. 132–33] Thus this expression is common in Scripture, that the wife is called a household building because she bears and brings up the offspring. The form which this building would have had in Paradise we have lost through sin so completely that we cannot even conceive of it in our thinking. But, as I said above, this present life of ours possesses some small and pitiable remnants of its culture and safeguards as well as of its dominion over the beasts. Sheep, oxen, geese, and hens we govern, although boars, bears, and lions pay no attention to our rule. Similarly some faint image of this building remains; for he who marries a wife has her as a nest and home where he stays at a certain place, just as birds do with their young in their little nest. Those who, like the impure papists, live as celibates do not have such a home.

This living-together of husband and wife – that they occupy the same home, that they take care of the household, that together they produce and bring up children – is a kind of faint image and a remnant, as it were, of that blessed living-together because of which Moses calls the woman a building. If Adam had continued in his innocence, his descendants would have married and wandered away from their father Adam to some little garden of their own. There they would have lived with their wives, and together they would have tilled the soil and brought up their children.

[P. 135] When I was a boy, the wicked and impure practice of celibacy had made marriage so disreputable that I believed I could not even think about the life of married people without sinning. Everybody was fully persuaded that anyone who intended to lead a holy life acceptable to God could not get married but had to live as a celibate and take the vow of celibacy. Thus many who had been husbands became either monks or priests after their wives had died. Therefore it was a work necessary and useful for the church when men saw to it that through the Word of God marriage again came to be respected and that it received the praises it deserved. As a result, by the grace of God now everyone declares that it is something good and holy to live with one's wife in harmony and peace even if one should have a wife who is barren or is troubled by other ills.

I do not deny, of course, that there are some who can live chastely without marriage. Because they have a greater gift than ordinary folk, such people can sail by their own wind...

[P. 137] Moreover, this designation [*woman*] carries with it a wonderful and pleasing description of marriage, in which, as the jurist says, the wife shines by reason of her husband's rays. Whatever the husband has, this the wife has and possesses in its entirety. Their partnership involves not only their means but children, food, bed, and dwelling; their purposes, too, are the same. The result is that the husband differs from the wife in no other respect than in sex; otherwise the woman is altogether a man. Whatever the man has in the home and is, this the woman has and is; she differs only in sex and in something that Paul mentions at 1 Tim. 2:13, namely, that she is a woman by origin, because the woman came from the man and not the man from the woman... For if the wife is honorable, virtuous, and pious, she shares in all the cares, endeavors, duties, and functions of her husband. With this end in view she was created in the beginning; and for this reason she is called woman, or, if we were able to say so in Latin, a "she-man"...

[P. 138] *Therefore a man will leave father and mother and will cling to his wife...*

[P. 139] This forsaking is not to be understood as though the married children would not have visited their parents at all. The reference is only to living together, namely, that the married children would dwell in their own little nest. Among the troubles caused by sin there is also this, that children are compelled to support their parents who have become feeble from age and are in need. But in Paradise our way of life would have been different and better, and yet then, too, this practice would have been kept: that because of his love for his mate the husband would choose his own little nest and give up living with his parents, just as the little birds are accustomed to do...

[P. 219] *And Adam called the name of his wife Eve, because she was the mother of all the living.*

We heard above that the punishment of being under her husband's power was inflicted on the woman. An indication of that power is given here. It is not God who gives her a name; it is Adam, as the lord of Eve, just as he had previously given names to the animals as creatures put under him. No animal thought out a name for itself; all were assigned their names and received the prestige and honor of a name from their lord Adam. Similarly even today, when a woman marries a man, she loses the name of her family

and is called by the name of her husband. It would be unnatural if a
husband wanted to be called by his wife's name. This is an indication and a
confirmation of the punishment or subjection which the woman incurred
through her sin. Likewise, if the husband changes his place of residence,
the woman is compelled to follow him as her lord. So manifold are the
traces in nature which remind us of sin and of our misfortune.

Martin Luther's introduction to Johannes Freder, Ein Dialogus//dem
Ehestand zu//ehren geschrieben . . . 1545, WA LIV, pp. 174–75
[Luther does not devote most of his attention to Freder but rather to
Sebastian Franck, with whose teachings on the Lord's Supper Luther disagreed. But he did also take great exception to Franck's collection of ancient
misogynist aphorisms. This is presumably what moved Johannes Freder to
write.] Just such a bumblebee is this Sebastian Franck, as you will see in
this booklet of M. Johann Freder. [Franck] crawls into the backside of all
women and brings together with his shameful proboscis every evil thing
that the devil has ever said about women or what they have done. He
titillates himself with it, laughs, and gives himself so much satisfaction
that he can say nothing good but everything bad about them . . . He holds
us besides by the nose and mouth as though we were supposed to thank
and praise him for passing such a stink and devil's filth under our nose,
or as though this great arse-bumblebee had daubed such a great dirt-heap
in our face by means of his books, and we were supposed to be happy
about it.

   I will give only one example in order to show that I have read his books
and am not against him without cause. Dear sir, tell me, is it becoming to
a writer of history to say, "Put out the light; [in the dark] all women are the
same"? And even if he had heard this saying from some frivolous person,
should he therefore write it in a book and confirm it with joy and pleasure?
Should he not at least – even if he forgets about the saints who were women
and virgins – think about his own mother, or about his own wife, and be
ashamed in his heart if he has a spark of reason or honor or an honest drop
of blood in his body? Or why are not all men, too, the same in the dark?

TABLE TALK

WA TR I, no. 7, p. 4
Marriage exists in all nature, for among all creatures there is the male and
the female. Even trees are married, likewise gemstones. Thus, among rocks
and stones there is also marriage.

WA TR I, no. 250, p. 104

Nothing is more delightful than the fellowship of a good spouse, nor is anything more bitter than the death of a good spouse. Next to it is the death of children, on which I am experienced – how painful it is. [He is referring to the death of Elisabeth Luther, b. 10 Dec. 1527, d. 3 Aug. 1528.]

WA TR I, no. 974, pp. 492–93

All the works of God are concealed from the world, and it does not perceive them or understand them. God is wonderful, who hides innumerable good things that we neither see nor pay attention to. For who can be adequately amazed by the married estate, which is God's gift and ordinance and which was founded and established by Him Himself. Out of this all the people in the world have come, regardless of their estate – whether spiritual, secular, or domestic. Where would we be if there were no marriage?

But the godless world is moved neither by God's ordinance nor by the sweet nature of little children who are produced in marriage; it sees only the shortcomings and hardships in marriage – it does not see the great treasure and benefit that is in it. Nevertheless, all of us have crawled out of our mother's body; emperor, kings, princes, even Christ himself, God's Son, was not ashamed to be born of a virgin.

Therefore, let the despisers and profaners of marriage ever go hang, like the garden-brothers [Anabaptists were reputed to meet in gardens], the Anabaptists that maintain no marriage but mix among themselves like animals, this one and that. Similarly, let the papists also have a good year, according to their taste with their unmarried life, who profane and insult the marital estate and have whores all the same. Even if they wanted to despise it in the devil's name, they ought to do so in a truthful way and not have whores.

WA TR I, no. 1046, p. 528

The wife governs the household – preserving without damage, however, the husband's right and jurisdiction. The dominion of women from the beginning of the world has never produced any good; as one is accustomed to saying: "Women's rule seldom comes to a good end." When God installed Adam as lord over all creatures, everything was still in good order and proper, and everything was governed in the best way. But when the wife came along and wanted to put her hand too in the simmering broth [*Sode*] and be clever, everything fell apart and became wildly disordered.

WA TR I, no. 1133, pp. 560–61

"Male and female created He them" ... Even though this verse mainly refers to human beings, still one can apply it to all the creatures in the world – the birds in the sky, the fish in the water, and all animals upon the earth. There one finds husband and wife ... who keep to one another and mate, raise young and increase themselves. God presents to our eyes the marital estate in all creatures, and we see the same image in trees, in the skies among the birds, on the land in the animals, and in the sea in fishes – even in stones. It is known to all that male and female are to be found among trees, such as apples and pears, where the apple tree is the male and the pear tree is the female, and similarly in other trees. If one plants them beside one another, they grow and develop better near each other than otherwise. The man stretches out his branches toward the woman, as though he wanted to take her in his arms; and the other way around, the woman raises her branches up toward the man. The sky is the man and the earth the woman; for the earth is made fruitful by the sky by means of the sun, the heat, rain, and wind, etc., so that from her all kinds of herbs and fruit grow. In keeping with this, one finds marriage reflected in the hard stones, especially precious gems such as corals, emeralds, and others. [Cf. TR IV, no. 4783, pp. 498–99.]

WA TR II, no. 1429, pp. 98–99

What Satan is not able to accomplish by himself he brings about by means of evil old women. When I was a young boy, a story was told of how Satan was unable with his slyness to sow discord between two married people who lived together in great unity and loved each other passionately. He attained his end by means of an old woman. She placed a knife under the pillow of each one and convinced each one separately that the other wished to kill him; each could obtain proof of the truth of this by looking under his pillow, where he would find a knife. The husband found the knife first and slit his wife's throat. The devil came to the old woman and handed her a pair of shoes on a long stick. She asked him why he did not bring them all the way to her. He replied, "You are more evil than I. What I could not achieve between these married people, you have accomplished." And so, you see what the devil does by means of his instruments.

WA TR II, no. 1656, p. 165

A person who has just married has unusual thoughts during the first year. When he sits at the table, he thinks, "Look, a while ago you were alone, and now there is another." In bed, he looks around and sees a braid there that earlier he did not see.

[Cf. WA TR III, no. 3178a, p. 211: adds that Käthe sat by him when they were first married, as he was studying, and asked him, "Herr Doctor, is the *Hochmeister* [of the Teutonic Knights] the brother of the margrave [of Brandenburg]?"]

WA TR II, no. 1657, pp. 165–66

I advise that when the engagement has taken place, one should hasten to hold the wedding and public church service. For it is dangerous to postpone and put off the wedding because Satan likes to create problems and defenses [against it] by means of evil gossips, slanderers, and the relatives of both parties... For that reason one should not delay but help to bring the couple together. And if I had not held my own wedding quickly and with the foreknowledge of only a few people, they all would have [tried to] hinder me, for all my best friends cried, "Not this one but another!"

WA TR II, no. 1658, p. 166

One has to have women. If one did not have this sex, womankind, house-keeping and everything that pertains to it would fall apart; and after it all worldly governance, cities, and order. In sum, the world cannot dispense with women even if men by themselves could bear children.

When we look backward and think about the past, marriage is not so bad, for by means of it the future and the world are maintained. For our parents, who were pious people within this ordinance of God, lived out their faith inasmuch as they obeyed God's command to raise children. Thus my children honor me as I did and behaved toward my parents.

Because I believe that my parents lived in sacred matrimony, why should I not also praise my own marriage? Can we condone what our parents did, but despise and reproach marriage for ourselves?

So too, when we look around us at brothers, sisters, and friends, we see nothing within marriage that is ungodly. But when we look at our own marriage, we are repelled by it; but my father slept with my mother just as I do with my wife, and he joked with her. They were pious people who did and were just like all the patriarchs, church fathers, and prophets.

[Cf. WA TR II, no. 1659, pp. 166–67; WA TR III, no. 3181a and 3181b, pp. 212–13.]

WA TR II, no. 2350b, p. 428 [together with no. 2350a, on the same subject]

He who takes a wife must surely be a pious man, but Hans Metzsch [*c.* 1490–1549, *Hauptmann* (electoral official) in Wittenberg] is not worthy of this divine gift; a good woman deserves to have a pious man. A spouse must be a pious person, someone who derives grace and peace from the marital estate. This gift is next to an understanding of the gospel. One finds many obstinate, queer married people who are estranged from one another, who fight, hit, argue, and bite one another and do not inquire after wife and children. They are not human.

[Also inserted here:] The greatest blessing is to have a pious, God-fearing, domesticated wife to whom one can entrust his property, even his body and life, with whom you can raise children. But God casts many of them into matrimony without their advice and particular consideration. Ketha, you have a pious husband who loves you, thanks be to God! [Cf. no. 2506, p. 497: "Ketha, you have a pious husband, you are an empress; give thanks to God!" This one gives a German version, too, that differs: "Ketha, you have a pious husband who loves you, you are an empress! I thank God."]

WA TR II, 2406a, p. 451
[Contrasting himself with papists:] I, however, shall die a lover of marriage. [Cf. no. 2406b, pp. 451–52.]

WA TR III, no. 2858b, pp. 29–30
That upright love between married people was seldom. A pretty young woman in a place that otherwise had many well-off suitors took a priest for the sake of money. Doctor Martin Luther said, "Money overcame the young queen."

Afterward they discussed how a very pretty little girl had been given to an old, eccentric cripple and greedy widower, who had previously treated his wife harshly and badly. And when he now often plagued her, she said, "Can't the devil get free of you? If he has had you in hell for such a long time, he should have grown tired of you." Then Dr. Luther said, "God the Lord give her His blessing and this little wedding song: that he [the widower] is zealous, as old men are accustomed to be in relation to young wives. Ah, dear Lord God, what a great and unusual thing it is, to love wife and children properly! We can easily love a sack, but not our wedded wife. It takes a pious husband and a pious wife to love one another and their children from the heart. Satan suppresses and extinguishes God's ordinance and the natural inclination and love in us. For what we ought to do, we cannot and do not wish to do."

WA TR III, no. 2867b, pp. 40–41
On New Year's Day the infant of Doctor Martin Luther cried and screamed so much that nobody could quiet it. The doctor with his housewife were sad and troubled for an entire hour. Afterward he said, "That is the

unpleasantness and hardship in marriage, on account of which everyone avoids it, is offended, and does not want to get married. We are too much afraid of the strange mood of women, of the howling and screaming of the children, of worry about the great expense and bad neighbors, etc. For that reason, we want to be free and untrammeled, to remain free lords and to do as it pleases us with whores, be idle, etc. Therefore, none of the [church] fathers wrote anything noticeably and especially good about marriage.

"Jerome was a proper blackguard [*Gardian*], wrote horridly enough – one could almost say, in an unchristian manner – about marriage. They see in marriage only the pleasure and flee in it nothing so much as the troubles of the flesh. They want to avoid every little drop of unpleasantness and have fallen into the sea of all voluptuousness and evil desires. Only St. Augustine wrote a good expression about marriage, when he said, 'He who cannot live chastely, let him take a wife and arrive safely at the Judgment of the Lord.' And again, 'If a man wants to be married not on account of children but because of necessity, in that without marrying he cannot be continent or live chastely, the same belongs to the forgiveness of sins on account of the faith and troth of marriage,' etc. The good Father could not say, 'For the sake of faith in the word.'

"But out of special grace God brought marriage, authority, and the preaching office in order, as He established and commanded it, before the Last Day by means of His word, so that we may see that they are His institutions...Married people were of the opinion that this compact, requiring them to be and stay with one another, was more of a custom that had been carried forward through use and practice rather than that God had ordained it so."

WA TR III, no. 2978b, p. 129
The pope, as one says, has extended his grace to all Lutherans [clergy] and their wives as long as they preach and teach what he wishes and hold their wives as whores and cooks. "Phooey to you!" said Dr. Martin. "What may the devil do? He leaves adultery unpunished! Not to respect marriage is human, but to damn it – that is indeed to despise God."

WA TR III, no. 3412a, pp. 307–8
A certain citizen of Torgau struck his wife, and often the neighbors ran to rebuke him. He said to them, "Let me exercise my right; this unhappiness arises on account of a nail on which she wants to hang her veil, but I hang my hat there." Evidently this is a cause of discord in marriage, that women obey their husbands in nothing.

Lucas Cranach the Elder had portrayed the wife of Doctor Martin Luther. When the painting hung on the wall and the doctor looked at it, he said, "I want to have a man painted in addition to that and the two images sent to the council in Mantua and ask the holy fathers who are gathered there if they would prefer marriage or celibacy, the unmarried life of the clergy." Now Doctor Martin Luther began to praise and extol marriage. [He said] "It is God's ordinance and without it the world would long since have become barren and waste, and all other creatures would have been created completely in vain and for nothing; for they were all created for the sake of human beings; there would [otherwise] have been no order or estates in the world. Thus, when Eve was brought to Adam, he was indeed filled with the Holy Spirit and gives her an especially splendid, beautiful name and calls her Eve, that is, the mother of all living things. He does not call her his wife but instead a mother, and he adds to that 'of all the living.' There you have the highest treasure, honor, and adornment of the women, namely that they are the fount of all living things, the spring and origin from which all living humans come. These may be short words, but they constitute a splendid encomium. And neither Demosthenes nor Cicero could ever speak splendidly about it; rather, the Holy Spirit is the orator about this, and he should claim and speak through our first father, Adam. And because this doctor and orator splendidly defines and praises the marital estate, we may properly cover everything over that is fragile about a woman. For the Lord Christ, the Son of God, did not despise marriage but was born of a woman. That is not a small praise of marriage. For that reason, St. Paul also saw and extolled marriage when he says in 1 Timothy 2, 'The woman is saved through the production of children, if she remains within the faith.' The woman is saved through bearing children if she stays in faith and in love and in sanctification together with modesty."

The rules of the household written by Doctor Martin Luther . . . : [in verse]
> The master must become the servant
> If he wants to find the house in order.
> The mistress must be the maid herself
> If she wants all in the house to run properly.
> The servants never take into account
> What is useful and harmful to the house;
> It has no bearing on them
> Because it does not belong to them.

They are the guests and the strangers in the house.
What is one's own does not go out [is not expended].

WA TR III, no. 3675, pp. 514–15

[Luther is quoted as saying] Dear God, what effort and work the matrimonial cases require! What it costs to bring married people [back] together! And after that it takes much more effort to keep them together. Adam's fall so dirtied, spoiled, and poisoned human nature that it is the most inconstant and flows hither and yon like quicksilver [mercury]. Oh, how good things are when married people are together at table and in bed! Even if they occasionally quarrel and complain, that does not hurt; marriage does not always run smoothly, it is a chancy thing. One has to commit oneself to it.

Adam and Eve will have fought with one another lustily indeed over nine hundred years. Eve will have said to Adam, "You ate the apple!" and he will have responded, "Why did you give it to me?" Over such a long lifetime, they will doubtless have regarded much evil and misfortune with pain and yearning in their marriage. All of this derived from their fall and disobedience and was caused by it...

WA TR III, no. 3755, p. 598

Doctor Martin Luther was at Hans Lufft's daughter's wedding. After the evening meal, he led the bride to bed and told the groom that he ought to adhere to the common pattern and usage and be the lord of the house, when the lady is not at home. And as a sign [of this], he removed one of [the groom's] shoes and laid it upon the canopy, so that he retained the dominance and the governance.

WA TR IV, no. 4064, p. 109

The whoring at court was considered, and how they [courtiers] shamelessly inquired everywhere after sluts and looked for them in [people's] houses. To this Dr. Martin Luther said, "Ah, Satan is the particular enemy of marriage, when in accordance with God's ordinance husband and wife come together. What is proper for us, we consider to be unpleasant and do not like it. All comedies and dramas that were rhymed and put together by the old heathens look at this and show how unpleasant marriage is to people. But they like whoring. The one who goes into the bath [of marriage] goes as in a dream and is not clever. One has probably helped [this attitude] with superstitions, the belief in loathsome celibacy and an unmarried way of life. Saint Jerome wrote a shameful book against Jovinian about widows who transgress against their first troth and fidelity – just as though it was improper for them to remarry, even though the text immediately afterward clearly presses on and says, 'I want young widows to marry,' etc. St. Paul says, 'It is good not to touch a woman.' From this Jerome concludes, 'Therefore, it is evil to marry'; even though Paul's word *evil* in that place means laborious, toilsome, or difficult."

WA TR IV, no. 4138, p. 163

After this he was asked whether Paul had been married. He said, "Presumably, for the Jews were accustomed to marrying early and young, and they still lived chastely and properly. For chastity suits virgins, widows, and married people, as the Letter to the Hebrews says: 'The marriage bed shall be kept unspotted by all.' But to be celibate and unmarried pertains actually to virgins and single people – to those who are not yet married."

Dr. M. Luther said further, "Bride and groom – one is accustomed to saying that the bride is given preeminence, which is a German way of speaking; for one says, 'Cheese and bread'; the cheese has to go first. Well, all right! With God's help, I want to carry out this wedding of my *Muhme* [Muhme Lehna, Magdalena von Bora, Käthe's aunt], perhaps the last one," etc. And he commanded that they should have the schoolmaster with the singers on the second day, "for music has small place and pertains to a great throng of people. *Venter caret auribus,* the belly has no ears."

WA TR IV, no. 4371, p. 267

[Cf. no. 4373, p. 269] Dr. M. Luther asked Dr. Basilius whether one might properly allow a married man whose wife gradually became sick and ill, such that no one could help her and she was simply a living cadaver and as though dead, and where the husband could not dispense with a wife because of his desire, to take another wife. He answered and said, "Law does not permit this easily, even though some cases might occur in which they permitted a man to have a mistress, concubine, and bedmate. But it happens seldom and not without great and important causes."

Dr. M. Luther said, "It is dangerous, for if one concedes and allows divorce on account of the most extreme illnesses and lets someone take another wife, one could think up many reasons every day for breaking marriage apart."

WA TR IV, no. 4408, p. 298

"Each person in the marriage shall fulfill his office, what pertains to him. The husband shall acquire, but the wife shall save. In this way, the wife can well make the husband rich, and not the husband the wife. For the penny saved is better than the penny earned. Being frugal is the best income. I should properly be entered in the registry of the poor," said Dr. Martin Luther, "for I keep too many servants."

WA TR IV, no. 4410, pp. 300–1

A woman had two husbands, one after the other. By the first she had a son, by the second a daughter. This son wishes to marry his stepsister, who is related to him in the third degree. The question is whether this is permissible. To this Dr. L. said, "We have turned this business over to the Elector. In a case of the fourth degree of relatedness, we permit it; but in the third grade we do not want to give in – not, to be sure, on grounds of conscience, but because of the bad example [it sets for] the greedy peasants, who for the sake of their property would marry their closest blood relation. If one allowed them to marry relatives of the third degree, they would accustom themselves to marrying in the second degree. There are girls enough; why should these be left sitting?

"Moses well commanded the rich to take those who were most closely related to them so that the poor girls were not left sitting. For that reason David and Solomon had many wives for the sake of their poor blood relations, so that these too would be cared for and nourished.

"But now our greedy peasants and those from the nobility gladly marry their closest blood relatives for their property's sake, so that the poor, miserable wenches are not considered or provided for. For that reason, we forbid [marrying] in this degree out of political and worldly need. But the pope has forbidden it out of sheer hypocrisy and grants dispensations and permits it for money."

WA TR IV, no. 4602, pp. 399–400

Doctor Martin Luther spoke of the unmarried life in popery, which had a great glory and regard in the eyes of the world; and by contrast marriage had much hardship, worry, and repugnance, etc. He said, "The leading causes of priestly celibacy are, first, that their children and descendants would become poor, abandoned orphans, and the fathers become greedy for their children to have something from which to nourish themselves – though they would have been greedy even without that. And the pope and the bishops could not flourish and increase [their wealth] without celibacy and the unmarried life. The second cause," he said, "is that the shortcomings of the priests' wives are aggravating; for if they criticized these faults [in others' wives], people would ask them why they didn't punish these in their own wives."

WA TR IV, no. 4736, pp. 459–60

In 1539 on 1 February Dr. Martin Luther had much to do with business and letters and said, "Today is a letter day and unpleasant. These matters [marriage cases] secretly steal away the time for studying, reading, preaching, writing, and praying. I am glad that the consistories have been founded, chiefly on account of the marriage matters."

WA TR IV, no. 4787, pp. 503–5

Doctor M. speaks about his wedding. "If I," he said, "had wanted to get married thirteen years ago, I would have chosen Eva Schönfeld, whom now Dr. Basilius, the physician in Prussia, has [as his wife]. I didn't love my Käthe at that time, for I regarded her with mistrust as someone proud and arrogant. But it pleased God, who wanted me to take pity on her. And, God be praised, this was well-advised, for I have a pious, faithful wife on whom her husband's heart can rely, as Solomon says, '. . . She does not spoil what is his.'

"Ah, dear God, marriage is not a thing of nature but a gift of God, the very sweetest and most lovely, indeed the most chaste life, superior to all celibacy . . . In spite of the fact that they [women] all collectively can practice the art of taking a man prisoner by means of crying, lying, [and] arguing, and can turn things around with the most skillful words, nonetheless, when these three things remain in marriage – namely, trust and faith, children and offspring, and sacrament, such that one regards it as a holy thing and godly estate – then it is truly a blessed condition.

"Oh, how heartily I yearned for my [family] when I lay deathly ill in Schmalkald! I thought that I would never see my wife and babies again. How much pain this being apart and separated caused me! Now I do believe that, in people who are dying, this affection and love that a husband feels for his wife and parents for their children is the very strongest. Because by God's grace I have become healthy again, I love my wife and children so much the more. No one is so spiritual that he does not feel this natural inclination and love. The bond and fellowship between a husband and wife is a great thing."

WA TR V, no. 5212, p. 10

Whether if a young man married an old woman who has had no children, this too is a proper marriage? "Why not? However, I would prefer that one left out the words of the blessing, 'Be fruitful and multiply.' But I am not to create ceremonies and ordinances, for once one begins, there is no end, and one ever comes after the other, as happened in popery."

WA TR V, no. 5524, p. 214

Lucas Maler [probably Lucas Cranach the Younger, 1515–86], when he had taken a wife and the wedding was over, wanted to be next to the bride. He had a good friend who told him, "My dear, do not behave this way! Before half a year has passed, you will have had enough. Whatever maid you have in the house you will prefer to your wife!" And so it goes. For we hate those things that are present, we love those that are absent. Ovid: what is permitted, etc.; what is not permitted burns more steadfastly. That is the weakness of our nature. The devil comes along and throws hatred, suspicion, [and] lust in the paths of both parties; and then one runs away. A wife is quickly taken. But to love her always, that is afterward difficult; and one who has this [ongoing love of his wife?] should well thank our Lord God. For that reason, when one desires to take a wife, let him be serious about it and ask our Lord God, "Dear Lord God, if it is your divine will that I should live without a wife, then help me; if not, grant me a good, pious little maid to spend my life with, so that I love her and she loves me." For the union of the flesh does not bring this about. There must also be a coming together of habits and character. Sexual intercourse does not make this.

WA TR V, no. 5578, pp. 258–59

There was a schoolmaster in Frankfurt an der Oder, a learned, godly man who had set his heart on theology and had preached several times to the great amazement of the listeners; [and] finally he was called to the post of deacon. But his wife, who had a haughty spirit and temperament, would by no means consent to his accepting it, saying that she did not want to be married to a cleric [*Pfaff*]. The question was what the good man was to do – whether he should leave his wife or the preachership. To this Dr. Martin Luther first said jokingly and laughing, "If he married a widow, as you say, then he has to do what she wants." Right after that he said, "If there was a proper authority there, they could compel the slut; for the wife is obliged to follow the husband, and not the husband the wife. It must be an evil wife, indeed a devil, who is ashamed of the office of preacher, which was occupied by the Lord Christ and the dear angels. The devil seeks out such a one, for he likes to slander and insult the preacher's post. I would say to her, if she were my wife, 'Will you follow me? Say quickly "No" or "Yes"!' If she said 'No,' I would take another wife and let this one go. This [situation] is the result of the authorities' not being there to enforce this and not supporting the office of preacher."

WA TR V, no. 5683, p. 319

...A maiden, as you wish; a widow, as she wills. Beware of her who has had two husbands; my horse will kick you!

WA TR V, no. 5733, p. 334

At weddings, when the groom and the bride are together in bed, one sticks to the old tradition that when they take off their shoes, they lay it [the groom's shoe] on the canopy as a sign of [his] power.

WA TR V, no. 5962, p. 411

In marriage one ought to consider these things: (1) God's commandment; (2) the confirmation of the Lord Christ; (3) the honor of Christ [that Christ paid to marriage]; (4) the first blessing; (5) the promise that comes with it; (6) the society and companionship; (7) the example of the holy patriarchs and fathers; (8) worldly laws and ordinances; (9) the rich benediction and blessing; (10) the examples of curses; (11) the threat of St. Paul; (12) natural law; (13) the nature and manner of the Creation; (14) the exercise of faith and hope.

WA TR V, no. 5963, p. 411

What frightens people away from marriage: (1) poverty; (2) age; (3) [social] class; (4) mockery; (5) the perpetual union; (6) the wife's behavior.

WA TR V, no. 6322, pp. 601–2

Marriage between like people is by far the best. An old man and a young maiden do not make sense together. Only money affects things. Just as in the past an old man bragged about all his wealth and showed it to a young woman. The servant pleased him [his master] and always added, "Dear maid, at night he has much more than this." In the end, as coughing plagued him, the servant said, "My lord has much more of this."

WA TR VI, no. 6908, p. 263

...Dr. Martin Luther said "Two young married people loved each other from the heart and got along very well. Now, the devil wanted to divide them so that these little people did not love each other so much. So he went to an old whore, to an evil gossiping woman, and offered her a pair of red shoes if she could divide this married couple. The old slut accepted this. She came first to the husband and said, 'Listen, your wife is looking to take your life.' The husband replied, 'That can't be true; I know that my wife loves me dearly.' 'No,' the old woman said, 'she has another love and wants to strangle you.' And she made things such that the man was afraid of the woman and was worried about all kinds of evil. Soon the old slut goes to the man's wife and says, 'Your husband does not love you.' The wife answers and says, 'Ah, I have a pious husband; I know that he loves me.' The old slut says, 'No, he wants another woman; so you do it before he does: take some scissors, put them under the pillow, and choke him!' The little wife believes it, develops suspicion (that crazy, poor little fool) toward her husband, believes the old, evil hag. The husband is hard toward his wife, and when he learns from the old whore that his wife has hidden scissors under the pillow, he waits until the wife has fallen asleep, finds the scissors, and throttles the wife. Then the old woman comes to the devil and demands the pair of red shoes. The devil reaches the shoes to her on a long stick, is afraid of her, and speaks, 'Take these; you are worse than I am!' That is what the evil tongue of the old woman does; the husband and wife easily believed her bad talk, which they should not have done. For this reason we say that married people in their marriage should diligently pray."

WA TR VI, no. 6910, pp. 264–65

When one time a person at Dr. Luther's table wanted to excuse the young men's wild and dissolute lives and whoring, Dr. L. answered and said, "They learn to despise the feminine sex, indeed to misuse women, for which they were not created." And he began after that to speak about marriage and said, "It is a great thing when a man can always love a girl, for the devil seldom permits it; if they are away from one another, he can't bear it; if they are together, he can't stand that either. As one is accustomed to saying: 'I can't live with you or without you.' For that reason, diligent prayer pertains to it [marriage]. I have seen many married couples who came together in such great passion that they wanted to eat each other up; but a half year later they ran away from one another. As that one said to Lucas Cranach [the younger], 'It is true, it goes that way, the devil drives [people] together in such an ardor that they cannot pray; first they yearn for the other sex, then they grow cold, then they hate.' In a city close to Wittenberg, there was a married couple more handsome than one could well have found in four principalities. They came together with such burning, but a year later she became a whore and hung around the worst lewd men, and he became a rogue and went around with the filthiest hags. It was a shame. Why? They didn't pray. The devil won the game. For that reason, my landlady in Eisenach was right to say to me when I went to school there, 'There is no more lovely thing on earth than the love of a woman, for those who can partake of it.' "

CHAPTER 6

Sexuality

Luther's ideas about women are tied to his ideas about sexuality. In some writings, such as the sermons and lectures on Genesis and particularly his comments about Eve, women's sexual nature is at the core of their being. He criticizes women, both prostitutes and other young women, for enticing young men into sexual relationships, with language that is much harsher than that discussing men enticing women. In other works, however, he concentrates more on male sexual desire and sexual activities, with women entering in primarily as desired objects rather than acting subjects. He regards sexual desire as extremely powerful in both men and women, but muses from time to time that women's weakness might make it even more difficult for them to control their desires than this was for men.

In Luther's opinion, the power of lust makes the truly chaste life impossible for all but a handful of individuals. Thus one of his earliest treatises attacks the value of vows of celibacy, and argues that the best Christian life is not one which fruitlessly attempts ascetic celibacy, but one in which sexual activity is channeled into marriage. Marriage is not a sacrament – Luther was adamant that it conferred no special grace – but it is the ideal state for almost everyone. Therefore the restrictions on marriage which had developed in the Middle Ages should be done away with, and everyone should marry, the earlier after puberty the better.

Because sexual desire is natural and created by God, it is a central part of marriage, and marriages in which it cannot be satisfied – such as those to impotent persons – are not truly marriages. Luther is faithful to Augustine's idea of the link between original sin and sexual desire, but also, and somewhat contradictorily, regards marital sex as a positive good in itself and not simply because it leads to procreation; sex increases affection between spouses and promotes harmony in domestic life. The centrality of sex to marriage leads Luther to advocate divorce in the case of impotence, adultery, desertion, absolute incompatibility, or the refusal of a spouse to have sex; reconciliation is preferable, but if this cannot be effected, the innocent party should be granted a divorce with the right to remarry. An even better solution might be bigamy, which Luther recommends as a solution to the marital difficulties of both King Henry VIII of England and Philip of Hesse, a prominent Protestant nobleman, though he advises that this be kept a secret.

Luther's advocacy of bigamy grows out of his harsh condemnation of all sex outside marriage, including prostitution, one of the few issues on which he explicitly broke with Augustine. During the late Middle Ages, most major cities in Europe and many of the smaller ones had an official brothel or section of the city in which selling sex for money was permitted. The women who lived in them were often termed "common women" (*gemeine Frauen* in German), because their services were held in common by many men and were not simply reserved for one, as was the case with married women. Cities justified the existence of brothels by noting that their residents protected honorable women and girls from the uncontrollable lust of young men, an argument that went back to Augustine, if not earlier. This toleration of prostitution began to change in the late fifteenth century, and cities imposed restrictions on the clothing and mobility of brothel residents. Selling sex came to be seen primarily as a moral issue rather than an economic one, described as one type of "whoredom," a term that also included premarital sex, adultery, and other unacceptable sexual activities. Luther discusses prostitution in almost every type of writing – lectures, sermons, letters, table talk – and also uses the word "whore" metaphorically when describing his theological opponents.

Luther's language regarding prostitutes is extremely harsh, as are his words about adulterers. Because adultery directly challenged the central link between marriage and procreation as well as impugning male honor, it was a very serious matter in legal codes as well as the writings of theologians. Many legal codes, including the criminal code of the Holy Roman Empire of 1532, called the *Carolina Constitutio Criminalis*, defined adultery as a capital offense. In a few cases individuals were indeed executed for adultery, though lesser punishments such as fines, prison sentences, corporal punishment, or banishment were more common. The status of the offender generally determined the punishment, with wealthier individuals fined and told to return to their spouses and poorer ones banished. Punishments also often involved public shaming; offenders were sentenced to sit in the stocks or on the "stool of correction," or to wear a large stone attached to a choker in a procession or around the marketplace. In contrast to many medieval law codes which defined adultery solely as sex between a married woman and a man not her husband, sexual relationships between a married man and an unmarried woman were defined as adultery in most sixteenth-century codes. Because adultery by a married man with a single woman did not threaten the family and lineage in the way that adultery by a married woman did, actual trials of married men were quite rare, however. This stands in contrast to Luther's statements about adultery, which are more often directed toward men than women, and warn about "adultery in the heart" as well as adultery in practice.

Luther comments directly and off-handedly about a variety of other sexual issues. He uses stories about complex cases of incest to make points about the centrality of marriage and the separation of world and secular power. Particularly in his later works, he uses highly sexualized language to describe the papacy, denouncing the popes and curia for what he regarded as "unnatural" sexual activity as well as incorrect doctrine. While his attacks on the sexual activities of lower-level clergy generally concentrate on heterosexual concubinage, attacks on the papal court describe a variety of same-sex behaviors. Sodomy had become a capital crime in the Holy Roman Empire during the 1530s, defined as relations between two men, two women, or any person and an animal. Sodomy was linked with heresy in the minds of many other theologians and jurists along with Luther, with the proper punishment for both regarded as death by fire. Despite such attitudes, however, the number of actual sodomy cases in the sixteenth century was very small, with many jurisdictions never seeing a single case in either ecclesiastical or secular courts. Almost all of the cases that did come to trial involved men; the handful involving women were generally brought after a woman had worn men's clothing, used a dildo or other device to effect penetration, or married another woman. The horror with which they were regarded sprang more from the fact that they had usurped a man's social role than that they had been attracted to another woman. This legal situation was reflected in Luther's writings, for though he often writes about the difficulties young nuns faced in resisting lust, he nowhere discusses attraction to other women as a possible outcome of this lust.

Because Luther – and other Protestants – expected good works as the fruit of saving faith, they regarded sexual morality as extremely important. Thus Luther spoke and wrote about sex regularly throughout his long career; because he said so much, however, his ideas about sexuality, like his ideas about women, often appear contradictory.

SEXUAL DESIRE

An Open Letter to Leonard Koppe, "Why Virgins Are Allowed to Leave the Convent in a Godly Way", 1523, WA XI, pp. 398–99

... The fourth reason for leaving the convent and the veil is probably the most important, although one must almost be ashamed of it: that is, that it is impossible that the gift of chastity is as common as the convent. A woman is not created to be a virgin, but to bear children. In Genesis 1 God was not speaking just to Adam, but also to Eve when He said, "Be fruitful and multiply," as the female sex organs of a woman's body, which God has created for this reason, prove. And this was not just said to one or two women, but to all of them, with no exceptions. God establishes this [i.e., chastity] not through our oaths or our free will, but through His own powerful means and will. Whenever He has not done this, a woman should remain a woman, and bear children, for God has created her for that; she should not make herself to be better than God has made her.

When He cursed Eve, He did not take her female body or her female sex organs; He did not take back the blessing that He had spoken to her, that she would be fruitful, but He reinforced this and said: "I will give you much trouble when you become pregnant." This misery was not just promised to one or two women, but to all of them. The words sound as if God knew that all women would become pregnant and would carry this curse, except for those that He Himself excepted. Against this no oaths or agreements can be maintained, for it is God's word and power ... if it were possible and saintly to abide by any oath you swore, then you might as well swear that you would become the Mother of God, like Mary.

Letter of Luther to three nuns, Wittenberg, 6 August 1524, WA BR III, no. 766, pp. 326–28

Grace and peace in Christ Jesus our Savior! Dear sisters! I have received your letters both times, and learned of your requests. I would have already answered, because I was concerned and there was a messenger at hand, but I have had much to do. First, you have understood correctly that there are two reasons to leave your convent life and your vows. The first is, when human law and convent life are maintained with force and are not a matter of choice, and the conscience is burdened through this. Then one should leave, and the convents and everything should be opened. If this is true for you, that you are not being allowed to decide freely about the convent, but your consciences are being constrained, then you should contact your relatives and let yourselves be assisted in leaving and (if the authorities will allow it) stay with them or stay somewhere else. If your relatives or parents do not want to do this, let other good people help you, without worrying about whether your parents become angry, die, or get over it, for the salvation of the soul and the will of God are above all. As Christ says: "Those who love father and mother more than me, are not worthy of me." If the sisters will let you free, or at least allow you to read and hear the word of God, you may stay in there, and do the work of the convent, such as spinning, cooking, and similar things, as long as you do not put your trust in such things.

The other reason is the flesh. Although women are ashamed to admit such things, both Scripture and experience teach that among many thousands there is not one to whom God gives the grace to maintain pure chastity. A woman does not have the power [to do this] herself. God created her body to be with a man, bear children and raise them, as Scripture makes clear in Genesis 1. Her bodily members, ordained by God for this, also demonstrate this. This is as natural as eating and drinking, sleeping and waking up. It is created by God, and He also wants what is natural, that is men and women being together in marriage. Therefore one should be contented and not be ashamed, for God created and made them for this. If one feels that one does not have the highly unusual gift [of chastity], one should leave, and do what one finds oneself created to do. You will read and learn much about this, when you come out and hear proper sermons. I have written a great deal about this in "On Monastic Vows," "Avoiding Human Teachings," and in the sermon "On Married Life." If you read these, you will find enough instructions about everything, whether it is confession or whatever else, so that I do not have to write at length here. I anticipate that you will leave the convent for these two reasons, or only one is enough, and you already mention the first. If it happens that in the future convents become matters of free choice, then you can certainly move back in again, if you have the grace and desire to do so. The city council of Berne in Switzerland opened the famous convent at Königfelden, and let the nuns leave, stay, or come in as they wished, and gave them what they brought into the convent. God be with you in this. And pray for me! Given at Wittenberg on the sixth of Martini 1524. Martin Luther. (Into the hands of the three nuns, my dear sisters in Christ, written in friendship.)

Sermon on Matthew 5:27–29, WA XXXII: Weekly Sermons on Matthew 5–7, 1530/32, pp. 369–75
You have heard that it was said to the ancients, "You shall not commit adultery." I say to you, however, that whoever looks at a woman in lust

has already committed adultery in his heart. If your right eye troubles you, rip it out and throw it away from you. It is better for you that you destroy one of your members rather than let your whole body be thrown into hell. If your right hand troubles you, cut it off and throw it away. It is better for you that you destroy one of your members than let your whole body be cast into hell."

This is truly a piece of salt against the teachings of the Pharisees, in which he [Jesus] considers two sorts of things: first adultery and afterwards divorce. In regard to adultery, they interpreted this exactly as the Fifth Commandment says and taught that nothing was forbidden except actually committing adultery in the deed. They did not consider it a sin, even if they were burned to death in their hearts with evil lust and love for another, and even if this showed itself openly with ugly words and shameful gestures. This did not affect their sense of their own holiness, as long as they otherwise did good works, made offerings industriously and prayed and so on. This does not mean that they are teaching God's commandments, but exactly the opposite; they do not make people pious through this but only make them angry, and give space and opportunity for all types of sin and immorality. But here you hear a different teacher, who makes their holiness into sin and shame, and shines a light on this commandment, showing that adultery can also be done with the eyes, ears, mouth, yes especially with the heart, such as when someone looks at or jokes with a woman and thinks about her with evil lust...

But you say: if it is true that marriage can be broken with a glance, what should we do? Men and women must live with one another and associate with each other every day, or should one run out of the world or poke out one's ears and eyes and have one's heart ripped out? Answer: Christ does not forbid that one lives with others, eats, drinks, or also laughs and is happy; all of this is without harm, except for the part of this that is your desires. Yes, the Jews wanted to help him in this, because they said it is not a sin if one loves another in one's thoughts or signs, just as they do not consider it a sin to be angry with one's neighbor or be his enemy in one's heart, so that they would not have to damn their whole people and many holy persons as if they were nothing but murderers and adulterers. For this reason they had to thumb their noses at this commandment, saying that it was not meant so strictly, but as our scholars said, certainly this is good advice in theory, but no one is bound to it. For this reason we have come so far that it is often doubted and disputed whether having a relationship with a whore outside marriage is also a sin. Actually now in Italy it is considered an honor among reasonable people, and they appear to consider them pious, and leave them alone. On the other hand there are also those who have made this commandment too strict, and want to be so holy that they have forbidden all looking at each other and teach that all contact between men and women should be forbidden. From this come the wonderful saints, who came out of the world into the deserts and cloisters, so that they gave up seeing or hearing anything, or having any contact with the world.

Christ is the opposite of both of these ways. He does not want to turn God's commandment upside down and give advice that would lead to unbridled immorality and whoredom. For he says with a few clear words that whoever looks at a woman with lust is an adulterer, and punishes him with hellfire. He says that it is better that a man pull out his eye than that the whole body be thrown into hell. But he also does not support the saints, who run away from people. For if that were the case, then the Ten Commandments would not apply to everyone. For if I am in a desert, separated from all other people, no one has to thank me that I do not commit adultery, murder or steal. Even if I think that I am holy, I have simply run away from the commandments, which were given by God to teach us how we should live correctly with our neighbors in the world.

For we are not created so that we should run away from each other, but should live with and next to each other, and experience good and bad. Because we are human, we must help each other bear all sorts of human misfortune and curses under which we were born. We must arm ourselves, so that we can live among evil people, so that everyone proves his holiness there in the world and does not let this make him so impatient that he flees away from it. For we must live on earth among thistles and thorns, in paths that are full of temptation, opposition, and disaster. And you do not help matters if you immediately run away from people and yet still carry the same villain with you, that is, of course, the passion and evil lust that is present in flesh and blood. For you cannot deny your father and mother, even if you are alone and locked in, nor can you throw away your flesh and blood and leave it there. This does not mean to throw away your foot and flee away from it, but to stay within it, to bravely stand and fight against all temptations and rip through and defeat them with great patience.

In this Christ is a good teacher. He does not teach you to run away from people or change your state, but to get hold of yourself and throw away the eye or the hand that annoys you, which means take away the cause of sin, which is the evil lust and desire that is within you and that comes out of your own heart. If this stays outside, you can live without sin among people and associate with everyone. He says clearly in regard to this (as I have said):

"If you look at a woman with desire, you have committed adultery in your heart." He does not forbid looking, for he is speaking to people who must live in the world among people, as the previous and subsequent chapters [of Matthew] make clear. However, he wants to separate looking and desire. You can certainly look at any woman or man, but be careful that desire does not follow. For this reason, God has ordained that everyone has his or her own wife or husband, to whom one's lust and desire should turn and should be limited. If you can stay with this, He certainly allows it, and gives this His blessing, letting it please Him as He has ordained and established it. But if you want to roam further, and are not satisfied with the one that God has given you and whom you should desire, if you gape at others, you have gone too far and have mixed up these two, so that looking has been destroyed by desire.

This is also the most common cause of adultery, that something always has to be added, that one cannot see God's word in one's spouse, see them as God's gift and blessing, but must always have one's eyes unlocked when one looks at others. And the heart quickly follows the eyes, so that the lust and desire that I am supposed to have for my spouse alone is given to another. Flesh and blood is always curious and quickly bored, not liking what it has and gaping after someone else. The devil plays on this, so that in one's own spouse one only sees what is wrong, and forgets what is good and praiseworthy. Out of this comes the idea that anyone is prettier and better in my eyes than mine. Many let themselves be deceived in this way who have perfectly lovely and pious wives; they become angry with them and become attached to a hideous and shameful tramp.

Thus the right way to combat this with strong weapons (as I have also said elsewhere when I have spoken about weddings and married life) is if everyone learned to see his own spouse correctly according to God's word, which is the most expensive treasure and most beautiful jewel, that one can find reflected in a husband or wife. Then he would certainly love his spouse and value her as a gift and jewel of God, and think, when he saw another (even if she were prettier than his): "She might be pretty, but she is not that pretty, and even if she were the most beautiful in the world, I already have at home a much more beautiful jewel in my spouse, who was given to me by God and who has adorned her above all others with His word, even if she is not beautiful in her body or is even deformed. Even if I look at all the women in the world, I find none except my own that I can praise in this way and with clear conscience say: 'God Himself has given her to me and put her in my arms, and it pleases Him and all the angels mightily when I keep myself to her with love and constancy. Why would I then despise a valuable gift of God and become attached to another, who would never be such a treasure or jewel?'

"See, I can look at all women and talk, laugh, and be pleasant with them, as long as lust and desire are not involved, and do not let any of them become so lovely or beautiful to me that I go against God's word and commandment. And if I am tormented by flesh and blood, I do not allow this or give in to it, but fight valiantly against it and defeat it through God's word, and therefore live in the world in a way that no one can say evil about me or tempt me to become an adulterer." If one does not pay attention to and follow God's word, it easily happens that one is bored by one's spouse and becomes angry with them and another becomes more attractive, so that lust and desire cannot be overcome. He does not have the art to see his spouse as the beautiful jewel that God has made her to be; he sees no further than his eyes, which see only deformity or weakness in his wife and see another as better and more beautiful. Thus you should understand that looking at another is a sin or not a sin depending on whether one is looking at another the way he should look at his wife...

Some people have argued and discussed in detail about whether it is a sin to desire a wife or husband in marriage, but this is foolish and against both Scripture and nature, for why should people marry unless they have desire and love for another? For this reason God has given such desire to the bride and bridegroom, for otherwise everyone would flee from marriage and avoid it. He has also commanded in Scripture that husband and wife are to love one another and shows that He takes great pleasure when things are well between a husband and wife. For this reason such desire and love must truly not remain outside, and one has luck and grace if they last a long time. For too easily for both [spouses], the flesh leads to their feeling bored, and they do not want to put up with the daily grind that they find themselves in. The devil also cannot stand it when he sees two married people who treat each other with love, and he is not satisfied until he has found a way to awaken impatience, discord, hate, and bitterness between them. Thus it is not only necessary, but also difficult and actually possible only for Christians to keep loving their wives or husbands, so that each does not find the other wanting and all sorts of misfortune come out of this. At first it happens that each one (as they say) wants to devour the other in love, but when their curiosity is sated, the devil is there with boredom. He wants to take your desire away from here, and make it flame elsewhere.

Thus it is, in short, regarding lust and desire. But what does it mean when Christ makes such harsh demands, when he says to tear out our eyes or cut off our hands, if they trouble us? Should one really harm oneself, and make oneself blind or lame? We must then also take our own lives and turn ourselves into suicides, for if we really cast away everything that troubled us, we would first of all have to rip out our hearts. But what would that be other than destroying all of nature and God's Creation? The answer: here you see that in this entire chapter Christ is not talking about the worldly order or condition; all such statements that are found here and there in the Gospels (such as deny yourself, do good to those who hate you, and so on) do not apply to the worldly kingdom or the realm of the emperor, nor are they to be understood as if they were the *Sachsenspiegel* [the code of law applying to Saxony], where jurists talk about poking out the eyes or cutting off the hands and similar things. How could life and government exist if this were so? They speak only to one's spiritual life and existence, so that one does not have to throw away one's eye or hand outwardly in the sight of the world, but only in one's heart before the eyes of God, and renounce and give up oneself and the things of the world. He does not teach about fists and swords, or about governing bodies and goods, but only about the heart and conscience [standing] before God. For that reason these words are not to be entered into the law books or applied to earthly governments.

In this way in Matthew 19 he also talks about castration, for he talks about three types of castrates or eunuchs: the first and second, who are born that way in nature or who are castrated by human hands, whom the world and legal scholars also call eunuchs; the third, however, who have castrated themselves for the sake of the heavenly kingdom. These are another type of eunuch, who have not castrated themselves outwardly in their bodies, but have done so spiritually in their hearts; they are not considered to be eunuchs in the worldly sense, but (as he says) in the heavenly kingdom. He does not have anything to do with the worldly realm. Therefore also here we should tear out our spiritual eyes, hand, or heart and let them go, so that they do not trouble us, but we should still live in the world.

So this is the meaning: if you feel that you are looking at a woman with evil lust (which is against God's commandment), rip your eye or glance out of your heart, not out of your body, for the desire and lust come out of your heart. Then you have understood this properly. For when evil lust is gone from the heart, the eye will not sin or trouble you. And if you see the same woman with the same bodily eyes without lust, it is just as if you had not seen her at all. For Christ is not really talking about your eyes that were already there, but eyes that are full of desire and lust; the eyes in your body are to stay undamaged. He also says in regard to eunuchs, when the heart decides to live chastely without marriage (if it has the grace to do this), it has castrated itself for the sake of the heavenly kingdom and does not need to damage any bodily member outwardly. In sum, such castration, cutting off or ripping out is not done with a sword or an executioner, but through God's word in one's heart.

Lectures on Genesis, LW I, V, and VII

From *Luther's Works*, vols. I, V and VII, edited by Jaroslav Pelikan, © 1968 Concordia Publishing Company. Used by permission of Concordia Publishing House

[I, pp. 118–19] It is a great favor that God has preserved woman for us – against our will and wish, as it were – both for procreation and also as a medicine against the sin of fornication. In Paradise woman would have been a help for a duty only. But now she is also, and for the greater part at that, an antidote and a medicine; we can hardly speak of her without a feeling of shame, and surely we cannot make use of her without shame. The reason is sin. In Paradise that union would have taken place without any bashfulness, as an activity created and blessed by God. It would have been accompanied by a noble delight, such as there was at that time in eating and drinking. Now, alas, it is so hideous and frightful a pleasure that physicians compare it with epilepsy or falling sickness. Thus an actual disease is linked with the very activity of procreation. We are in the state of sin and of death; therefore we also undergo this punishment, that we cannot make use of woman without the horrible passion of lust, and, so to speak, without epilepsy...

[v, p. 35] I recall that before these times of the revival of the Gospel husbands at confession frequently deplored conjugal fun as a most serious sin. Indeed, what is most disgraceful and an affront to the Creator, if at any time some honorable matron or virgin had crossed the cemetery of the Franciscans, the monks immediately cleaned it with brooms and purified the sacred place with fire. Yet they are our mothers. Nor can the flame of lust that results from original sin be purged out with brooms or fire; but it is kindled more and more and stirred up in this way, and a woman who has been denied increases the madness. But these hypocrites had no knowledge of original sin. Therefore they had no knowledge of the remedies which God had pointed out. In the first place, Christ wants us to be baptized, in order that the heart may be set right and cleansed. Then, if you cannot have the gift of virginal chastity, at least choose that of a widow or a spouse; for in both sexes, male and female, there is flesh. Consequently, they [i.e., women] also have seed and the passion that arouses to procreation...

[v, p. 37] But from this one can take an admonition concerning the modesty and continence of married people. For some are such swine that they think that in marriage they are permitted to do anything they please with their wives. But they are decidedly in error. And they should know that they may indulge only in that wretched pleasure and embracing – not as though it were clean in the flesh, for both spouses are infected with original sin and the disease and frenzy of lust...

[VII, p. 76] For girls, too, are aware of this evil [lust] and if they spend time in the company of young men, they turn the hearts of these young men in various directions to entice them to love, especially if the youths are outstanding because of their good looks and strength of body. Therefore it is often more difficult for the latter to withstand such enticements than to resist their own lusts.

TABLE TALK

WA TR III, no. 3182a, p. 213 (1532)

Someone asked whether marriage satisfied all men's [sexual] appetite, therefore enabling them from then onward to abstain and resist their appetites for rape or secret love affairs, and resist being inflamed by feelings of lust. He answered: "Marriage is the means of creation, but labor is the means of resisting the hidden sin of lust. But desire for a woman is the creation of God, as long as its nature is pure and not corrupted as it has been by the Italians and Turks."

WA TR III, no. 3508, p. 368 (1536)

The burden of the married state. "He who takes a wife," said Doctor Martin Luther, may not be idle, for it gives him plenty to do. But keeping oneself chaste and pious without being married is not the smallest temptation, as those who have attempted and experienced this know. But the repugnance and burdens of marriage are unbearable to some people. For this reason the wise pagan Socrates gave a good answer to someone who asked him whether or not he should marry. 'Whichever of these two you decide to do,' he said, 'you will regret it.'

Ah, in paradise, if humans had remained in their innocent state, then marriage would have been a pleasant and happy thing; then there would not have been such burning and frenzy, but our flesh and blood would have been different. But we are poisoned through original sin, so that there is no condition on earth, even those established and ordained by God, in which those who are in it do not have regrets. That is the fault of our original sin, that shit on and laid waste to human nature. But despite this I think to myself that the most pleasant life is an average home life, living with a godly, willing, obedient wife in peace and unity, contenting oneself with little, being happy and thanking God." And as he, Doctor Martin, said this, he looked toward the heavens and said, "Oh, dear Lord God, how will you make it so that things can please us?"

WA TR V, no. 6316, p. 599
A girl of eighteen is ready for marriage, for this age feels the burning of the flesh; for this reason this is a suitable and appropriate age.

ADULTERY

Sermon on the Sixth Commandment WA XXX/1: Catechism sermons, 1528
[P. 37] The primary commandment is that you should do no harm to your neighbors, but help them. Next in order after your neighbor, you cannot come any closer to a man than to bring his wife to shame. Be sure that you do not do any harm to the neighbor of your neighbor. And this speaks about adultery, for all of the Israelites were married. But it not only prohibits the act of adultery, but also talking about it, desiring it, or similar things. For if you do this, or you give advice and assist in the adultery, it is the same as if you do it yourself. We are also responsible for taking care that our wives, children, and families are kept chaste and maintain their honor. For if you could stop this with a word and do not do this, you are guilty. If you were to say, however, "How does this concern me?," your neighbor might care for his wife in the same way. No: it is commanded that you not look through your fingers [i.e., that you do not tolerate this]. In sum: God wants you to live chastely and to help others live the same way, as far as is possible. This is also a rule that is easy. Certainly anyone will look after his wife, for otherwise he is a scoundrel. But people do not pay enough attention when someone else steps over the line, but we are to both avoid [adultery] and help others avoid it...
[Pp. 75–77] Adultery includes all immorality. Yet nevertheless the worst is expressly adultery that is committed publicly. The Jews were all married; none of them were clergy. God created men and women, not so that whoring would happen because of rules of celibacy, but He gave the body its nature and form, in order to be fruitful and multiply. It is a very excellent gift, that no human heart considered or put in motion. But God wanted through this to keep the bodies of men and women in chastity, to be given up [to each other]. For this same reason He ordained that each man should have

his own wife, and each one should stay with her. Married life is not a joke, but the marital estate is excellent. God saw that everything in the earth was good. He honored this so greatly, that He put everything under their dominion [Genesis 1:28], so that people will be raised within marriage, and so on. He saw to it that each one stayed with his wife or her husband, and also that both kept their bodies pure, not only in terms of actions, but also that they did not fall in love with someone else. "You are one flesh," He said. And this is the First Commandment: Fear God. You say: "Can't I have any room to stray over the line?" Yet this is what God says: "Fear." The emperor does not say this, but God, who is above all. Therefore say: "Oh God, give me grace and do not fail, so that I keep my marriage pure." That is, you should live chastely in your marriage with love, kind words, a pleasant demeanor, and your heart. Therefore He gives everyone his own wife, and I do not need to mention the other sins of restlessness, such as raping or seducing young women. Now I consider God's grace, that we have brought it to this, that this state [i.e., marriage] is honored, which is the best and the highest. Now the bishops and emperor, if they wish to have territories full of life, should concern themselves with marriage, and start with this estate. Blessed be he who acts in a way that public whoredom does not enter in. "Do not knock anyone down," that is, you should do no harm to your neighbor through a sign, word, act, or wish, or demand or advise this, whether to your friend or your enemy. But all works of mercy come together. You should keep yourself chaste in your words and works and stay with your wife, love and honor her. Stay away from immorality with another's wife or daughter, and keep yourself united with the one whom God has brought near to you.

A wedding sermon on the verse Hebrews 13:4, "Marriage should be held in honor among all, and let the marriage bed be undefiled; for God will punish whores and adulterers," WA XXXIV/1, Sermons from the Year 1531, pp. 69–75
The apostle says here that married life should be kept honorable and the marriage bed undefiled. He sets these two verses against these temptations, namely that our flesh is full of shameful lust, and our curiosity and boredom are both great, with the result that boredom pursues me here, and curiosity drives me there, and lasciviousness throws me somewhere else. This is not to be understood as referring to washing the bed and bedclothes, but this uncleanness and dirt in the marriage bed are nothing else – as the author himself makes clear – than whoredom and adultery. These are the true stains that dirty the marriage bed, making it impure and dishonorable. Those who are outside the [marital] estate and lead immoral lives, such

as pimps, think marriage is nothing, but they despise and denigrate both God's word and this estate, no matter how pious they pretend to be. Those who are married but do not regard it seriously and instead break God's word and commandment do the same.

All those who regard married life as if it were an estate that is almost coarse, and practically enter into it by accident, shame it. For they do not see that married couples are contained within God's word and they cannot understand that husband and wife are clothed and adorned with God's word. For that reason it is not an honorable estate for them, but they lay all sorts of shame on it. For they let their shameful, immoral lives please themselves better than the godly and honorable life. For this reason He warns them here, so that they will pay attention to this and live so that they regard marriage as splendid and as ordained and established by God in all honor. In addition, [He warns them so] that they leave their whore's life and enter into marriage. After they do this, they are to make sure that they are careful to keep the marital bed pure and unstained, which means that the wife keeps to her husband and the husband lets himself be contented with his wife. Where this does not happen, God's word, the beautiful jewel, is befouled with the devil's filth and the marital bed is stained and (we might as well say) shit in.

Therefore take care, when the devil comes to you with curiosity and boredom, that you are smart and hold onto God's word and think: God has created me as a man and put me in this estate; He has placed her in my arms so that she will be mine. If you do that, you can keep your marital bed pure more easily. For the word will create fear and hesitation, or actually loathing and horror, toward others in you. It will adorn your wife, so that even if she is hideous and hostile, impatient and obstinate, she will be more dear to you because of the word, and will please you better than if she were adorned in vanity with gold. There is no veil more valuable than a bridal veil and no hat more bejeweled than a bridegroom's hat for those who can keep themselves in this. This means that they honor and maintain marriage, and keep the marital bed pure. For there is no honor nor ornament more beautiful, nor any purity that is above God's word.

There are some clever ones who seek exceptions so that they do not get married, and drown themselves in whoredom. They say that much that is bad happens in marriage, and that there is great sin through anger, impatience, evil lust, etc. No one denies this, or says that it is pure and without sin. But, on the other hand, give me any godly estate in which there is no sin! If we were to be held to this, I would not be able to preach any longer, no servant or maid would be able to serve, no authorities would be able to govern, no noble would be able to ride a horse. Not yet, my dear; in this life we will never be so pure that we can do any good work without sin. This point remains: I believe in the forgiveness of sins. And daily I say the Lord's Prayer: "Forgive us our trespasses."

So do not make an exception for marriage – sin here, sin there – for if you put one estate in sin, so you must put all others there as well. If you pull one out, so pull the others out as well. I have never preached nor will ever be able to preach a sermon without sin. I remain a sinner and will remain with and not deny the point about the forgiveness of sins. If you are sometimes angry with someone, that is sin and incorrect. But the forgiveness of sins is so much greater than this when you stay and do not run away, but remain in the estate to which God has called you. For even though you cannot be without sin, God's word is so great that according to His will this estate can be pure and godly. I also want to say: when you see that since Adam we are all born in sin, every marriage, even one that is well kept and correct, is sinful and impure, just as God regards all life and actions by heathens and disbelievers as sinful and damning.

It is important to note that here [the author] talks about marriage and speaks as if out of God's mouth, that it should be kept pure and honorable, which among Christians means more than simply avoiding adultery and whoredom. If one looks at the fall of Adam and our nature correctly, it is not pure or honorable to God. Fleshly lust and other sinful desires were not there in paradise. No person had to be shy or ashamed in front of another person, or clothe and adorn themselves, but man and woman joined together without evil lust and desire. Children were born and raised easily and without trouble, as easily as one picks an apple from a tree. But now, no man or woman can come together without shameful desire. For this reason Psalm 51 says: "I was conceived by sinful seed, and my mother bore me in sin." And all the saints that were married must acknowledge that they did not want to have this desire but had it anyway. For this reason Christ himself did not want to be born in the natural way from a man and a woman, but chose a virgin for his mother and sanctified her flesh and blood for this, so that his birth would be a pure and holy birth.

[The author] says here that God graced this estate so that even though it was impure in its nature, it would not be impure among those who are Christians and who have belief, but should from this point on be called "a pure marital bed." It was not so in itself or because of our nature, but because God covered it with His grace and will not judge us according to the natural sin and impurity that the devil planted in us. He also purifies this [marital] estate with His word, so that it becomes a holy and blessed estate. He does not do this by taking away desire or love for one's bride, or by forbidding marital intercourse, even though this cannot occur without sin, so that the popes teach and regard this estate as impure. [Marriage] is instead purified because God through His grace has made it pure, and has not attributed to us the sin that is in our nature...

We see with our own eyes how God holds in honor this miserable flesh and blood, born and living in sin, for He blesses it over and over and makes it fruitful. All saints come from marriage and all of life springs out of it. For that reason the first mother is given the name "Eve," which means "living" or "mother of the living." And how could He praise it any higher than by calling it pure and blessed in the New Testament as well?

Therefore we should honor and praise this estate and not do as the filthy sows do who think and talk about nothing else other than shameful whoredom and adultery. They are abominable filthy beasts, who soil their own nests and love to root around in the filth with their dirty snouts and roll around in their own excrement. Christians, however, should regard this estate as honorable and good, for they see that God Himself does this. If they see something impure, they should cover this up and adorn it just as God does, who takes what is sinful and impure in its nature but does not count it as sin but pulls a blanket over it and makes it beautiful and honorable.

We should also not do as the hostile clever ones do, who rebuke this dear estate and criticize it because there is much dissatisfaction, strife, trouble, and toil in it, and who say "God keep me from this estate – he who takes a wife gets a devil." People like this are rabid dogs who shame this dear estate with their vicious muzzles and tear at it with their poisonous teeth, dirtying it just as the sows do with their snouts. The devil always finds a pretext to be against this estate, for he sees both the original sin and the unhappiness, trouble, and toil that are ascribed to it. He can use these two things well, and wants to make marital life more difficult for everyone or even destroy it. For that reason we must lift this estate even higher, praise and honor it even more, adorn and embellish it, just as God Himself does. Let the devil shame and defame it through his sows and dogs as he will, and let them praise whatever it is that their God, the devil, has given to them. You, however, should learn to honor and keep it [marriage] as it has been cleansed and purified by God's word and as His works are to be honored. Those who are married should take comfort in this and thank God that He has let it please Him, covered over the marriage bed or the blanket on it, and has adorned and praised it so beautifully. This is said to honor weddings and marriage; God give us the grace to believe this and to live it, Amen.

WA TR I, no. 183, p. 82

The pope's punishment for those who have committed adultery. "The punishment with which the pope condemns married people who have sinned is bad, that is, that the man who has committed adultery may not demand the marital debt, but only render it. [The "marital debt" refers to the obligation spouses have to engage in sexual relations with their spouse when he or she wishes it; according to Catholic doctrine, adulterers could not require a spouse to engage in sexual relations, though they were required to have sex if the innocent spouse wished it.] This gives cause for whoredom. I would rather that they are punished by having to carry a sign of their shame, or having to eat bread and water, or something similar."

WA TR II, no. 2542b, pp. 513–14

An unfaithful wife is a man's greatest sorrow. "I have the greatest sympathy for the pious man M. A. [perhaps Mattheus Aurogallus] who has an unfaithful wife but does not want to divorce her. If he brings it [the case] to us, we will divorce them. Even if she is not an open adulterer, she is unchaste, disobedient to her husband, does nothing to please him but goes everywhere she wants to when she wants, does only what she wants, which are signs of adultery. And he has a bad illness, and problems with his kidneys.

"It is a poor and sad thing to have an untrue companion, whom one must be with one's whole life, but in whom one has no trust. Even if one does not know for sure, it still causes suffering; but to knowingly and openly tolerate an adulterer who sleeps with one's wife, that is certain pain. People say that peacocks cannot stand to have other peacocks near them who also breed with the same peahen; even if it is only seeing the shadow of the other on the water, they will drown themselves over this. The dear, glorious, excellent words of the Holy Spirit also refer to this: "The heart of the husband trusts in her" (Proverbs 31:11).

"Is it not a terrible evil and deception of Satan that he so shamefully brings distress and confusion, and then destroys this ordinance of God [i.e., marriage], that is supported by divine and natural law, bound together with body and goods, bearing and raising children? Yes, [and the devil wants to] strike this dead! For this reason this is the advice that I would give anyone who would be free of this. Do not joke, and do not follow or hang on the desires in your breast. Pray, pray! He who gets a pious wife gains a good dowry. Only pray, it is absolutely necessary! And even if your wife is somewhat bitter, you should have patience with her, for she belongs in the house."

WA TR III, no. 3510, pp. 368–69 (1536)
Of two types of adultery. Doctor M. L. said once, "There are two types of adultery. The first is spiritual, before God, when someone desires the husband or wife of another, as in Matthew 5. No one can avoid this. The other is bodily, as in the eighth chapter of John, when a wife is caught in open adultery. This is a terrible vice, but sometimes in the world it is seen as an honor. An admirable man said to me once, 'I never understood that adultery was such a great sin.' It is a sin against God and against order in the state, city, and household, and an adulterous woman brings a foreign heir into the house and deceives her husband."

WA TR V, no. 5381, pp. 117–18
On adultery. A shoemaker who had caught his wife in the act of adultery had cut off part of her lover's nose, and Mrs. Luther asked, "Is this the way to bring an end to adultery? He was just a young man." Doctor Luther responded, "I'm afraid I would have stabbed him!" His wife asked, "How can people be so bad and stain themselves with such sins?" He answered, "Dear Katie, people don't pray. The devil is not lazy; for that reason we should always pray against the whoring-devil: 'Lead us not into temptation, but deliver us from evil.'" He said further to his table-mates, "I think that if God had ordered that a woman had to accept any man who came to her [for sex] and a man accept any woman who came to him, people would get very tired of this life and would sigh in longing for marriage. That this was a young man is no wonder to me, for children are children when you place them together. When fire and straw lie down with each other, all will soon be burned up. I praise Philip Melanchthon's brother, who, when Philip admonished him to guard against immorality, answered, 'I will take a wife, so that whores and other men's wives will stay away from me.' Thus young men should decide to take their own wives and avoid immorality."

WA TR V, no. 6327, pp. 604–5
A princess left her lord and spouse out of boldness and moved away from him. "If I had been in his place," said Dr. Martin Luther, "I would not have

looked through my fingers so long but would have taken the advice of her brother and all her blood relatives and compelled her with blows.

"This is a great disobedience that is full of aggravation. I have said it to her in plain enough German, until she has grown hostile toward me. She showed me [a list of] twenty articles, which I read and said to her that she should burn it and let it pass under no one's eyes, or she would lose her honor and indulgence [*Glimpf*]. And in case there was some truth in them, she should bear it with patience, as a Christian. Finally I said, 'Gracious Lady, you will not be able to stop up everyone's mouth and prevent them from speaking ill of you; rather, they will regard you as guilty of adultery. Even if you are honorable [have not actually committed adultery], the example you set is similar to adultery.'"

PROSTITUTION

Letter to the German Nobility, 1520, WA VI, p. 467

Finally, is it not a lamentable thing that we Christians maintain open and common brothels among us, when we are all baptized into chastity? I certainly know what some say about this, that it is not simply the custom of one people and that it would be difficult to end it, that it is better to have such [houses] than to bring married women or maidens or even more honorable people to dishonor. But should not the temporal and Christian government recognize that such evil is not to be prevented in this heathen way? If the people of Israel could exist without such an abomination, why cannot Christian people do as much? In fact, how do the many cities, market towns, and villages which do not have such houses stand it? Why cannot the large cities also do without them?

Treatise on Good Works, 1520, WA VI, p. 262

O would to God in heaven that such a government would be established as it was among the people of Israel, that would do away with the common houses of prostitution! It is certainly an unchristian picture that a public house of sin is maintained among Christians, and unheard of earlier. It should be a rule that young men and women are to be brought together in marriage in good time, and vice like this would be prevented. Both the spiritual and the temporal authorities should strive for such a rule and practice. If this was possible among the Jews, why should it not be possible also among Christians? Indeed, if it is possible in villages, market towns and some cities, as we have seen, why is it not possible everywhere?

Lectures on Genesis 19:9, 1539, LW III, p. 259
From *Luther's Works*, vol. III, edited by Jaroslav Pelikan, © 1968
Concordia Publishing Company. Used by permission of
Concordia Publishing House

The example concerning the houses of ill fame which are tolerated in large cities does not deserve to be discussed, for it is clearly in conflict with the Law of God, and those who publicly tolerate this disgrace should be regarded as heathen. It is silly for them to suppose that outcroppings of debauchery and adultery are reduced by this means. Once a young man who associates with prostitutes has surrendered his modesty, he will, when the occasion arises, keep away neither from married women nor from virgins. Therefore lust is increased rather than cured by this means, and it becomes a warrant to sin for those who otherwise would be continent if this opportunity had been denied them. Other and better remedies have been pointed out and commanded by God, namely, marriage. Therefore a government which tolerates houses of ill fame should be regarded as heathenish. For a godly government should not tolerate fornication, especially manifest licentiousness. Even against the will of the officers of the state and in spite of their prohibition this evil nevertheless prevails and cannot be completely abolished.

TABLE TALK

WA TR IV, no. 4857, pp. 552–54
Against the whores and greasy students. Out of special hatred for our faith, the devil has sent some whores here to destroy our poor young men. Against this, dear children, I give you my fatherly request, as an old and faithful preacher, that you will certainly believe that the evil spirit has sent such whores here, who are scabby, scratchy, stinking, nasty, and syphilitic, as one can unfortunately discover every day. If only a good young man would warn his mates! For such a syphilitic whore can poison ten, twenty, thirty or more of the children of good people, and thus is to be considered as a murderer, or worse, as a poisoner. Everyone should help those who are in such a poisonous dung-heap with true advice and warnings, as you wish would be done for you!

If, however, you despise my fatherly warning, we have (God be praised) such a praiseworthy ruler, who is honorable and moral, an enemy to all immorality and vice. With a heavy hand, armed with the sword, he will clean out the outlying areas [where students meet prostitutes], and also the whole city, to honor the word of God, which his Electoral Grace has taken on in all seriousness and to which he has stayed loyal at great cost despite great danger. Therefore I advise you greasy students to trundle off before the ruler discovers what you are doing with whores. For his Electoral Grace would not tolerate this in the army camp near Wolfenbuettel, and how much less would he tolerate it in his forests, towns, and land. Be off, I advise you, and the earlier, the better! He who cannot live without whores can move home or go wherever he wants. He who wants to become a pimp can do it elsewhere. Our lord Elector has not endowed this university for pimps or brothels, you can count on that!

And I must speak plainly. If I were a judge, I would have such a poisonous syphilitic whore tortured by being broken on the wheel and having her veins lacerated, for it is not to be denied what damage such a filthy whore does to young blood, so that it is unspeakably damaged before it is even fully grown and destroyed in the blood [poisoned]. The young fools think that they must not hold out; as soon as they feel lust, a whore should be there! The [church] fathers called this the impatience of sexual desire, secretly suffered. But what one desires does not have to be made good so soon. That is, if I were you, I would not follow after lust (Ecclesiasticus 18, 30). You cannot enter into marriage so immediately. To conclude: guard yourself from whores, and ask God who has created you to give you a pious child [to marry]. As you will, according to the words of God. 1 Corinthians 10:8, Numbers 25:9.

Letter to Hieronymus Weller, 3 September 1540, WA, BR IX, no. 3532,
pp. 228–29. Translated into German and reprinted in Table Talk,
WA TR VI, pp. 272–73

My dear Hieronymus:

You should have nothing to do with nor be involved with those who want to reopen the public brothel. It would have been better and more tolerable not to have driven the devil out, than to let him in again and acknowledge him. Those who want to open such houses again have denied the name of Christ, and confessed that they are not Christians but heathens who know nothing of God. We who would otherwise wish to be Christians have a clear command in God's word, for St. Paul says: "God will judge whores and adulterers." He will punish even more those who promote, protect, or help them in word or deed. How can one teach publicly against whoredom and punish this, if one praises the authorities that tolerate and allow it? "Yes," they say and boast, "but those [people] from N. do this, as if we were the only ones who did wrong in this way; the world would become full of whoredom if we did not allow such houses." [My] answer: there is a good remedy for this from God's grace, that is, marriage or the hope of becoming married. Who would need the hope or remedy of marriage, if we let whoredom go on unpunished?

We have certainly experienced that when such houses stood in full bloom and were preserved under the devil, things were not helped or aided by this; rather through the example of freely permitted prostitution, whoring and the raping of maidens and women increases and is unashamedly publicly known. Because whoredom is now forbidden according to God's grace, there is also less of such immorality and adultery, especially in public. The authorities, if they want to be Christian, punish all severely – whoredom, the dishonoring and rape of maidens and women, and adultery – at least that which is public. If these still occur in private, then the authorities are to be excused once they have been energetic [in their duties]. In sum, we cannot do, allow, or tolerate anything that is against God! We should do what is right, even if the world is destroyed because of this.

Letter to an unknown addressee, 1539, WA BR XII, no. 4274, pp. 295–98
First we must differentiate between a land or people who want to consider themselves and be considered Christians or God's people, and those who are heathens and want to be considered as such. If they want to be and to be called heathens, to deny and turn away from Christendom, God, and the Christian name, then they can allow, open, and live in not only one, but as many brothels as they would like. But if they want to be called Christians and live under God's name, belonging to Him and becoming blessed, they are required for the salvation of their souls not to tolerate such houses, and even less to open them or allow them to be opened. Instead they are required to prevent this with word and deed, as much as they can. Here are the reasons:

First: because they themselves confess that this is a sinful business and against God's commandment. It is also against the honor of God's name that His people should tolerate, allow, or protect such things that are against God and still be called His people. For in this they serve the devil and his realm against the realm of God, and they do this as Christians, under Christ's and God's name! This is taking God's name in vain, as forbidden by the Second Commandment. None of them can then pray the "Our Father" in good conscience – "Hallowed be thy name" – for lying is its own punishment.

St. Paul also writes in Ephesians [5:3] that whoredom should not be tolerated among Christians, and in 1 Corinthians [7:2] he says that in order to avoid whoredom, everyone should have his own wife. In all of the Epistles he forcefully forbids whoredom. If a Christian realm or community wants to be called Christian and nevertheless knowingly tolerates or protects something shameful like this, which is openly against God's word and commandment, that is so corrupt that it would also be shameful for heathens and against natural reason.

If they say that they do not know about it or advise it, but simply let it happen and tolerate it, then I answer that this is just as bad as if they did it themselves. Paul says in Romans [1:32] that all merit death, both those who do things and those who let them happen, for those who can prevent something and allow it to happen or tolerate it are just the same to God as those who do it themselves. We have a good example of this in 1 Kings 5, where God punishes Eli the priest more harshly when he did not resist his sons than at any other time, for God complained that he honored his sons more than he did Him. How much more would Christ say about this, when whores and pimps are honored more than he is?

It is clear that the authorities permit and protect the whorehouses, and give them privileges. Without such permissions, protections, and privileges, such houses cannot be established or continue. Thus they [the authorities] are guilty of all sins and vices that happen there. It is also clear that the authorities could resist and stop them; if they do not, then they are again guilty of all sins. Let them themselves judge whether they who have indulged and allowed something are to be considered innocent, if they have not done an act, but have known that someone else did it and could have prevented it – if they themselves did not rape their wife or child, or murder, or rob a house or farm, but they also did not stop or prevent this, but looked on; even more, if they protected the one who did this, housed and sheltered him, let him do whatever he wanted in his house. How much more serious is this, for they have sworn to honor God, and still tolerate such enemies in their territory, protect them, and against God's word let them do what they want, though they could certainly stop them. If whorehouses are to be tolerated, so murderers' houses and thieves' houses should also be established and condoned.

But, they say: "We must tolerate a lesser evil, in order to prevent a greater evil; this happens according to God's will." Against this is Paul, in Romans 3[:8]: One should not do evil so that good comes of it, for otherwise God would say in Psalm 50[:18]: "You run with the thieves, etc." You should resist others' evildoing with righteousness, and not with sinning. [You should] not sin in order to keep others from sinning or you will be paying more attention to the sin of your neighbors than to the honor of God. So God says also in Exodus 23[:2]: "You should not follow the crowd to do evil."

But, they say: "Christendom has tolerated this until now." We say no to this. Augustine did write that one tolerates whorehouses in which everything is not stained with sin, but he was speaking of pagan states, for Christians at that time were not in power. But the Christians did not do this, as we see in the writings of all the church fathers: Cyprian, Chrysostom, Jerome, Augustine have all punished public sinning, which is why there are so many penitential canons about this. The heathen Pliny also wrote to the Emperor Trajan about Christians, that they would not tolerate whoredom and other sins and punished them severely. For Christ, in Matthew 18[:16–18], has given the [power of] the keys and [provided] the way [*Schlüssel und Bahn*] for Christians to punish such sins, and those who do not want to improve themselves should be regarded as pagans and let go. One does a disservice to Christianity to say that they tolerate such things. False Christians, who let God's word and commandment go and are whores themselves, certainly tolerate this, including almost all clergy up to this point.

But it is yet more unchristian and devilish that the universities are not left in peace. For there one lets the evil go against God and promotes the realm of the devil. Here one opposes the good and destroys the realm of God – that is the devil himself. We are instructed to raise young men in the fear of God's word, and if it becomes difficult for them to account for this, to help them; we could do this, but we do not. What will they say, who would gladly do otherwise and prevent or hinder this?

[To the argument] that whorehouses defend against other vices, I can easily argue the opposite: how much are other vices also contained within them? I see that whorehouses are really the cause and provocation of all sins and evils and wild living. There would be much that would not take place if the public houses of shame did not serve as schools of immorality. I do not know how a man could honor his wife and children if he kept a whore in his house for young men. One preserves morality and honor in a community just as much when one opens a public house of immorality and sets the example of all sins before the citizens, giving permission to this and allowing every man to go in and learn and practice such immorality. Bah – it is too vulgar when the worst heathens do this, so I will say nothing more about Christians.

OTHER SEXUAL ISSUES

Lectures on Genesis, LW III
From *Luther's Works*, vol. III, edited by Jaroslav Pelikan, © 1968
Concordia Publishing Company. Used by permission of
Concordia Publishing House

[Pp. 251–52, commenting on Genesis 19:4–5: But before they lay down, the men of the city, the men of Sodom, both young and old, all the people to the last man, surrounded the house; and they called to Lot: "Where are the men who came to you tonight? Bring them out to us, that we may know them."] Moses proceeds with a description of this terrible sin. I for my part do not enjoy dealing with this passage, because so far the ears of the Germans are innocent of and uncontaminated by this monstrous depravity; for even though this disgrace, like other sins, has crept in through an ungodly soldier and a lewd merchant, still the rest of the people are unaware of what is being done in secret. The Carthusian monks deserve to be hated because they were the first to bring this terrible pollution into Germany from the monasteries of Italy. Of course, they were trained and educated in such a praiseworthy manner at Rome...

[P. 254] But what shall we suppose was in the mind of godly Lot, toward whose house everybody was going during this uproar in the whole city? He alone feared God, and in his house he maintained discipline and chastity to the utmost of his ability, while the others indulged freely and without shame in adultery, fornication, effeminacy, and even incest to such an extent that these were not regarded as sins but as some pastime, just as today among the nobility and the lower classes of Germany fornication is regarded as a pastime, not as a sin, and for this reason is also entirely unpunished.

First in Italy and then by some canons in Germany it was argued that simple fornication of an unattached man with an unattached woman is not a sin but is a cleansing of nature, which seeks an outlet. Let this be said with due respect for innocent ears, for I do not relish dealing with these matters. Yet we must be on our guard lest such shocking utterances carry away and ruin the age that is rash and is in general inclined to sin...

[P. 255] The heinous conduct of the people of Sodom is extraordinary, for inasmuch as they departed from the natural passion and longing of the male for the female, which was implanted into nature by God, and desired what is altogether contrary to nature. Whence comes this perversity? Undoubtedly from Satan, who, after people have once turned away from the fear of God, so powerfully suppresses nature that he blots out the natural desire and stirs up a desire that is contrary to nature.

Lectures on Genesis, *LW VII*
From *Luther's Works*, vol. VII, edited by Jaroslav Pelikan, © 1968 Concordia Publishing Company. Used by permission of Concordia Publishing House

[Pp. 20–21, commenting on Genesis 38:9, Onan spilling his semen on the ground rather than impregnating Tamar, the widow of his brother] Onan must have been a malicious and incorrigible scoundrel. This is a most disgraceful sin. It is far more atrocious than incest and adultery. We call it unchastity, yes, a Sodomitic sin. For Onan goes in to her; that is, he lies with her and copulates, and when it comes to the point of insemination, spills the semen, lest the woman conceive. Surely at such a time the order of nature established by God in procreation should be followed. Accordingly it was a most disgraceful crime to produce semen and excite the woman, and to frustrate her at that very moment.

Letter to Eberhard von der Thann, a government official at the Wartburg and Eisenach, 27 June 1540, *WA BR IX*, no. 3507, p. 162

[On the bigamy of Philip of Hesse, whose second wedding took place on 4 March 1540, with Philip Melanchthon and Martin Bucer in attendance] I do not know of anything better than that you would write [to the emperor], that His Princely Grace [i.e., Philip of Hesse] intends to write to the emperor himself regarding this matter, and say that he has taken a concubine and intends to send her away again, as other princes and lords have also done before. Such a letter would raise a fuss, but people would come to some agreement, and the matter would be covered up again and made secret, and the mouths that are yammering now would be shut. It is absolutely not advisable for His Grace to make a public report and explain the whole thing openly, for then the debating and suspicions would be endless and immeasurable. If the emperor were to regard her as a concubine, however, no one would dare to speak or think about it in any other way.

Letter to the Hessian Chancellor Johan Feige (sometime after 16 July 1540), *WA BR IX*, pp. 178–79

[Luther defends his refusal to reveal whether he gave Philip of Hesse permission for the second marriage, saying that this is a matter of private confessional advice.] For what is secretly a yes can not be made a public yes, for then secret and public would be the same . . . Even if I advise a troubled conscience in secret need to use the model or law of Moses, I have not established, and indeed could not establish, a public law or legal model, for I am a confessor, who must treat everything as if it were a private matter of conscience and not a public matter of law or model.

It must not be a matter of public law or model unless the authorities make it so, even though it [bigamy] was allowed in the earlier times of the dear patriarchs in the law of Moses. I will not even mention that one can also find examples after the birth of Christ of a man secretly having two wives because of the needs of his conscience, without the approval of the authorities, as many say about the emperor Charlemagne or about Valentinian. But no public model, example, or tradition may be derived from these. For it is not valid that what you do out of necessity I can do out of right. A thief steals bread out of hunger and is not punished; killing in self-defense is murder, but it is not damned. But these do not create a model or give one the right to steal and murder freely. Necessity surpasses models and rights, but it does not make models and rights.

But this ingenious argument [about the distinction between public and private] will nevertheless leave a thorn in the conscience, as long as the duke publicly has two wives and just tries to cover this over with words; the debate will not easily be ended. For that reason I would like (as far as this is possible) the duke to return to secrecy, to a private "yes" and a public "no," to let it be spoken and preached that no one can find any right or model for taking more than one wife, except for matters of secret advice and need that take place in confession. I would let the record [of the marriage] be deferred, for there can be no record stating that one is allowed to have two wives, but only fuss about him (that is, the duke as an individual). So one can leave talk to work against talk; preaching against this will easily silence talk in favor of it as time passes, especially as one public sermon can easily prevail over rumors and gossip from a hundred taverns or alleys.

I think this will be the easiest way. And as long as he does this secretly, even though he is guilty, because the duke has sworn so fervently that he needs this young woman so much and thus cannot let her go, theologians and confessors can help to defend him before God. They can argue that it is a matter of necessity, and explain it away with the example of Moses. But we can and will not defend it before the world and the rules of law nowadays.

Against the papacy in Rome, established by the devil, 1545, WA LIV, p. 287
... I appeal and demand of the Roman See, that is of those who decide whether the popes are men or women, in the name of all of us. If they are men, they should show their witnesses [or "show their testicles" – the words for testicles and witnesses are the same in Latin, and the two were related, as testifying in court in Roman law was limited to those who had testicles, i.e., to men] against us heretics. If they are women, then Paul says to them: "Women should keep silent in church." It is necessary to know this because of the common rumor, known throughout all of Europe, that honorable morality has been eradicated. It is said and well known that the kings and queens of the Roman curia are great hermaphrodites, androgynes, boy prostitutes [*cynaedi*], and sodomites [*pedicones*]. These are all not competent to make a judgment about heretics.

TABLE TALK

WA TR I, no. 913, p. 464

Doctor Martin Luther's prayer of thanks for marriage. When I am by myself, I thank the Lord God for the knowledge of marriage, especially when I compare this estate [i.e., marriage] to the godless, incestuous, shameful celibacy among the papists and to the abominable "Italian marriages" [sodomitical relationships].

WA TR II, no. 1316, p. 39

About clerical concubinage. Someone said to Luther that if there was a reformation of the canons in Zeitz and Naumburg, they would be forced to dismiss their "cooks" and send them away. They would concede this for only two weeks, for they could not do without them for any longer, or hold themselves back. Thus they took them back again. But the "cooks" did not want to come back to them, but they promised them that they would support and protect them. And they bought new clothes for them, so that people did not recognize them.

And people said that a locksmith was supposed to have said that he had had much work during these two weeks, day and night, just making keys. For every woman wanted a key to the parsonage now that they [the canons] had sent their whores away.

To this, Doctor Martin said, "I wish that people did not insult our Lord God like this! One should not act so frivolously regarding God's order and commandments. Those who are blessed can hardly endure this, so how will it be for the godless, mockers, and blasphemers? But the godless papists have their god, the pope. As a famous doctor [of the church] said, 'When I serve the pope truthfully, I become blessed, and have enough left over for everlasting salvation. When someone puts a monk's cowl on me, as I am dying, the left-over good works of the monks heal me, and I trust in this, and will be saved.'

"And I also thought, when I was a monk, that if I left my cell without a scapular I had committed a terrible mortal sin, and I was thrown into doubt. I shudder at the thought of this, that people trust in this foolishness and depend on it, when this honor should only be given to the Lord Jesus Christ. One should be angry with the papacy for just this one piece of error and foolishness!"

WA TR II, no. 1647, pp. 162–63

On fornication. Doctor Hennike, a learned theologian from Bohemia, asked Doctor Luther, while at the table, whether fornication is also a sin when it involves an unmarried young man and an unmarried young woman and not someone else's wife. Luther answered, "Paul answers this question when he says, 'Neither whores nor adulterers will inherit the kingdom of God.' In this he makes a distinction between the fornicators and the adulterers."

Again Doctor Martin Luther was asked whether simple fornication was also wrong and a sin, for many jurists say that it is not, and that it should not be punished. To this Doctor Martin Luther answered, "What do you mean, not a sin? Saint Paul speaks loud and clear, that both fornicators and adulterers will not inherit the kingdom of heaven."

WA TR III, no. 2978b, pp. 129–30 (1533)

It is said that the pope would graciously accept all Lutherans and their wives if they would just preach and teach what he wants them to and regard their wives as whores and concubines. "Shame on that," said Doctor Martin, "what will the devil do next? He lets adultery go unpunished! Not to honor marriage is human, but to damn it is to despise God. Witzel [Wicelius?] wants to do this with his wife. I would not advise any pious woman to follow him for this reason. The pope mocks both God and humans, because he despises and laughs at religion, worldly authorities, and all honor. He proves this in that his son, the child of a whore, has now become engaged to the emperor's illegitimate daughter, and has been made a duke; he is not ashamed and now wants to be glorified as honorable! He should more appropriately be ashamed in his heart, yet he wants to be praised as a pastor! [Luther is here speaking of Pope Alexander VII and Allesandro Medici, who was actually the pope's nephew (the son of Lorenzo Medici) and not his son. In 1530 Emperor Charles V established Alessandro Medici as the Duke of Florence, and arranged for him to be married to his illegitimate daughter Margarete; the marriage took place in 1536.]

WA TR III, no. 3807, pp. 630–31

Italian marriage [same-sex relations, though the Weimar edition glosses this as "pederasty"]. Next there was a discussion about that which is called Italian marriage, which for a long time has exceeded every lewdness and the adulteries of the Germans; though these sins are human, their filthiness is satanic. [Doctor Martin Luther said:] "God protect us from this devil! For by the grace of God there is no mother tongue in Germany that knows anything about such wickedness."

WA TR III, no. 3665b, pp. 501–2

A strange and terrible marital case. Doctor Martin Luther told about a case that had taken place, "in which a mother was made pregnant by her own son. The son wanted to sleep with the maid, and she reported this to her mistress, who said, 'He is too young; I don't believe it.' But the son persisted with the maid, and the mother lay down in the maid's bed. The son thought it was the maid, slept with her and made her pregnant. The mother remained silent, however, keeping it a secret and telling her son nothing about it. After that she [secretly] gave birth to a daughter, raised her and kept her for her maid. When the girl grew up, she married the son, who did not know that she was his sister. In this case both the son and the daughter were relieved of guilt, as both did not know anything about these things, but the guilt is on the mother. One should not rip apart this marriage or make [the situation] known to those who do not know about it. This happened according to our memory."

WA TR IV, no. 4099, p. 135

A question. If someone abducts a young woman that he loves and steals her from her parents, and she agrees to this, the question is asked, "Does he sin and commit a wrong, because this injury was done willingly? Is something harmful that was done with good intentions?" Doctor Martin Luther answered: "The violent deed of abduction and theft was not carried out against the one who agreed to this, but against her parents; harm was done to them against their will, for their child was forcibly abducted, stolen

and taken away [or raped – the word *Raub* can mean either rape or theft].
One should understand this injury in reference to them. This type of theft
and robbery [or rape] is stringently forbidden and a high punishment set
in the imperial law code. But the pope, the Antichrist, views such action
as allowable in his decretals."

WA TR IV, no. 4474, p. 332

An old man and a young maiden. If an old man takes a young wife, this
is a very ugly spectacle, for there is no pride or lust in such a man, for the
opportunities for this are past. There is nothing attractive or strong about
him any more. For this reason an old man with a young wife is contrary to
nature. It is best if like and like are paired together.

WA TR IV, no. 5116, pp. 678–79

Marriage is mocked by worldly people. Doctor Martin Luther said in 1540,
when he was at the table, that the world was becoming godless, for many
people do not consider whoredom and adultery to be sins. Regarding this
the Bishop of Lünden said to Philip Melanchthon, "I wonder why you feel
forced into marriage, for all the other nations mock you about this." And
Doctor Martin Luther said, "Let it go! We must be like Lot, whose soul was
tortured day and night at Sodom. We must let ourselves and our marriage
be mocked, as we have smoothed it out and praised it in our sermons,
writings, and in the examples we have set. But an Epicureanism seeks to
spread in the German lands, which comes from Italy, and we Germans fall
right into it. Such Epicureanism also predominates in Turkey, so that no
one asks about the estate of marriage, but everyone takes as many wives as
he wants to, then afterwards pushes and drives them away, or barters and
sells these wives. For they do not know what the estate of marriage is; but
with our books we put marriage on its feet again. I fear very much that in
twenty years all good books will be forbidden, that no one will be able to
think this in the pulpit, and the pure word of God will be followed only
a little by pure hearts. Our Lord Jesus Christ help us; only he is just and
accepts us, the others mock us just as they mocked Noah before the flood
when he was building the ark; just as the Sodomites mocked Lot, and as
they mocked Isaiah by sticking out their tongues."

WA TR VI, no. 6939 p. 282

How unchastity is punished. Doctor Martin Luther thought of the canons
of Naumburg, and said, "Once they had a whore from the nobility, with
whom they did many immoral things. Because she was also very haughty

and always wanted to take precedence over other honorable wives of citizens, the city council of Naumburg lay in wait for her, grabbed her in the street and took her to the common city brothel. This annoyed the canons badly, and they let her out again quickly. Then she thought about how she would take revenge on the Naumbergers for their scorn and mockery. As she was invited to a wedding, she went in front of her mirror to beautify herself, and a devil possessed her. It tormented her very badly and she died after three days.

WA TR VI, no. 6941, pp. 283–84

The fruits of the celibate life of priests, nuns, and monks. Doctor Martin Luther said once in a sermon, "I have read that Saint Ulrich, who was once the bishop of Augsburg, wrote in a letter and complained, as Pope Gregory [VII, 1073–85] was establishing and strengthening clerical celibacy, and also would not allow those who had been married before his decree had been issued to remain married. Shortly afterwards the pope wanted to fish in a deep pond that lay right next to a convent of nuns. The water was let out of the pond, and the heads of six thousand children were found who had been thrown into the pond and drowned. These are the fruits of celibacy! And St. Ulrich wrote that Pope Gregory was very shocked by this spectacle and lifted the rule of celibacy. But the other popes that succeeded Gregory established celibacy again."

And Doctor Luther said, "In our time it also happened in Austria. In Neuburg convent there were nuns whom people wanted to force out of the convent because of their godless and immoral life; they sent them to another place, and then Franciscan monks were put in this convent. And as these monks wanted to expand their monastery and dug out the foundation, they found twelve pots in the ground, and in every pot there was the dead carcass of a young child. Pope Gregory did something that was right and good when he allowed clerics to marry and applied the words of St. Paul, 'It is better to marry than burn.' I say as well that it is better to be free [to marry] than to give cause for so many innocent children to be strangled and killed.

"In Rome, there are so many whores' children born that a special convent was built for these foundlings where they could be raised, and the pope is called their father. And when there are major processions in Rome, all these foundlings precede the pope in the procession."

And Doctor Luther said, "When I was a young boy, people considered weddings and marriages as sinful and dishonorable, and had the opinion that when you thought about married people's lives, you were sinning.

Whoever wanted to lead a life that was holy and pleasing to God was not to take a wife, but to live chastely or praise chastity, and many men whose wives died became monks or priests. But those who went to the trouble to maintain and honor their marriages through God's word truly served the Christian Church. For now we know that it is holy and precious when a man and woman live peacefully with each other in marriage, even if God does not grant them children or if the woman has some other sort of infirmity."

CHAPTER 7

Childbirth

Bearing children was to Luther's mind women's paramount function. Without the creation of Eve, humankind would have died out with Adam. There was at the outset no human counterpart to the female of every other species, with which the bucks, boars, bulls, and billy goats were able to reproduce their kind. Eve had other salient duties, such as to assist Adam in all his tasks and to be his companion. In these he could theoretically have been aided by another man. But only with a woman could he "be fruitful and multiply and replenish the earth."

Luther does not reveal conclusively whether he thought Adam and Eve actually had progeny before the Fall. We are not told how much time elapsed between the creation of Eve and her seduction by the serpent. Luther thought that without the Fall mating would have taken place without "evil lust" but rather calmly, matter-of-factly, without shame or self-consciousness. People would have had many more offspring than the one that women now ordinarily bore at a time, and mothers would have experienced none of the common maladies of pregnancy, parturition, nursing, or babyhood. God had added all the travails of reproduction and child-tending to women's lot when Eve disobeyed.

In addition to remembering what Luther said about bearing children in a narrow sense, we must also consider his teaching on "vocation." Based on the Latin word *vocare* (to call), the term designates not something that a person chooses but what God has called her to be. The German word *Beruf* (vocation) has the same connotation, based, as it is, on the verb *rufen* (to call). Luther was certain that women were not called to preach, teach, or govern, but to "bear fruit." In the terminology of the sixteenth and seventeenth centuries, a baby could be called a *fruit* – as it could in early modern English, when, during the Visitation, Mary's kinswoman Elizabeth exclaims to the Virgin, "Blessed is the fruit of thy womb!"[1] Women's vocation was to be mothers.

---

[1] Luke 1:42.

From this dual perspective, we can understand Luther's apparent callousness in giving advice to the woman in labor: "Bring the child forth
and do it with all your might! If you die in the process, then pass on over,
good for you! For you actually die in a noble work and in obedience to
God."[2] The Reformer's intention here was to bring encouragement and
consolation to the woman in childbed. To fulfill one's vocation was to conform to God's demand of every individual. He wanted to assure mothers
that God had ordained their afflictions and that in accepting these they
pleased Him.

Luther's primary concern – and he attributed this to the mothers as well –
was that their children should survive. As faithful, baptized Christians, the
mothers themselves should be content to place their trust in God. A baby
not yet born into the world, much less christened, had to rely on others.
Luther's thought and action on baptism were occasionally contradictory.
Although he believed that one could do nothing to effect salvation, which
lay in God's hands alone, an uninitiated infant was a "child of wrath" and
could not with certainty be saved. Luther harbored some doubt whether
an unbaptized baby could go to heaven. His provisions for the church
speak as loudly as his learned statements, for he felt it necessary to retain
emergency baptism and to have the pertinent clergy ascertain afterward
whether the midwife had administered a valid sacrament. Thus, the need
to decide on the viability of the newborn and act accordingly, without
delay, may have heightened the tension in the birthing chamber. Toward
the end of his life, however, he wrote for the sake of mothers whose children
had died without baptism that God would indeed hear their prayers. "One
ought not to regard such infants as damned" for whom devout women
prayed.

TREATISES AND SERMONS

On Married Life, 1522, WA X/2, p. 296

One should also consider the woman in her tasks, when she nurses the
child, rocks it, bathes and does other things to it, and when she otherwise
works and helps her husband and is obedient. One should also comfort
and strengthen a woman who is in labor – not with St. Margaret's legend or
go around doing other foolish women's deeds, but say as follows: "Think,
dear Greta, that you are a woman and that this work of yours [giving birth]
is pleasing to God. Console yourself happily by [thinking of] His will, and

---

[2] "Vom ehelichen Leben. 1522," WA X/2, p. 296.

let Him do with you what is His right. Bring that child forth, and do it with all your might! If you die in the process, so pass on over, good for you! For you actually die in a noble work and in obedience to God. Indeed, if you were not a woman, you should wish that you were for the sake of this work alone, so that in the course of this precious and godly task you could suffer pain and die. For this is the word of God, who has created you [and] implanted such pain in you..."

Sermons from the Year 1531, 30 April, WA XXXVI, pp. 351–52
See how much is expected of a woman in labor. It is not a laughing matter; she bites into a sour apple. No woman is able to say, "I am certain of a happy birth," but she thinks, "God help [me and] give advice! I stand in God's power"... She is not able to say, "It [the pain] will be moderate." She cannot [fore]see that; and then she bears and is weakened by severe pain such that she could not bear any more. It happens to you. You will have a time of moderate temptation, and then you will be relieved again. And we are more certain than she. For we have this promise: "You will see me again." [Paradoxically] no woman has this certitude, and yet the one having this certitude is saved. It should go this way and happen that you lack nothing.

LECTURES

Lectures on Genesis, LW I
From *Luther's Works*, vol. I, edited by Jaroslav Pelikan, © 1968
Concordia Publishing Company. Used by permission of Concordia
Publishing House

[Pp. 104–5] But who can describe in words the glory of the innocence we have lost [through the Fall]? There still remains in nature the longing of the male for the female, likewise the fruit of procreation; but these are combined with the awful hideousness of lust and the frightful pain of birth. Shame, ignominy, and embarrassment arise even among married people when they wish to enjoy their legitimate intercourse. So universal is the most oppressive evil of original sin! The creation indeed is good, and the blessing is good; but through sin they are so corrupted that married people cannot make use of them without shame. All these things would not have existed in Adam's state of innocence; but just as married people eat and drink together without shame, so there would have been a transcendent decency, not shame and embarrassment, in procreation and birth...

[P. 126] Thus it is a great miracle that a small seed is planted and that out of it grows a very tall oak. But because these are daily occurrences, they have become of little importance, like the very process of our procreation. Surely it is most worthy of wonder that a woman receives semen, that this semen becomes thick and, as Job elegantly said (Job 10:10), is congealed and then is given shape and nourished until the fetus is ready for breathing air. When the fetus has been brought into the world by birth, no new nourishment appears, but a new way and method: from the two breasts, as from a fountain, there flows milk by which the baby is nourished. All these developments afford the fullest occasion for wonderment and are wholly beyond our understanding, but because of their continued recurrence they have come to be regarded as commonplace, and we have verily become deaf to this lovely music of nature...

[P. 128] Indeed, we see a man and a woman being joined; we see the woman made pregnant by a droplet of blood; and later, at a definite, fixed time, a baby is brought into the world. These are the facts that lie before the eyes of all and are well known; and yet without the reminder and instruction of the Word you have no actual knowledge of the very activity which you are carrying on consciously and with open eyes...

[P. 130] Just as Adam was made from a clod, so I was made from a droplet of my father's blood. How my mother conceived me, how I was formed in the womb, and how my growth took place – all this I leave to the glory of the Creator. For it is truly unbelievable that a human being comes into existence from a drop of blood; and yet it is true...

[P. 133] Similarly, there are also some remnants [of the time before the Fall] in the instance of procreation, although in the state of innocence women would not only have given birth without pain, but their fertility would also have been far greater. Procreation is now hindered by a thousand diseases, and it happens either that unborn children do not survive the period of gestation or that at times marriages are altogether barren. These are flaws and punishments resulting from Adam's awful fall and from original sin...

[P. 194] Women gave birth up to the Flood and later until the time of Mary; but their seed could not in truth be called the seed of the woman, but rather the seed of a man. But what is born from Mary was conceived by the Holy Spirit and is the true Seed of Mary, just as the other promises given to Abraham and David testify, according to which Christ is called the Son of Abraham and the Son of David...

[P. 195] This very clear promise ["I shall put enmity between you and the woman"] is at the same time also very obscure, because God speaks in general of "the seed of the woman." Thus at the same time He makes all women suspect to Satan and worries him with endless concern and care. It is, therefore, an amazing instance of synecdoche [a figure of speech by which the species is used for the genus]. "The woman's seed," He says. This means all individuals in general; and yet He is speaking of only one individual, of the Seed of Mary, who is a mother without union with a male....

[P. 198] *But to the woman He said: I will greatly multiply your sorrow when you are pregnant. In pain you will bear children, and you will be under your husband's power; and he will rule over you.*

This punishment is inflicted on the woman, but it is a happy and joyful punishment, because it is not out of harmony with the earlier verdict that was pronounced upon Satan. If this stands, that the head of the serpent must be crushed, the hope for resurrection from the dead is sure. Then whatever is inflicted on the human race is bearable, provided this hope remains unshaken.

Moreover, this is also why Holy Scripture is so careful not to say anything in connection with the punishment meted out to the woman that is opposed to the verdict earlier pronounced upon Satan. It inflicts punishment on the woman, and yet it leaves the hope of resurrection and of eternal life. But it assigns death, which she had deserved through her sin, to the other and less noble part of the human being, namely, to the flesh, so that because of faith the spirit may live in righteousness.

Therefore the woman is subject to death so far as the flesh is concerned; but so far as hope is concerned, she is free from death. The verdict remains sure; God threatens that the devil's head will be crushed. The physical body has its cross and death here, as St. Paul also says (1 Cor. 15:44): "The natural body dies, but the spiritual one will rise." Thus in this natural life marriages continue, and the woman experiences the punishments which the Lord here inflicts because of sin. From the time of conception, during birth, and during all the rest of her life, while she devotes herself to her children, she will encounter various dangers. But all these things pertain only to the natural life or to the flesh itself, and meanwhile the hope of a spiritual and eternal life after this life endures.

[P. 199] Therefore truly happy and joyful is this punishment if we correctly appraise the matter. Although these burdens are troublesome for the flesh, yet the hope for a better life is strengthened, together with those very burdens or punishments, because Eve hears that she is not being repudiated by God. Furthermore, she also hears that in this punishment she is not being deprived of the blessing of procreation, which was promised and granted before sin. She sees that she is keeping her sex and that she remains a woman. She sees that she is not being separated from Adam to remain alone and apart from her husband. She sees that she may keep the glory of motherhood, if I may use the phrase. All these things are in addition to the eternal hope, and without a doubt they greatly encouraged Eve. Above all, there remains also a greater and more genuine glory. Not only does she keep the blessing of fruitfulness and remain united with her husband, but she has the sure promise that from her will come the Seed who will crush the head of Satan...

[P. 200] Therefore this is indeed a threat in which the Lord threatens Eve with definite punishments... The threat is directed particularly at birth and conception. But conception designates the entire time during which the fetus, after being conceived, is carried in the womb, a time beset with severe and sundry ailments. From the beginning of that time a woman suffers very painful headaches, dizziness, nausea, an amazing loathing of food and drink, frequent and difficult vomiting, toothache, and a stomach disorder which produces a craving, called pica, for foods from which nature normally shrinks. Moreover, when the fetus has matured and birth is imminent, there follows the most awful distress, because only with utmost peril and almost at the cost of her life does she give birth to her offspring...

[P. 201] Even among those physical misfortunes there still remains that outstanding glory of motherhood and the blessing of the womb which the wiser among the heathen have also wondered at and gloriously extolled. There still remain the other gifts: that we are all nourished, kept warm, and carried in the womb of our mothers; that we nurse at their breasts and are protected by their effort and care...

[P. 202] To me it is often a source of great pleasure and wonderment to see that the entire female body was created for the purpose of nurturing children. How prettily even little girls carry babies on their bosom! As for the mothers themselves, how deftly they move whenever the whimpering baby either has to be quieted or is to be placed into its cradle! Get a man to do the same things, and you will say that a camel is dancing, so clumsily will he do the simplest tasks around the baby! I say nothing about the other duties which mothers alone can perform...

If Eve had not sinned, she would not only have given birth without pain, but her union with her husband would have been just as honorable as it is today to eat or converse with one's wife at the table. Rearing children would also have been very easy and would have abounded in joy. These benefits have been lost through sin, and there have followed those familiar evils of pain and work that are connected with gestation, birth, and nurturing. Just as a pretty girl, without any inconvenience, nay, even with great pleasure and some pride, wears on her head a beautiful wreath woven from flowers, so, if she had not sinned, Eve would have carried her child in her womb without any inconvenience and with great joy. Now there is also added to those sorrows of gestation and birth [the fact] that Eve has been placed under the power of her husband – she who previously was very free and, as the sharer of all the gifts of God, was in no respect inferior to her husband.

This punishment, too, springs from original sin; and the woman bears it just as unwillingly as she bears those pains and inconveniences that have been placed upon her flesh. The rule remains with the husband, and the wife is compelled to obey him by God's command. He rules the home and the state, wages wars, defends his possessions, tills the soil, builds, plants, etc. The woman, on the other hand, is like a nail driven into the wall. She sits at home...

[P. 203] The pagans have depicted Venus as standing on a seashell; for just as the snail carries its house with it, so the wife should stay at home and look after the affairs of the household, as one who has been deprived of the ability of administering those affairs that are outside and that concern the state...

[P. 217] Since a wife becomes pregnant and gives birth only once in a year, the question is raised: Is it also a punishment to become pregnant only once? Likewise, why does God say here that He wants to multiply her conception? Now so far as the latter is concerned, I think the correct explanation is: "I shall multiply conception, that is, the pains and inconveniences which follow conception. The punishment is that though no more than one child is conceived in a year, she is burdened with countless inconveniences." If the human race had continued to remain in innocence, the fertility of the women would have been far greater. We see some traces of this when in one birth twins, often triplets, and sometimes even quadruplets, are brought into the world.

And of this fertility there are examples among the rest of the beasts. The fertility of birds and fish is great. Dogs, cats, and pigs also give birth to a large number of young. Although some larger animals give birth to only one at a time, I nevertheless have no doubt that if there were no sin, women would have given birth to a much more numerous offspring. Now those who are most fertile give birth at most to one child in a single year, and that shameful and heinous lust has been added to it. All this reminds us of the enormity of sin.

Lectures on Genesis, LW V, pp. 380–82
From *Luther's Works*, vol. V, edited by Jaroslav Pelikan, © 1968
Concordia Publishing Company. Used by permission of
Concordia Publishing House

[Commenting on Genesis 30] It is an established fact and in agreement with the teachings of physicians, who state that in the conception of all living beings, not only of dumb animals but also of human beings, special forms or marks are imprinted on the young, both as a result of a mental image and as a result of various objects that appear to the heart or the eyes, not only in the very heat of conception but also after impregnation has taken place.

Jerome and the naturalists relate the example of a queen who gave birth to a child with the form and face of an Ethiopian as a result of a strong mental image of an Ethiopian painted on a tablet near her bed. They also tell of another woman who was accused of adultery because, although she herself was ugly, she had given birth to a beautiful infant unlike both parents and the whole relationship. She would have been condemned, they say, had Hippocrates not obtained her liberation by giving the advice to ask her whether in her bedchamber she had had a painted tablet which had given her pleasure when she looked at it. When this had been found, she was absolved by the judges. Thus we sometimes see bloody spots or spots of another color scattered on the face, on the eyes, on the cheeks, and on the neck of infants, namely, when pregnant women have been suddenly excited by the sight and the fear of something unusual and have moved their hands to those members. Here at Wittenberg we have seen a citizen with a face like a corpse who stated that while his mother was pregnant, she was suddenly confronted by the sight of a corpse and was so terrified that the face of the fetus in her womb took on the form of a corpse.

The same custom is carefully observed when cattle and beasts of burden are mated. Thus Jerome states that among the Spaniards horses of the noblest stock are placed before the mares when mating takes place, in order that foals like them may be produced. Therefore there should be no joking with pregnant women, but they should receive careful attention because of the fetus. For there are countless dangers of miscarriages, monsters, and various deformities. Therefore a husband should live "considerately" with his wife at this time most of all, as Peter says (1 Peter 3:17). I remember that when I was a boy at Eisenach, a beautiful and virtuous matron gave birth to a dormouse. This happened because one of the neighbors had hung a little bell on a dormouse in order that the rest might be put to flight when the bell made a sound. This dormouse met the pregnant woman, who, ignorant of the matter, was so terrified by the sudden meeting and sight of the dormouse that the fetus in her womb degenerated into the shape of the little beast. Such examples are all too common when pregnant women are often excited by sudden emotions and fears at the risk of their life.

Accordingly, one must be on guard, lest they experience both bodily and mental disturbances that are rather violent. For those who pay no attention to pregnant women and do not spare the tender fetus become murderers and parricides. Thus some men are so cruel that they vent their rage on pregnant women even with blows. Of course, they are brave and full of courage against the weak sex! Otherwise, however, they are complete cowards. We heard recently that a certain prince, noted for many other crimes and outrages, drew his sword against his wife when she was sick and bedfast [bedridden]. Truly an outstanding hero and a mighty soldier! But this is by no means heroic; it is outrageous and most disgraceful. For if you are a man, you will find your equal with whom you may clash. Heroes are brave against the brave and weak against the weak. For why is it that you stir up a fight against a child or a pregnant woman? Even in the company of temperate husbands this sex has dangers enough and more than enough in other respects from neighbors, from the devil, and from various apparitions and pictures of dumb animals. It is an outrage if they are increased by your cruelty.

Indeed, even the heathen have praised this virtue in their heroes, namely, that they were gentle and pleasant toward their wives. For the description of Achilles and Hector, etc., in Homer bear[s] this out. Armed Hector kisses his little son. Thus they were women with women, so much so that nothing seemed more womanish than those heroes in the company of their wives. But in battle Achilles conducts himself differently against Hector from the way he conducts himself when he amuses himself with Briseis. Therefore those who are brave and pugnacious against the unarmed and weak sex are worthy of hatred. We men are born not to harm but to defend the weaker sex. For a woman has a body created for pregnancy, for the nourishment of the fetus, and she is exposed to very many dangers. Therefore she must be treated with wisdom and moderation.

ADVICE BOOKS

A Consolation to Those Women Who Have Had Difficulties in Bearing Children, 1542, WA LIII, pp. 205–8

It often happens that we are sought for consolation by a number of pious parents, and in particular by the wives to whom it happened, without their

consent, indeed against their wishes, and who with heartfelt pain have had
to suffer because their giving birth has gone wrong and improperly, such
that the child has died while being born or has come forth dead.

Here one ought not to frighten or trouble such mothers with inconsider-
ate words, for it is not their fault nor the result of their neglect or carelessness
that the child has been injured. One should distinguish these from those
women or females who do not want to bear a child, intentionally injure it,
or even wickedly smother and kill it. Instead, one should speak to them in
this manner:

First of all, although one should not and cannot know God's secret
judgment in such a case, and why, despite every possible effort, He has not
allowed it to be born alive and baptized, the mothers should be content
with this and believe that at all times God's will is better than our own, even
though according to our fleshly opinion things look very different. Above
all, we should not think that God is angry with the mothers or others who
have taken part, but rather that He is urging us to be patient. We also know
that such cases from the very beginning have not been unusual, and the
Scripture itself gives examples such as Psalm 58; and St. Paul himself calls
a miscarriage or untimely birth an *abortivum*.

Secondly, it is also to be hoped that because the mother is a Christian and
faithful, her heartfelt sighing and complete yearning to bring the child to
baptism is accepted as a genuine prayer by God. For although it is true that
a Christian, in his great distress, cannot name or wish or dare to hope, as it
seems to him, what he so deeply desires and would gladly purchase with his
own life, if this were possible and could be given him as a consolation, here
the verse of St. Paul to the Romans (8[:26]) is pertinent: "The Spirit helps
our weakness, for we do not know what we ought to pray" – that is, as said
above, we dare not wish it, as is proper, but the Spirit itself represents us
powerfully, with unspeakable longing. Whoever examines his heart knows
what the Spirit means or wishes, etc. Another example, Ephesians 3[:20]:
"The Immeasurable does more than we either ask or conceive," etc.

Ah, one should not esteem a Christian so little, like a Turk, heathen,
or godless person! He is precious in God's sight, and his prayer is an all-
powerfully great thing. For he has been saved by Christ's blood and anointed
by the Spirit of God. What he sincerely requests, particularly with the
unspeakable yearning of his heart, that is a great and intolerable cry in
God's ears. He must hear it, just as he speaks to Moses in Exodus 14[:15]:
"What are you crying out to me?" Out of worry and trembling, Moses
could hardly whisper, for he was in the greatest distress. But this longing
and the fundamental crying out of his heart divided even the Red Sea and

made it dry. He led the children of Israel through it and drowned Pharaoh with all his power, etc. That and still more a spiritual yearning can do and does, for Moses too did not know what and how he ought to pray. He did not know how his salvation would take place, but he cried out in his heart.

Isaiah did this too, against King Sennacherib, and many other kings and prophets who by means of their unarticulated prayers accomplished impossible things that amazed them afterward, even though beforehand they could not properly have expected or wished these things of God. That means to achieve higher and more than we either pray or understand, as St. Paul says in Ephesians 3[:20], etc. St. Augustine writes about his mother that she prays, sighs, and weeps for him, though she desires nothing more than that he turn away from the error of the Manichees and become a Christian. God gave her not only what she wanted, but also what St. Augustine calls *Cardinem desiderii eius* [the main part of her desire], that is, what she wished for with an unspeakable longing, namely that Augustine become not only a Christian but also a teacher above all teachers in all Christendom, such that Christianity, apart from the apostles, does not possess his equal.

And who would doubt that the children of Israel who died uncircumcised before the eighth day, upon the prayer of their parents, based on the assurance that He wanted to be their God, were saved? God, one says, did not bind His power to the sacraments, but He bound Himself to us by means of His word. Because of that, we ought to speak otherwise and more consolingly with Christians than with the heathen or (of whom there are many) wicked people, including in those cases where we do not know His secret judgment. For He speaks and does not lie: "All things are possible to those who have faith," even if they have not prayed, thought of, or wished everything that they would like to see happen, of which enough has now been said. Therefore, we should present such cases to God and console ourselves that He assuredly hears our unspoken longings and has done everything better than we have been able to put into words.

In sum, take special care to be a true Christian and thus to pray in proper faith to God and learn to yearn from your heart, whether in this or any other distress. Then do not be sorry and do not worry, either for your child or for yourself. Know that your prayer is pleasing and that God will do everything much better than you can grasp or desire. "Call upon me," He says in Psalm 50, "and I will help you; you should praise and thank me." Consequently, one ought not to regard such infants as damned, with and over whom such longing, wishing, [and] praying is done by Christians or the faithful – unlike those with whom no Christians or faithful people have believed, prayed, or sighed. He does not want to despise or reject our prayer or yearning that are founded upon His promise; He wants to regard them highly and as precious. I have said above and otherwise preached sufficiently how God does much for people, even if they themselves do not believe, for whom others approach Him in faith and yearning and make requests. In the Gospel, Christ awoke the son of the widow of Nain because of the mother's longing, even though the son did not have faith himself. And he freed the little daughter of the Canaanite woman from the devil because of the mother's faith and not because of the daughter's own belief; and also the royal officer's son in John 4; and the man afflicted with gout [*Gichtbruechtigen*, Matt. 9:2], and many more, of which I shall speak no longer here.

TABLE TALK

WA TR I, no. 251, p. 157

Papists have given us evil thoughts about children who die. Here one must proceed cautiously. Women are mischievous and the maids too: they smother them [the infants] secretly, and the mothers injure them and often also the midwives... For that reason it would not hurt to keep them in fear. Otherwise, they could well let the children be wantonly destroyed. There is misfortune enough [without that]. Therefore, we say and we admonish them to hurry to baptism.

WA TR II, no. 1554, p. 130

Mothers' milk and female breasts. Their mothers' milk is children's best nourishment, drink, and food, for it feeds them well. Just as young calves, too, put on more weight from the milk that they suck than from any other fodder. Those babies grow stronger who have been nursed for a long time.

Breasts are a women's adornment when they are well proportioned. Large and fleshy ones are not the best, do not look as good, promise much but give little. But those breasts that are full of veins and nerves, even if they are small, look attractive even on small women, and have much milk so that they could nurse many children.

...It is unfriendly and unnatural for a mother not to nurse her child, for God has given her breasts and milk for that purpose, for the sake of the infant – unless she is not able to nurse. Necessity breaks iron, as one says.

WA TR II, no. 1668, p. 171
A pregnant woman is a divine work, giving birth, etc. Marriage is the fount of the entire human race, and nevertheless this sacred origin of life is concealed and held in contempt, such that it has the reputation of being a fleshly, worldly way of life. If all the leaves in the meadow of Torgau were to speak in tongues, they could not adequately preach the praise of marriage or the turpitude of celibacy, etc.

WA TR II, no. 2564, p. 526
Giving birth is the most difficult task and is hard and dangerous for the pregnant woman. For the infant must come out through the pelvic bones, which have to be forced apart; otherwise, when they are in their usual place, hardly an apple could go through. It is a great, incomprehensible miracle of God.

WA TR II, no. 2578, p. 530
Taking his own infant [in his arms], Martin said, "Oh, God has put these black eyes in a piece of flesh that comes out of a stinking sack [the mother's body]! It reminds me of making a blintz and setting lovely eyes in it. It is also an art to make a nose, mouth, hands, and feet out of a little piece of flesh in the mother's body."

WA TR II, no. 2764a, also 2764b, pp. 643–44
Doctor Luther's wife was ill in the afternoon, and Luther said to her, "Dear Kethe, don't die!" He said that she contravened the rule: women [in her state of advanced pregnancy] were cold, but she was hot. "A woman is a poor thing, but she nevertheless excels if she bears children. It is the greatest honor of a woman that all people are born through them. To reproduce is a gift of God".

WA TR III, no. 3319b, pp. 265–66
Martin Luther happily looked at his pregnant wife, saying, "My dear Käthe, you do this to honor me, for by the blessing of God and your fertility you have made me the father of six children..." [The editors of WA note that the number 'six' was an error introduced later by Anton Lauterbach, for she had only been pregnant five times at that time; n. 4.]

WA TR VI, no. 6758, pp. 167–69
When it happens to a woman that the child cannot entirely emerge from her but an arm or other members comes forth, one should not baptize

that member, as though in this way the entire child is baptized. Much less should one baptize a child that is still in the mother's body and has not and cannot come out, such that one would wish to pour water over the mother's belly etc. For that is not proper and not in accordance with divine Scripture [as] clearly appears in the words of Christ when he says about baptism, "Unless the person has been born into the world."

For that reason if a baby is supposed to be baptized, it is necessary that it first be born and come into the world; and this does not happen if only one little member comes out of the mother. So we should always adhere to the rule of Christ: "Unless the person is born into the world," etc. But those who are present should kneel down [and] pray to our Lord God that he permit this infant to partake of his suffering and death, and not doubt therefore that he will know what to do in accordance with his godly grace and mercy.

Because the baby is brought to Christ by means of our prayer and such prayer is spoken in faith, it is certain that God hears what we ask [and] that he gladly receives [it, the child]. For he says, "Let the little children come unto me, for of these is the kingdom of heaven," etc. So we should regard it as certain that this little child, even if it has not attained proper baptism, is not thereby lost.

Another thing. If it quickly turns out that the baby, as soon as it comes into the world, is so very ill and weak that it might die before it could be brought to public baptism in the church, the women are permitted to baptize it themselves with the appropriate words, namely, "I baptize thee in the name of the Father, the Son, and the Holy Spirit."

In this case one should diligently observe the following distinction, namely that the mother of the child should always have at least two or three women or persons called in such an emergency who can bear witness that the child has been baptized. Just as the holy Scripture says, "In the mouths of two or three is all witness."

Afterward, if the child remains alive, they should bring it into the church to the pastor or the deacon and indicate to him that the baby, in an emergency, was baptized by them; and they should request that he confirm and validate their emergency baptism by laying his hands on the infant's head. If this does not occur, as though the baptism performed by the women were improper and invalid, it is nonetheless in and of itself a proper baptism. Still, there should be public testimony, which is given by the servants of the church in the manner just described.

Therefore, if one finds a child in the street or elsewhere and does not know to whom it pertains and belongs [or] whether it has been baptized or not, even if it were already baptized, because there is no public witness available, one should have it baptized again in the church. And such a baptism should not be regarded as Anabaptism, for the Anabaptists attack public infant baptism alone.

Should it occur that, unforeseen, a woman is overtaken by sudden birth and the child is so weak that she is concerned that it might depart and die before she could call somebody – in this case she may baptize the child herself. If it should then die, it has died well and has received the proper baptism, which the mother should not doubt.

If the infant stays alive, the mother should tell no person about this baptism but be quiet about it and bring that child again to public baptism, in accordance with Christian ordinance and custom. And this second baptism should and may not be counted as rebaptism, as is said above about the foundlings. For it might happen, especially in such an important matter as the salvation of souls, that the mother, as one single person, might not be believed, and her baptism has no witness. For that reason, the public baptism is highly necessary. [Cf. no. 6763, p. 172.]

WA TR VI, no. 6764, pp. 172–73 [a version of Luther's letter of 8 February
1536, to Anton Lauterbach, pastor in Pirna]
About the parturients who are in labor, there is no doubt that, if they die in faith, they are saved, for they die in the office and vocation that God created them for. And the faith in the work is effective, indeed will be found perfect in the cross, to her who is certain and waits for the Day of Judgment, yes, of Consolation.

For that reason, one should admonish the women to cooperate and work with all their might when they are in labor so that they may be delivered of their fruit and infant and recover, even if they should die in the midst of it. However, one should be moderate in this matter and not drive them too far. For some women are accustomed to advise and help themselves more than the fruit because they are worried and fear that they might die, or [they are afraid] to suffer great pains and hurt.

CHAPTER 8

Katharina von Bora, Luther's wife

While Martin Luther became something of a saint, such that images of him were "incombustible" and could occasionally work miracles, Luther's wife Käthe down through the centuries has borne the brunt of criticism until, in the second half of the twentieth century, her star began to rise, particularly among women.[1] Beginning soon after their marriage, which took place on 13 June 1523, Luther referred to his *Hausfrau* in letters to a wide circle of friends, adding her greeting to his. Perhaps this was a technique for reconciling his inner circle to his wife. Initial reserve among Martin's colleagues turned to acceptance if not love.

The facts of their contented life together are well known. An equally significant result of Luther's lack of restraint, in comparison to any other Reformer, in describing his domestic life is that the Luthers as a couple quickly became a model of the Evangelical clerical marriage. Pointedly rejecting celibacy, Luther lived out the revolution within the parsonage that marked one of the Reformation's starkest departures from the Catholic ideal of priestly behavior.

Because of the ample record, including the observations written down by guests at the Luthers' dining table, we gain insight into Luther's dual concept of marriage as a source of satisfaction and, simultaneously, as a *cross* – a torment and burden. We are permitted to witness the pair's deep affection for one another and their children, Martin's happiness when Käthe was pregnant, their yearning to be together when one of them was traveling, Käthe's mastery as a brewer of beer – even, obliquely, their pleasure in sexual

---

[1] R. W. Scribner, "'Incombustible Luther': The Image of the Reformer in Early Modern Germany," *Past and Present* 110 (1986): 38–68. See Jeanette C. Smith, "Katharina von Bora through Five Centuries: A Historiography," *Sixteenth Century Journal* 30,3 (1999): 745–74. Down to the present, artists and writers have envisioned Katharina Lutheryn. See the catalogue of the exhibition in honor of Katharina's five-hundredth birthday by Martin Treu, *"Lieber Herr Käthe" – Katharina von Bora, die Lutherin: Rundgang durch die Ausstellung* (Wittenberg: Stiftung Luthergedenkstätten in Sachsen-Anhalt, 1999), especially pp. 90–99. On the persistent criticism, see Richard Friedenthal, *Luther*, trans. John Nowell (London: Weidenfeld and Nicolson, 1967), p. 439.

congress. At the same time, we see the burdensome side of marriage: Käthe's morning sickness, Martin's anxiety that she might die, his impatience when in his opinion she talked too much or tried to dominate him, hers when he spent money too freely, their profound grief on the deaths of their daughters Elisabeth and Magdalena. Martin thought that the common awareness of the inevitability of such tribulations encouraged some men to avoid marriage, but he countered this sentiment by insisting that God had instituted the marital estate and wanted nearly every person, male and female, to enter it. The Luther who wed to bear witness to his faith, to thwart the devil, and to please his father, Hans (who hoped for the continuation of his line), quickly moved from simple esteem for his bride to a deep emotional bond with her. Even though throughout their lives together, she addressed him in formal language as "Sir Doctor," while he used the familiar *Du* and called her by her first name, there was a high degree of mutuality in their relationship. Indeed, Martin realized that he could not carry out his many tasks as writer, preacher, and teacher without Käthe's unstinting, efficient labor in household and garden. So much did he value her judgment that in private he occasionally consulted her about matters of running the church.[2]

Her life focused on him and on their children. When Martin died in February 1546, Käthe's loss was horrendous. Despite Martin's explicit wish that she should administer her own estate and remain in charge of her children – which was contrary to Saxon law and practice – guardians were named for her and for them. The outbreak of the Schmalkaldic War soon rendered her a refugee as she tried in vain to migrate to the court of Christian III of Denmark. She returned to Wittenberg and ultimately died in Torgau on 20 December 1552, after falling from a wagon. She was fifty-three years old, nine years younger than her husband at the time of his own demise.

LUTHER'S LETTERS TO HIS WIFE

From Torgau, 27 February 1532, WA BR VI, no. 1908, pp. 270–71
To my beloved housewife, Katharin Lutherin, for her own hands.

God greet you in Christ! My sweetheart Käte! I hope that if Doctor Brück gets permission to leave, as he consoles me [that he will], I will be able to come with him tomorrow or the day after. Pray to God that he brings us home fresh and healthy! I sleep altogether well, about six or seven

[2] For example, WA BR IX, no. 3509, July 1540, p. 168.

hours without waking, and after that two or three hours more. It is the
beer's fault, in my opinion. But I am sober, just as in Wittenberg... His
Electoral Grace is as healthy as a little fish in his body as a whole, but the
devil has bitten and stung him on the foot. Pray, pray on! I hope that God
will hear us, as He has already begun to do. For Dr. Caspar [Cruciger] is
of the opinion that God must help here.

Because Johannes [a servant] is moving away, necessity and honor demand that I let him depart from me in an honorable condition. For you
know that he has served faithfully and diligently and has humbly and truly
kept to the gospel and done everything and suffered. For that reason, think
over how often we have been generous with evil knaves and ungrateful
schoolboys, on whom everything has been lost. So dip into your purse, and
do not let such a pious fellow lack for anything. For you know that it is
well invested and pleasing to God. I am well aware that there is little there;
but I would happily give him 10 gulden if I had it. But you should not give
him less than 5 gulden, for we are not providing him with new clothes.
Whatever you are able to give him above that, I ask you to do it. To be sure,
the community chest could well give something to such a servant of mine,
in honor of me, in view of the fact that I have to maintain my servant at
my own expense, but for the service and use of their church; but as they
wish. Do not fail to do it as long as there is a cup there [a silver cup that
could be sold]. Think of where you get everything. God will provide you
with more, that I know. Herewith I commend you to God, Amen.

... Kiss young Hans for me, and tell little Hans, Lenchen [Magdalena,
one or two years old], and Aunt Lena to pray for our dear prince and for
me. Even though it is the annual market here in this city [Torgau], I cannot
find anything to buy for the children. If I do not bring anything special,
have something on hand for me to give them. [Date]

D. Martinus Luther.

From Dessau, 29 July 1534, WA BR VII, no. 2130, p. 91
Grace and peace in Christ! Dear Lord Kethe! I do not know what to write to
you because Master Philipp [Melanchthon] himself, along with the others,
is coming home. I have to stay here longer for the sake of the pious prince.
You may wonder how long I will stay here or how you can set me free. My
view is that Master Franciscus will make me free again, just as I have freed
him, but not so soon. Yesterday I had a drink of bad beer and had to sing.
When I do not drink well, I am sorry. I would so have enjoyed it. And
I thought what good wine and beer I have at home, and in addition a
beautiful lady, or should I say lord. And you would do well if you sent the

whole cellar full of my wine over here to me, and a keg of your beer, as soon as you can. Otherwise, I will not be home until the new beer is ready. I commend you to God, along with our young ones and all the servants, Amen. [Date]

Your little Love,
Mart. LutheR D. [*sic*]

From Tambach [place], 27 February 1537 at 3:00 a.m., WA BR VIII, no. 3140, pp. 50–51

Grace and peace in Christ! For the time being, you may rent whatever horses you need, dear Käte, for My Gracious Lord will keep your horse and send Master Philipp home on it. I myself left Schmalkald yesterday in My Gracious Lord's own wagon. The reason for this is that I have not been in good health longer than three days. From the first Sunday [n. 3 says ML was exaggerating that his retention of urine began on 11 Feb., but Philip Melanchthon reported that it began on 19 Feb.] until tonight, no drop of water has passed out of me, I have not rested or slept and have not been able to retain either drink or food. In sum, I have been dead. I have commended you together with our little children to God and My Gracious Lord, as though I would not see you again in this mortal life... But now people have prayed to God so hard for me that the tears of many brought it about that God tonight opened the way out of my bladder, and in two hours probably a *Stüdigen* [n. 4 says 3–4 liters] came out of me. It seems to me that I have been reborn.

On this account, thank God and have our dear children along with Aunt Lena thank our true Father; for you would certainly have lost this father. The pious prince had people run, ride, fetch, and did his utmost to see whether anything would help me; but it just did not want to be. Your [medical] arts with the manure did not help me either. God performed a miracle on me tonight, and He continues to do it because of pious people's petitions.

I am writing this to you because I believe that My Gracious Lord has commanded his bailiff to send you out to meet me in case I died on the way, so that you could speak with me or see me. This is not necessary, and you might as well stay home. God has so generously helped me that I anticipate coming happily to you. Today we are staying in Gotha. Other than this, I have written four times, and I am surprised that nothing has reached you. [Date]

Martinus Luther.

From Weimar, July 1540, WA BR IX, no. 3509, p. 168

To my beloved Kethe, Mrs. Doctor Lutherin, etc., lady of the new sow-market, for her hands.

Grace and peace! Dear maiden Kethe, gracious lady of Zölsdorf (and whatever else Your Grace is called)! I submissively give you and Your Grace to know that things are going well with me here. I eat like a Bohemian and drink like a German, God be thanked, Amen. This comes from the fact that Master Philipp was truly dead and just like Lazarus has arisen from the dead. God the dear Father hears our prayer – that we see and grasp. But nevertheless we still do not believe. Let no one say Amen to our shameful unbelief. I have written to Dr. Pomeranus, the pastor, that the Count of Schwartzburg asks for a pastor for Greussen. As a clever lady and Mrs. Doctor, you may help to advise Master George Maior and Master Ambrosio about which of the three whom I indicated to Pomeranus may let himself be persuaded. It is not a bad parish...

Here in Arnstadt the pastor in proper Christian fashion drove a devil out of a little girl. About that we can say that if God, who still lives, wills it, it should bring pain to the devil.

I have received the children's letters and also that of the B.A. [Baccalarien = man with bachelor's degree] (who is no child)...but from Your Grace I have received nothing. The fourth letter [this one] would you, God willing, answer for once with your own hand.

Herewith I send Master Paul [Eber] the silver apple that My Gracious Lord presented to me. As I said before, you may divide it among the children and ask them how many cherries and apples they would take for it...

Convey to our dear boarders, especially Doctor Severus or Schiefer, my friendly feeling and good will, and ask them to tend to all matters in the churches, schools, house, and whatever needs their attention. Also ask Master George Maior and Master Ambrosio to be a consolation to you at home. If God is willing, we will set out by Sunday from Weimar to Eisenach, and Philipp with us. Herewith be commended to God... All of you, be of good cheer and pray, Amen. [Date]

Martinus Luther.
Your sweetheart.

From Eisenach, 10 July 1540, WA BR IX, no. 3511, pp. 171–73

To Lady Katherin Luderin in Wittenberg, etc., my dear housewife, etc.

Grace and peace! Dear Maiden Kethe! I am sending you hereby, with the wagoner of Dr. Blickard, etc....42 *taler*, my salary that falls due next

St. Michael's Day, and also the 40 *florin* of Georg Schnell on account. You may use it until we come. We have not been able to get at court one penny of small coin; we have just as little as you have in Wittenberg. The small denominations have come to Georg Schnell from Duke George's land of Weissensee... You might see if Hans von Taubenheim at Torgau could or would exchange smaller money for the taler. There is nothing new, except that here, too, in these lands, the devil rages with horrifying examples of his evil, and drives the people to arson, suicide, etc. But they are caught in the act and executed. Thereby God admonishes us to believe, to fear Him, and to pray. For this is God's punishment for our ingratitude and contempt for His dear word. Master Philipp is coming to life again out of the grave, still looks sick and jaundiced, but he jokes and laughs again with us and eats and drinks as he used to do at the table. God be praised! You as well as we should thank the dear Father in heaven, who awakens the dead and who alone gives all grace and good things; may He be blessed in eternity! Pray assiduously, as you are obligated to do, for our Lord Christ, that is for all of us who believe in him, against the devil's swarms that presently rage in Hagenau and rebel against the Lord and his anointed ones and who want to break their bonds, as the second Psalm says, so that they mock God, but in the end shatter like a potter's vessel, Amen... [Date]

Mart. Luther.

From Eisenach, 16 July 1540, WA BR IX, no. 3512, pp. 174–75
To my gracious Maiden Katherin Lutherin von Bora and Zölsdorf in Wittenberg, my little dear,

Grace and peace! My dear maid and lady Kethe! Your Grace should know that we here (God be praised!) are fresh and healthy, feast like the Bohemians (but not too much), drink like the Germans (but not often). We are cheerful, for our gracious lord of Magdeburg, Bishop Amsdorf, is our table companion. We do not know any other news except that Dr. Caspar, Mecum, and Menius have allowed themselves to be well cared for and have gone on foot from Hagenau to Strasbourg, in the service and honor of Hans von Jena. Master Philipp is fine again. Praise be to God! Tell my dear Dr. Schiefer that his King Ferdinand is rumored to want to invite Turks to be godparents in preference to Evangelical princes. I hope that this is not true. It would be too gross. Write to me too to let me know if you have received everything that I have sent, such as, recently, the 90 florins in care of Wolff Furman, etc. Herewith be commended to God, Amen. And have the children pray. Over here there is such heat and drought that it bespeaks

evil and is unbearable day and night. Come, dear Last Day, Amen! [Date]
The Bishop of Magdeburg sends you friendly greetings.

Your little love
Martin Luther.

From Eisenach, 26 July 1540, WA BR X, no. 3519, p. 205

To the rich lady of Zölsdorf, Lady Mrs. Doctor Katherin Lüdherin, physically resident in Wittenberg but mentally sojourning in Zulsdorf, to the
hands of my little love,

... We [ML and D. Pomeranus (Johannes Bugenhagen)] wanted to
arrange to find a good drink of beer in the house. For if God is willing,
we want to depart for Wittenberg tomorrow, Tuesday. Things are such
a mess with the imperial diet in Hagenau. So much effort and work is
lost and expense incurred, all in vain. On the other hand, if we have not
accomplished anything else, we have brought Master Philipp back from hell
and want to bring him out of the grave and joyfully home, if God is willing,
and with His grace, Amen. Out here the devil himself is possessed by nine
other devils. He burns and damages things horribly. My Gracious Lord has
lost more than a thousand acres [*ackers*, not equal to an English acre] of
woods to forest fire, which is still burning. There is additional news today
that the forest by Werdau has also caught fire. And many other places; no
effort to extinguish it helps. That will make wood expensive. Pray and have
others pray against the dreadful Satan, who rages most vehemently against
not only our soul and body, but also against our property and honor. May
Christ our Lord come down from heaven and blow up a little fire under
the devil and his companions that he could not put out, Amen. I have
not been certain whether these letters would find you in Wittenberg or
Zölsdorf. Otherwise, I would have written about more things. Herewith I
commend you to God. Greet our children, boarders, and all. [Date]

Your little love,
<M. LutheR D. [*sic*]

From Wittenberg to Zölsdorf, 18 September 1541, WA BR X,
no. 3670, pp. 518–19

To my dear housewife, Käthe Ludern von Bora, for her hands.

Grace and peace. Dear Kethe! I hereby hurry Urban off to you so that
you will not be frightened in case an alarm about the Turks should reach
you. I am surprised that you do not write or send instructions home at
all. You well know that we here are not without concern for you, because
Mainz, Heintz, and many of the nobility in Meissen are very hostile toward

us. Sell and purchase what you can, and come home. For in my opinion, filth is about to rain down. God will repay our sin with the rod of His anger. Herewith be commended to God, Amen. [Date]

M LutheR [*sic*]

From Eisleben, 1 February 1545, WA BR XI, no. 4195, pp. 275–76
To my beloved housewife, Katherin Lutherin, Mrs. Doctor, resident of Zölsdorf and of the Sowmarket, and whatever else she can be,

Grace and peace in Christ, and my old, poor love, and as Your Grace knows, impotent. Dear Kethe. I was weak along the way, just before we got to Eisleben. It was my fault. But if you had been there, you would have said that it was the Jews' fault or the fault of their god [! *sic*]. For we had to travel through a village close to Eisleben where many Jews live, and perhaps they blew hard upon me. At this very hour over fifty Jews are resident here in the city of Eisleben. And it is the truth that, as I went past the village, such a cold wind blew back into the wagon onto my head and through my hat, as though it wanted to turn my brain to ice. This may have helped me to become dizzy. But now, God be praised, I am in good shape, with the exception that the beautiful women cannot tempt me as much, and I have neither concern for nor fear of unchastity.

If the main issues were settled, I would have to devote myself to driving out the Jews. Count Albrecht is hostile to them and has already abandoned them. I am drinking Naumburger beer, which almost has the taste of the Mansfeld beer that you once praised to me. It pleases me well and in the morning gives me probably three stools in three hours. Your little sons traveled to Mansfeld the day before yesterday because Hans von Jena so humbly asked them to. I do not know what they will do there if it is cold except help to freeze. Now it is warm, and they could do or bear whatever pleases them. Herewith be commended to God, along with the whole house, and greet all the table companions. [Date]

M. Luth. Your old little love

From Zeitz, 28 July 1545, WA BR XI, no. 4139, pp. 149–50
To my friendly, dear housewife Catharina of Luther, von Bora, preacher, brewer, gardener, and whatever else she can be.

Grace and peace! Dear Kethe, How our trip has gone, Hans will well tell you all about – although I am not yet certain whether he will stay with me. Dr. Caspar Creutziger and Ferdinand might well inform us. Ernst von Schonfeld has already entertained us in Lobnitz, and much more lavishly Heintz Scherle in Leipzig. I would gladly arrange things so that I did not have to come back to Wittenberg. My heart is chilled, so that I do not like to be there anymore. I wish, too, that you would sell the garden and the field, house and yard. Then I would return the big house to My Most Gracious Lord. And it would be best for you if you moved to Zölsdorf while I am still living; I could help you with my salary to improve that little estate. For I hope that My Most Gracious Lord will allow me to have the salary for at least a year at the end of my life. After my death, the four elements in Wittenberg will probably not tolerate you. For that reason, it would be better to do what needs to be done while I am still alive. Perhaps Wittenberg will – as its government gives occasion for – contract, not St. Vitus's dance nor St. John's dance, but the beggars' dance or Beelzebub's dance. And this already starts: the women and maidens bare themselves behind and in the front, and there is nobody to punish or resist this; and God's word is mocked. The only thing to do is to get away and out of this Sodom. [Moral transgressions of their servants.] ... In the countryside I have heard more than I learn in Wittenberg. For that reason, I am tired of the city and do not want to come back, if God will assist me.

The day after tomorrow, I will go to Merseburg, for Prince George [von Anhalt] has strongly requested my presence. I shall, therefore, ramble around and sooner eat the bread of beggary than spend my poor, old, last days being martyred and worked up about the disorderly behavior in Wittenberg, and [endure] the loss of my hard, precious work. If you wish, you may convey this to Doctor Pomeranus and Master Philipp, and perhaps Doctor Pomeranus would bless Wittenberg on my behalf. For I can no longer bear the anger and dislike. [The editors of the WA think that this means that Luther cannot hold back his own anger and dislike. It could also be that as he becomes more and more judgmental, the people express their anger and dislike to him.] Herewith be commended to God. Amen. [Date]

Martinus LutheR D.

From Eisleben, 7 February 1546, WA BR XI, no. 4201, pp. 286–87
To my dear housewife Katherin Ludherin, Mrs. Doctor, resident of the Sowmarket in Wittenberg, my gracious lady, to her hands and at her feet.

Grace and peace in the Lord! Read the Gospel of John and the small catechism, dear Kethe, about which you once said, "But I have said everything that is in that book." For you want to worry about your God just as if He were not almighty, He who could create ten Doctor Martins in case the old one should drown in the Saale ... Leave me alone with your worry! I have a caretaker who is better than you and all the angels, who lies in the manger and hangs on the tits of a virgin, but who sits even so at the right hand of God the Father Almighty. Therefore, be content, Amen.

I think that hell and the whole world must now be empty of all devils, which perhaps on my account have come together here in Eisleben, so firm and hard is this matter. There are also fifty Jews here in one house, as I wrote to you before. Now it is said that in Risdorf, which is right by Eisleben, where I became ill on driving through, four hundred Jews ride and walk in and out. Count Albrecht, who is in charge of all the borders around Eisleben, banned those Jews who were seized on his properties, but still no one is doing anything to them. The Countess of Mansfeld, widow von Solmis, is regarded as the protectress of the Jews. I do not know if it is true. But I let people hear my opinion today, coarsely enough, in case anybody wanted to take note, and if it would help. Pray, pray, pray and help us make it good... You should let Master Philipp read this letter – for I did not have time to write to him – so that you can console yourself that I would gladly love you if I could, as you know. Perhaps he too knows and well understands in relation to his wife.

We live well here, and the city council gives me at each mealtime a half measure of Reinfal, which is very good. Sometimes I drink with my companions. The wine of this country is also good, and Naumburger beer is very good, though I do not think it fills my chest with phlegm... The devil has spoiled the beer of the whole world with his pitch, and at home the wine with sulphur. But here the wine is pure...

And know that all the letters you have written have arrived. And today, with Master Philipp's letters, those came that you wrote last Friday, so that you do not make a mistake. [Date]

Your little love
Martinus LutheR D.

From Eisleben, 10 February 1546, WA BR XI, no. 4203, p. 291
To the holy, worried lady, Lady Katherin Lutherin, Mrs. Doctor, resident of Zölsdorf in Wittenberg, my gracious, dear housewife.

Grace and peace in Christ! Most holy Lady Doctor! We thank you in a most friendly way for your great concern, because of which you could not sleep. For since that time that you have worried about us, fire wanted to consume us in our accommodations, right up to the door of my room. And yesterday – doubtless because of the power of your concern – a stone would have struck us on the head and crushed us like a mouse. For in our apartment for two days limestone crumbled down over our head until we called some people who took hold of the stone with two fingers. A piece as long as a long cushion and a large hand wide fell out. This was probably thanks to the worry of Your Holiness, in case the dear angels had not prevented it. I worry that if you do not stop worrying, the earth will finally swallow us up and all the elements follow. Do you teach the catechism and the creed? Pray, and let God worry. You are not commanded to be anxious for me or for yourself. It says, "Cast your desires upon the Lord, He will take care of you" (Ps. 55) and many other places.

We are, God be praised, fresh and healthy, with the exception that the matters at hand are unpleasant, and that Jonas dearly wanted to have a bad leg, which he more or less struck on a chest. So great is people's envy that he could not permit me alone to have a bad leg. Herewith be commended to God. We would like to get out of here and travel home, if God wills, Amen. [Date]

Your Holiness's willing servant
M. L.

LETTERS TO OTHERS

After 1525, unknown location and addressee, WA BR XII, no. 4303, p. 379
My Ketha asks me to give you a friendly warning that by your body you do not marry a peasant clod [*Klöppel*], for they are coarse and proud, do not keep men well, and also can neither cook nor make wine. Thus Ketha, 4 o'clock.

Luther to Nicolaus Hausmann, pastor in Zwickau, Wittenberg (early February 1530), WA BR V, no. 1527, p. 237
...My empress Ketha reverently greets you.

LUTHER'S WILL IN THE WITTENBERG COURTBOOK

Attachment to WA BR IX, no. 3699, pp. 574–76, 1 February 1544
[This is actually an additional statement, for his original will was 6 January 1542; the editors of the WA, 574–75, think his intention was to emphasize that he wanted to leave his wife in control of various properties under the governance of Wittenberg.]

Court held on Friday, the eighth day after the feast of the Conversion of St. Paul in the 1544th year.

The honorable Hans Lufft as attorney, and at the command of the venerable, highly learned Lord Martin Luther, Doctor of Holy Scripture, has given, transferred, and released in the very best form, manner, and style that he with the utmost constancy and efficacy could or might do before the law: to his wedded housewife Catharina, if she should survive him, the following pieces of real property as her own, to have and to employ in accordance with her pleasure, for her use and service [*Frommen*] without any contradiction, as namely:

First: the little house or shanty by Bruno Brauhers brewery at the Elster Gate, in its entirety, just as it was purchased;

Second: the garden and the spread [of land] which was bought from Claus Heffener the sculptor, next to each other at the Elster Gate;

Third: another garden, which was bought from the wife of Jakob Gehemann and paid for, located near the Speck Wood;

Fourth and fifth: a hide of land called the Kabelhufe, outside Wittenberg, together with a garden lying in the Egelpfuhl, pertaining to the same hide, which were bought from Andreßen Mebeße and paid for.

All these enumerated pieces of real property, which are within the city council's jurisdiction and the municipal precincts, shall as stated above lie within the power of aforesaid Frau Catharina to use for her own benefit, wellbeing, and pleasure without any contradiction or hindrance by her children. To this end, Wolfgang Seberger has been accepted by her to take on this assignment in her place, and inasmuch as she has sworn with hand and word, as is customary, and this has taken place without any contradiction, she is in judgment and law recognized as [the] valid [owner], and this is to be indicated at the command of the judge and the jurymen.

TABLE TALK

WA TR II, no. 2589, p. 534

"Muhme Lehna, would you like to go back to the convent and become a nun [again]?" She replied, "No! No!" [Felicitas von Selbitz] said, "Why don't you want to go back?" The doctor [ML] asked, "And, I wonder, why don't women choose to be made virgins?" Everyone was silent and smiled.

WA TR III, no. 2847b, p. 26

Complaining to his wife, he said, "You persuade me of anything you will; you have the dominion. In the household I concede to you the governance, saving only my right. For the rule of women never accomplished anything good. God made Adam the lord of all creatures so that he might rule all living things. But when Eve persuaded him that he was a lord above God, he thereby spoiled it all. We have that to thank you women for..."

WA TR III, no. 3612, p. 457

In 1536, 18 July, after the sermon, D. M. L. went to visit an honorable, pious
matron who had been driven out of Leipzig. On account of her husband's
having drowned, she fell into such distress and pain that she became sick
over it and in one night became unconscious fifteen times. As the doctor
came, she received him in a friendly manner and said, "Oh, my dear Herr
Doctor, how shall I deserve this?" D. M. answered and said, "It has long
been deserved. Christ Jesus with his blood did and earned much more."

After this he asked her how she was and how she kept herself. He admonished her to let God's will be pleasing to her and to endure it with patience
when He, as a father, punished her whom He had previously redeemed
from the greatest evil, from Satan and the abomination of popery. "Dear
daughter," he said, "be satisfied and bear the father's punishment, whether
it ends in life or death, as it may please the dear God. For we belong to
the Lord whether we live or we die. He Himself says, 'I live, and you will
also live.' He sent you indeed a precious treasure to suffer [Christ]; He will
enable you to bear this with patience. To this end pray diligently!" To this
she replied in a very Christian manner that she was satisfied; that God ever
intends what is good and fatherly toward her and would lend her patience
and help her to bear this cross, etc. With that the doctor departed from
her, blessed her, and commended her to the protection of our dear God.

WA TR V, no. 5490, pp. 185–87
[Luther's epitaph for his daughter Magdalena]
5490a [version 1]
   Here sleep I, Magdalena, Doctor Luther's daughter,
      I rest in my little bed with the saints.
      I was born in sin and had to die,
   But now I live, redeemed by Thy blood, Christ Jesus.
5490b [version 2]
     Magdalena, Luther's dear child,
     Is found sleeping among the saints,
     And her bed here is the earth,
   For we all together have nothing better.
     A daughter was born to die
     And was lost on account of sin,
     But because of Christ's blood,
     Death is turned to life and good.
5490c [version 3]
     I, Lena, Luther's dear child
     Sleep easily here with all the saints

And lie in my peace and rest.
Now I am God's guest.
To be sure, I was a child of death,
From mortal seed my mother bore me.
Now I live in the kingdom of God;
For that I thank Christ's blood and death.

[Added to 5490c] Because his wife was very sad [and] cried and howled, Dr. Martin Luther said to her, "Dear Käthe, think about where she is going! She comes to good! But flesh fleshes [a verb Luther made-up] and blood bleeds; they behave according to their nature. The spirit lives and is willing. Children do not dispute [about things]; they believe what they are told. With children everything is simple – dying without pain and anxiety, without argument, without the temptation of death, without physical pain, just as they go to sleep."

WA TR V, no. 5494, pp. 189–90

When his daughter still lay very sick, Dr. Martinus spoke: "I love her very much; but, dear God, if it is your will to take her away, so I will gladly know that she is with you." And as she was lying in bed, he spoke to her: "Magdalenchen, my little daughter, you would gladly stay here with your father, and you also go gladly to that Father!" She replied, "Yes, dear father, as God wishes." Then the father said, "You dear little daughter, the spirit is willing but the flesh is weak!" And he turned around and said, "I love her very much; if the flesh is so strong, what will the spirit be?" And among other things, he said, "In a thousand years God has given no bishop as great gifts as he has given me, for one ought to extol God's gifts. I am angry at myself because I do not rejoice in them from my heart, nor can I be thankful, even if from time to time I sing our Lord God a little song and thank Him a little bit."

* * *

As Magdalenchen lay at her last breath and was ready to die, her father fell upon his knee beside the bed, cried bitterly, and prayed that God would redeem her. Then she departed and went to sleep in her father's hands. Her mother was probably in the same room but was further back because of her grief. This happened a little after nine o'clock on Wednesday, the 17th Sunday after Trinity in the year 1542.

He, the doctor, often repeated what is told above, and said, "I would gladly have kept my daughter, for I love her very much, if God had wanted to leave her with me. However, His will be done! Of course, nothing better can happen to her!" When she was still alive, he said to her, "Dear daughter, you have another Father in heaven, and to Him you will go." Master Philipp said, "The love of parents resembles and is an image of the Divine that is impressed upon the human heart. God's love for the human race is as great as the love of parents for their children, as the Scripture says; it is truly great and hot."

When she was lying in the coffin, he said, "Dear Lenichen, such good has happened to you!" He looked upon her lying there and said, "Oh, you dear Lenichen, you will arise again and shine like a star – yes, like the sun!" Because someone had made her coffin too narrow and too short, he said, "This bed is too small for her because she has now died. I am happy in my spirit, but in the flesh I am very sad; the flesh does not want to go forth, [for] the separation vexes one way beyond all measure. It is a marvelous thing to know that she is certainly in peace and that all is well with her and yet to be so sad!"

And when the people came to help to bury the corpse, and said to the doctor, in accordance with common practice and custom, that his grief pained them, he said, "It should make you happy! I have sent a saint to heaven, yes, a living saint! Oh, if we could have such a death! Such a death I would undergo at this very hour!" Someone said, "Yes, that is well the truth; nonetheless, one would like to keep his own." Dr. Martin answered, "Flesh is flesh and blood is blood! I am happy that she is over there; she has no sadness of the flesh." Again he spoke to others who came: "Do not be sorry! I have sent a saint to heaven. Indeed, I have sent two of them!" Among others who came to the corpse, where one sings, "Lord, remember not our past misdeeds!" he said, "I say, 'O Lord, Lord, not only our past and old ones, but also our current and present sins; for we are usurers, cheaters, misers, etc. Yes, the abomination of the Mass is still in the world!"

As they put her in the ground and buried her, he said, "It is the resurrection of the body!" And when one returned from the burial, he said, "My daughter has now been sent off, both in body and soul, etc. We Christians have nothing to complain about; we know that it has to be this way. We are the very most assured of eternal life, for God, who has promised us this through and because of his dear Son's will, cannot ever lie."

* * *

When Magdalena, Dr. M. Luther's daughter, died in the year 1542, the night before Dr. Martin Luther's wife had a dream ... that two handsome, young, well-adorned young men had come and wanted to take her daughter to the wedding. When in the morning Philipp Melanchthon came into the cloister ["Black Cloister"; their house] and asked her how her daughter was doing, she told him about the dream. He was frightened and said to other people, "The young men were the dear angels who will come and take this maiden to heaven, to the real wedding." And on that same day she died.

[Cf. no. 5496, p. 192; no. 5497, pp. 192–93; no. 5498, p. 193; no. 5499, pp. 193–94; no. 5500, p. 194; no. 5501, p. 194; no. 5502, pp. 194–95.]

WA TR V, no. 6117, p. 496

He inquired of his wife whether she desired to be the wife of a prince for the sake of luxuries. "Oh, dear Käthe, there are few joys in their good days. They are always tormented by cases, events, and their own wisdom. Things never go as they plan. However, I am happy in my condition [and] would not be tempted if the devil did not annoy me. When he does too much, I present him with a fart as a walking stick; he has often had to take that from me."

WA TR V, no. 6328, p. 606

Dr. M. L. complained a great deal about the disobedience of the son of his sister, and it pained him that he had become engaged without [the participation of] his relatives. For this reason, he said, "I will write a severe letter to the parents of the young woman."

WA TR VI, no. 6927, p. 274

Dr. M. Luther's prayer for his marriage. "Dear heavenly Father, because You in Your name and in the honor of Your office have ordained and want to name and honor me as father, grant me the grace and bless me so that I may govern and nourish my dear wife, children, and servants in a godly and Christian manner. Give me the wisdom and strength to govern and raise them well, and give them a good heart and the will to follow your teaching and to be obedient. Amen."

CHAPTER 9

Luther and other contemporary women

Women were visible in early modern Germany. Although lesser creatures than men in theory, law, and official life, because their labor was essential, they were present nearly everywhere. When Martin Luther gathered with boarders and dinner guests at the table in his home, the Black Cloister in Wittenberg, some of the guests were female, usually the wives of theologians and other scholars. Katharina Lutheryn served the meal, aided by women relatives such as "Muhme" Lehna, and by servants. The Luther children were also present. Although the men conversed in Latin on learned topics, often their discourse involved plain concepts best expressed in the vernacular tongue. At least to this extent, the women had access to such exchanges; Katharina herself is reputed to have learned some Latin while a nun. Although women appear seldom to have initiated conversations, we must recall that Luther's adoring followers wrote down exclusively what *he* said. Where women's remarks appear, it is because Luther interacted with them. Certainly Katharina and women guests talked with their table-mates, and domestic happenstance frequently diverted the men from their lofty plane. Despite Luther's conviction that women lacked the mental acumen of men, he was glad to engage them on matters of mutual interest.

The Reformer's correspondence likewise reveals his sympathy for women in their human predicaments. Martin rendered advice to literate women concerning their marriages and their spiritual afflictions. The recipients' very literacy increased the likelihood that they were members of Germany's higher urban and noble classes. Only a woman of this rank, like Barbara Lißkirchen of Freiberg, would probably have been preoccupied with the possibility that God had not elected her to salvation and have sought consolation from the Reformer.[1] As for Germany's farming citizens, even though his father had been a peasant's son, Luther frequently expressed the prejudices that were characteristic of the more privileged levels of society.

---

[1] WA BR XII, no. 4244a, pp. 135–36.

Martin's letter to his mother in her final illness stands as a monument of filial devotion. Yet, to the modern sensibility it is surprising for its docent attention to doctrine; he wanted his mother to pass away in full confidence of God's saving love for her. Likewise, his expressions of grief on the deaths of Elisabeth and Magdalena rend our hearts. His bereavement would have been no greater had the deceased been sons.

Luther lived his public as well as his private life among women. Such was the nature of northern European society, where women walked un-accompanied in the lanes, hawked wares in the marketplace, and spoke openly with men to whom they were not related. Even as Luther carried on a tradition of esteeming females less than males, he could regard himself as a friend of women.

LETTER TO HIS MOTHER

Luther to his mother Margarethe, from Wittenberg, 20 May 1531,
WA BR VI, no. 1820, pp. 103–6

Grace and peace in Christ Jesus, our Lord and Savior, Amen. My beloved mother! I have received the writing of my brother Jacob about your illness, and I am heartily sorry, especially that I cannot be with you physically as I would so much like to be. But I appear physically here in this letter, and I will not be away from you in spirit nor from all our others.

Even though I hope that your heart without any further help has been long and richly enough instructed, and (God be praised) that His com-forting word is contained therein, and that it is in addition provided on all sides with preachers and comforters, nonetheless, I want to do my part and acknowledge my duty as your child to you as my mother. For your and my God and Creator has made us and obligated us to one another, and therefore I add myself to the throngs of those who comfort you.

First of all, dear Mother, you well know now about God's grace, that our illness is His fatherly, gracious rod, and a very slight rod compared to those that He uses on the cornerstone Jesus Christ, who will not falter or fail us, and who cannot let us sink or go under. For He is the Savior and is called the Savior of all poor sinners and of all those who are stuck in distress and death, if they rely upon Him and call upon His name.

He says, "Be comforted: I have overcome the world." If He has overcome the world, then surely He has also overcome the prince of the world with all his power. What is this prince's power other than death, with which he throws us under himself and holds us captive on account of our sin? But now death and sin are overcome, and in joy and consolation we may hear that sweet word: "Be comforted: I have overcome the world." And we should not doubt that it is absolutely true, and not only that, but we are also commanded to accept this reassurance with joy and with all thanksgiving. And anyone who does not want to let himself be comforted commits an injustice and the greatest dishonor upon the dear Comforter, just as though asserting that it were not true that He had told us to be comforted, or as if it were not true that He had overcome the world...

Therefore, we may now rejoice with all certainty and pleasure; and if thoughts of sin or death sometimes frighten us, we should lift up our hearts and say: "See, dear soul, what you are doing? Dear death, dear sin, how do you live and frighten me? Do you not know that you are conquered, and that you, death, are in fact dead? Do you not know the one who says about you: 'I have overcome the world'? It is not proper for me to pay attention to your scaring nor accept it, but instead [to hearken to] the consolation of my Savior: 'Be comforted, be comforted, I have overcome the world.'"

That is the Victor, the true Hero who gives and dedicates to me His victory: "Be comforted!" I stick with that, I hold myself to His word and comfort; after that I stay here or I pass over there, but He does not lie to me. Your [the devil's] false fright would like to betray me and, with false thoughts, tear me away from such a Victor and Savior – but this is a lie. What is true is that He has overcome you and has commanded us to be comforted.

In this way St. Paul praises too, and he defies the terror of death. Death is consumed in victory: "Death, where is thy victory? Hell, where is thy sting?" You can frighten and excite, like a wooden image of death, but you have no power to strangle. For your victory, sting, and power are swallowed up in the victory of Christ; you can show your teeth, but you cannot eat us up. For God has given us the victory over you, through Jesus Christ our Lord, to whom be praise and thanks, Amen.

With such words and thoughts, dear Mother, let your heart be occupied, and with none other; and be thankful that God has brought you to such recognition. Be thankful that He has not allowed you to remain stuck in papist error, according to which we were taught to build upon our works and upon the holiness of monks, and not to regard Christ as our one Comforter, our Savior, but as a gruesome judge and tyrant, from whom we had to flee to Mary and the saints and from whom we could receive no grace or consolation.

But now we know otherwise. We know about the boundless goodness and mercy of our heavenly Father, that Jesus Christ is our mediator, our throne of mercy, and our bishop in heaven before God. He daily represents us and reconciles all those who only believe on him and call upon him. He is not a judge nor gruesome, except alone to those who do not believe in him and who do not want to accept his comfort and grace. He is not the man who accuses or threatens us, but rather he who reconciles us and represents us by means of his own death and blood, shed for us, so that we are not afraid of him but come to him and in all security call upon him: "Dear Savior, you sweet Comforter, you true Bishop of our souls, etc."

To such a recognition I say God has graciously called you. On that you have His seal and His letters, namely the gospel, baptism and the Sacrament, which you hear preached. Therefore, you should experience neither danger nor distress. Only be comforted and thank God with joy for such a great favor! He has begun this [work] in you, and He will graciously complete it. We cannot assist ourselves in such great matters. We are not able to free ourselves from sins, death, and devil by means of our works. For that reason, another person is there in our place and for us, someone who can do it better and gives us the victory and commands us to accept it and not to doubt it. He says, "Be comforted, I have overcome the world"; and again, "I live and you shall also live"; and "No one shall take your joy away from you."

May the Father and God of all consolation give you through His holy word and Spirit a firm, joyful, and thankful faith, so that you are able blessedly to overcome this and every distress, and finally taste and experience that it is the truth that He Himself speaks: "Be comforted: I have overcome the world." And I herewith commend your body and soul to His mercy, Amen. All your children and my Käte pray for you. Some weep, some eat and say, "Grandmother is very sick." God's grace be with us all, Amen. [Date]

Your dear son
Mart. Luther.

LETTERS TO OTHER WOMEN

Luther to the noblemaidens Janna von Draschwitz, Milia von Ölsnitz,
and Ursula von Feilitzsch, from Wittenberg, 18 June 1523,
WA BR III, no. 625, pp. 93–94

To the honorable, virtuous maidens Janna von Draschwitz, Milia von Olßnitz, and Ursula von Feylitzin, my special friends in Christ.

Grace and peace in Christ! Honorable virgins, dear maidens! Mr. Nicolas von Amsdorf has reported your request to me and the abuse that you have experienced on account of my books from the court at Freiberg; and in addition he requested me to write you a letter of consolation. Even though

I suspect that you do not need my comforting, and although I do not write gladly to people with whom I am not acquainted, I have not known how to turn him away.

First of all, it is my true, friendly request that you should set your hearts at ease and not bear a grudge or wish anything unpleasant upon those who have used you badly in this way, but rather, as St. Paul teaches and says, "If we are oppressed, we should praise"; and in addition, Christ at Matthew 6: "Bless those who slander you, pray for those who insult you, and do good to those who persecute you."

Do this also in view of the fact that you are enlightened by God's grace, and they are blind and obdurate, and in addition they do much more damage to their souls than all the world could do. Unfortunately, you are all too set in opposition to them because they wrong you, and in this way you rage against God and gruesomely accumulate offenses. It is proper for you to take pity on them as raving, senseless people who do not perceive how grievously they ruin themselves even as they intend to do you wrong.

But instead remain faithful and let Christ do the work! The insults that you bear will be richly repaid, and more times over than you could have wished if you had taken on the matter; turn it over to him.

And even if it weighs on your conscience that you might have given cause, you should still not shrink back. For it is precious evidence that Christ quickly drew you into repentance. You should consider that even though you wanted to do much against them, you did not carry anything out. For it is a divine matter in which you suffer, which God lets nobody judge or avenge than Him Himself, as He says through the prophets: "Whoever touches you, touches the apple of my eye." I can well imagine that the miserable, blind head, Doctor Wolff Stehlin, is the leader in this, but he is described in other [Biblical] passages than he imagines, and unfortunately it will go all too hard with him. Therefore, act, my dear sisters, and hold your friends to it as well. If you do, God's grace and peace will be with you. Amen. And take my writing in a good way! [Date]

Martinus Luther.

To Katharina Zell, from Wittenberg, 17 December 1524,
WA BR III, no. 808, pp. 405–6
To the virtuous lady, Katharin Schützin, my dear sister and friend in Christ, in Strassburg.

Grace and peace in Christ! My dear! That God has so richly given you His grace so that you not only personally see and are acquainted with His kingdom, which is concealed from so many people, but also that He has given you such a husband, through whom you daily and unceasingly are better able to learn and hear this – [because of this] I wish you well, and also desire for you the grace and strength to retain all this with thanksgiving until that day when we shall all see one another and rejoice, if God wills it.

No more just now. Pray to God for me, and give my greeting to your lord, Mr. [*Herr*] Matthias Zell! Be commended herewith to God! [Date]

Martinus Luther.

Luther to an unknown woman, from Wittenberg, 31 July 1525,
WA BR III, no. 909, p. 552

A letter of Doctor Martin Lutter, most useful to those who are weak in faith.

Grace and peace in Christ! My dear lady! I hear it said that you are suffering great challenges to your faith. I am very sorry, and I ask God to graciously strengthen you, as I do not doubt that with time He will do so. He gives you all things, as we know, according to His will, but for a while yet He wants to leave you and have you [as you are]. Consider that weak faith is also faith; and Christ is close to the weak person as well as the strong, as Paul says in Romans 14... And Paul everywhere commands us to receive the weak, from which we can well note that the weak also sit in the lap of Christ... Woe to them that are completely crazy and lack nothing! For that reason be comforted, and as Joel says, "The weak shall say, 'I am strong,'" and Paul, 2 Corinthians 12: "Strength increases through weakness." This must be true. I have also suffered illness such that I was of the opinion that I meant nothing to either God or Christ; I wondered why such a thing had happened to me, [and] I was more certain of everything [else] than of my own life. God tries us, but He does not leave us... Herewith I commend you to Christ, who makes you weak in your own strength so that he can strengthen you with his power, Amen. [Date]

[No signature]

To the honorable and virtuous Maiden Else von Kanitz, presently at the oak
[presumably a pun on the town of Eicha, near Leipzig, where she was],
my dear friend in Christ. From Wittenberg, 22 August 1527,
WA BR IV, no. 1133, p. 236

Grace and peace in Christ Jesus! Honorable, virtuous maiden Else! I have asked your dear kinswoman Hanna von Plausig in writing to send you to me for a period of time, for I have in mind using you in the instruction of little girls. I want by means of you to introduce your work as an example to others. You would stay and eat in my house, so that you would have no danger and no worry. And so I ask you now not to reject my request. I hear too that the evil enemy [the devil] tempts you with heavy thoughts. O dear maiden, do not let yourself be frightened! For whoever suffers from the devil here will not have to suffer there; this is, then, a good sign. Christ himself also had to suffer everything in this way, and also many holy prophets and apostles, as the Psalter demonstrates. Therefore, be comforted and gladly endure this chastisement from the Father. He will most probably help you out of it in His own time. When you arrive, I will speak to you further about this. Herewith be commended to God, Amen. [Date]

To Katharina Jonas in Wittenberg, from Koburg, 23 April 1530,
WA BR V, no. 1551, p. 284

Grace and peace in Christ! I have read the letter that you wrote to your lord Doctor Jonas, dear Mrs. Doctor and little godmother. It pleases me well that God has given you an easy spirit and good hope, both on account of the fruit of your body and the destruction of your house. Your lord is not in such a light mood but worries very much about you. He is angry, frowns and curses on account of the razing of the house . . . But you should be comforted: you will suffer no distress on account of the house, for this matter has found a solution. And so I hope that God will also graciously help you in the unburdening of your body. Would to God that you would have twins. I think, however, that it will be a little daughter, for they are so strange, they do not want to come out, [and] already find the great house [of the world] too small for them, just as the mothers also do who make the world too narrow for their poor husbands. Greet for me your dear [son] Jost and the grandmother, and yourselves too. Herewith be commended to God, Amen. [Place and date]

Martinus Luther.

Luther to Barbara Lißkirchen in Freiberg, from Wittenberg, 30 April 1531,
WA BR XII, no. 4244a, pp. 135–36

To the honorable, virtuous lady Barbara Lyskirchnerin in Freyberg, my kind, good friend.

Grace and peace in Christ. Virtuous dear lady. Your dear brother Hieronymus Weller has informed me that you are troubled by temptation concerning eternal Providence. I am truly sorry to hear that, and may Christ our Lord free you from this, Amen. I know this affliction well and have lain in the hospital to the point of eternal death. I would like to comfort and advise you by [telling you] about my prayer. In such matters, writing is a weak instrument, but nevertheless, as far as I am able, I shall not give up if God gives me the grace. I will tell you how God helped me out of this [predicament] and by what means I daily hold out against it.

First of all, you must hold fast in your heart that these thoughts are assuredly the devil's hot air and fiery arrow. The Scripture says as much, as in Ecclesiastes [*sic*; perhaps Proverbs 25]: "Whoever investigates the High Majesty, he will be suppressed." Such thoughts are idle examination of the divine Majesty and want to look into his high Providence. And Ecclesiasticus 3[:21–24] says, "Altiora te ne quaesieris," etc.: "You shall not look into that which is too high for you." Instead, think continually about those things that God has asked of you. And David laments in Psalm 130 that things had gone badly with him when he wanted to examine lofty matters. Therefore, it is certain that the question that torments your heart is from the devil, and not from God, in order to make a person hostile to God and despairing. God strictly forbade this in the First Commandment and desires that one trust, love, and praise Him; and from this we draw our life.

Secondly, when such thoughts occur to us, you should learn to ask yourself, "My dear, in which commandment does it say that I should think about this or deal with it?" If there is no such commandment, you should learn to say, "Oh, get up [and get out], you disagreeable devil, you want to drive me to worry about myself. But God often says that I should let Him care for me. He says, 'I am your God,' which means, 'I am taking care of you. Rely on me and attend to what I say, and let me provide.'" St. Peter teaches, "Cast your worries upon Him, and He will care for you," and David, "Lay your concerns upon the Lord, who will provide for you."

Thirdly, even if the thoughts do not immediately let up – for the devil does not happily let go – you yourself should not give in, but you should always turn your heart away. You should say, "Don't you hear, devil, that I don't want to have such thoughts, and God has forbidden them! Get up! I must now think about His commandments and let Him take care of me. If you are so clever in such matters, go up to heaven and dispute with God Himself! He can give you an adequate answer!" And you should therefore continually push him away from you and return your heart to God's command.

Fourth, of all God's commands the highest is that one should imitate His dear Son, our Lord Jesus Christ. Every day He should be our heart's foremost mirror, in which we see how much God loves us and how highly He, as a pious God, is concerned for us, so much so that He even gave His

Son for us. Precisely here, here, I say, one learns the true meaning of [divine] Providence and nowhere else. It is found when one believes in Christ. If you believe, then you are called. If you are called, then you are certainly saved [*versehen*]. Do not allow this mirror and throne of grace to be torn from the eye of your heart; rather, when such thoughts come and bite you like the fiery serpent, do not notice either the thoughts or the serpent. Instead, turn your eyes away and look upon the brazen serpent, which is Christ, who was given for us. Then it will get better, if God wills. As is said, you must always struggle and put these things from your mind. When you think about them, let them go away again, just as you would quickly spit out a piece of excrement that fell into your mouth. This is the way God helped me. For it is God's earnest command that we keep His Son before us, through whom He has richly revealed Himself to be our God, as the First Commandment teaches, who helps us and provides for us. Accordingly, He will not tolerate that we help ourselves or want to provide for ourselves. This would be to deny God and the First Commandment, and Christ besides. In opposition to the First Commandment, the unpleasant devil, who is the enemy of God and Christ, wants by means of such thoughts to tear us away from Christ and God and [make us rely] upon ourselves and our own provision. This is to intrude on God's office (that is, to care for us and be our God), [and to ask] how he wanted to make Adam in paradise into God, [and to assert] that Adam himself was God and should have cared for himself – and [in sum] to rob God of such provision and divine work. For this Adam so horribly fell.

This much I do want to recommend this time. I have further indicated to Hieronymus that he diligently warn and admonish you to learn to let such thoughts go and send them back to the devil so that *he* can look into them. He well knows how his circumstances befell him, namely, that he fell from heaven into the abyss of hell. In sum, whatever is not commanded of us we should not allow to lead us astray or trouble us. It is the devil's doing and not God's. May our dear Lord Jesus Christ show you his feet and hands and greet you in a friendly way in your heart, so that you see and hear him alone until you are joyfully joined with him. [Date]

Martinus Luthe R. [*sic*]

To Dorothea Jörger, who had given him 500 gulden, from Wittenberg,
27 April 1534, WA BR VII, no. 2109, p. 61
Grace and peace in Christ! Honorable, very virtuous lady! I hereby inform you that your charitable gift, praise God, has been very well invested and has helped and continues to help many poor people. I cannot doubt that

the God who assigned you this task will openly show His pleasure in this thank-offering, so that you confess and praise that grace which He has shown to you through His dear Son Jesus Christ. May God strengthen you in firm faith and blessedly fulfil in you the work that He has begun, Amen. I myself was unaware and would not have believed that in this little city and poor school there were so many pious, able fellows who throughout the year have survived on water and bread and have suffered frost and cold, so that they might study the Holy Scripture and the word of God. To these your gift has become a great comfort and refreshment. I have already given out over half and have received their written signatures [as testimony that the recipients] are honest fellows and no loose knaves. I have not wanted to withhold this from you, for I wanted you to know how things were going and how they stood with your money. To Andreas [Hügel] I have given more than to the others, indeed 10 florins and then again 10 florins; among the others, 2, 3, and 4 florins, in accordance with the advice of good friends, and all are happy and grateful. As a sign [of appreciation?] I have requested, via Michel Stiefel, this little booklet, which I have attached [to this letter]. Because he has had to be without a parish, I have given him 10 florins. He asks me to give you his enthusiastic greetings. May Christ be with you and all your family, Amen. [Date]

Martinus Luther D.

To Barbara Lißkirchen in Freiberg, from Wittenberg, 7 March 1535,
WA BR VII, no. 2184, pp. 167–68
To the honorable, virtuous lady Barbara Lyskirchnerin in Freyberg, my kind, good friend.

Grace and peace in Christ! Honorable, virtuous lady! Your dear brother Hieronymus Weller has indicated to me that you are desirous of the Holy Sacrament in both kinds and consider whether it might be secretly so received at home. Now, even though in popery the custom existed of having portable [equipage] in their houses for their own masses, etc., nevertheless, for the sake of example and other reasons, I cannot recommend it. For with time, everybody might want to do this, and in this way withdraw from the communal church and congregation, which would waste away. So it should remain a public and communal confession. If you otherwise (if it can be done) occasionally bring it [have it brought to your home] and want to risk it, because your conscience desires it and is convinced, so you might do this in the name of God, to whom I commend you with my poor prayer. [Date]

Martinus Luther D.

To Agnes Lauterbach in Leisnig, from Wittenberg, 25 October 1535,
WA BR VII, no. 2265, p. 305

To the honorable, virtuous lady Agnes Lauterbachin in Leisnig, wife of the preacher, my good friend and relation [*Gevattern*].

Grace and peace in the Lord! My dear kinswoman [*Gevatter*]! Mr. Antonius has indicated to me that you are very troubled because of the son whom God gave you and then so quickly took away again. What can we make out of this? We have to learn to recognize God's will and that He alone is good and holy, even though it seems much otherwise to our will, which is an erring, transitory darkness.

You have certainly often read and heard that God's work is hidden, and that under the cross all grace is covered over until the time of the revelation, when we shall see, and will harvest with joy, what we now sow with tears, as David says in Psalm 126: "They go out and weep, and strew their seed"...

Therefore, be moderate in your grieving! God still lives, and He has more [pain] than He has ever given out. May He comfort you in Christ, His dear Son, Amen. [Date]

Mart. Luther.

To Else Agricola in Eisleben, from Wittenberg, 13 November 1536,
WA BR VII, no. 3102, p. 587

To my friendly, dear kinswoman [*Gevatter*] Else, wife of the Magister in Eisleben, the virtuous lady and special patroness of all pious people.

My poor Lord's Prayer, dear Else, dear kinswoman, indeed almost my dear daughter! My lord Käte asks me to say many good things to you. She is inclined toward you with her whole heart, for she has not forgotten your good deed. And I can add something myself (as I have great hope), [namely] that you come again to us in Wittenberg – that I will not leave out. For I am considering bringing help to your Master [her husband] as best I can, as he will probably tell you. Be herewith commended to God. You may believe that my intention is true toward you and yours, as far as it lies within my ability. May God help us (as He does everybody, and hears our prayers), Amen. [Date]

Greet on my and our behalf your dear son and daughter and your sister.

Martinus Lutherus D.

To the widowed princess, Margarete von Anhalt, from Wittenberg,
9 January 1538, WA BR VIII, no. 3211, p. 190

Grace and peace in Christ Jesus, our Lord and Savior! Serene Princess, gracious lady! It has been conveyed to me, including through Your Princessly Grace's dear son, My Gracious Lord, Prince Wolfgang, etc., in writing, that

Your Princessly Grace is supposed to be quite weak, so that it would have been proper for me to have written a letter of consolation to Your Princessly Grace long before now. However, until now, through no fault or desire of mine, I have been prevented [from doing so]. All right, what is past is past. But now Your Princessly Grace is being afflicted and burdened with illness by our dear Father in heaven, who made and gave us both body and soul, and afterward redeemed us from the fall and death of Adam by means of His dear Son Jesus Christ, and who through His Holy Ghost in our hearts has given us the hope of eternal life. Your Princessly Grace should not be troubled but should rather accept such gracious affliction with thanksgiving. Your Princessly Grace has often heard reported, and you know, that all those who believe in the dear Son of the Father cannot die eternally, as he himself says: "Whoever believes in me will not die, and even if he dies, yet does he live" (John 11); and St. Paul (Romans 15 [in the modern Bible it is Romans 14:7–8]) says: "Whether we live or die, we belong to the Lord; nobody lives in himself, nobody dies in himself, but in him alone who died for us all." For that reason, we who believe in him ought to be comforted, for we know that we do not belong to ourselves but rather to him who died for us. If we are sick, we are not sick for ourselves; if we are healthy, we are not healthy for ourselves; if we are in distress, we are not in distress for ourselves; if we are happy, we are not happy for ourselves. In sum, may it go with us as it will, this does not happen for ourselves but rather for him who died for us and received us as his own. A pious child, if it is ill or in distress, afflicts its parents more than it is afflicted itself – for it affects the parents far more than the child – for the child does not belong to itself but to its parents. Therefore, Your Princessly Grace should be consoled and yield yourself, whether it be to life, to illness, or to death, and not doubt that Your Princessly Grace does not experience this for yourself but instead for him who acquired Your Princessly Grace together with us with his blood and death. We believe in him, and if we have this faith we do not die, even if we should die, but instead we live; likewise, we are not sick even if we are sick, but we are healthy in Christ, in whom all are healthy, fresh, alive, and blessed – even if we think, in accordance with the flesh, that we are ill, sick, dead, and lost. The One in whom we believe is almighty. May God maintain such comfort and recognition of the dear God in Your Princessly Grace's heart until that blessed day. To Him I hereby faithfully want to have commended [this is literally what it says] Your Princessly Grace, Amen. [Date]

Your Princessly Grace's
Willing
M. Luther

To Ursula Schneidewein, from Wittenberg, 4 June 1539, WA BR VIII,
no. 3344, pp. 454–55 [her son lived in Luther's house for nearly ten years]
To the honorable, virtuous lady Ursula Schneidewin, widow, citizen of
Stolberg, my kind good friend.

Grace and Peace in Christ! Honorable, virtuous, dear lady! I have written
to you about your son Johannes, how he is bound in great love with an
honorable maiden. I had hoped to have a good answer to my thoughts and
perceptions. But this delay in the matter of your son is growing too long, and
it causes me to act further. For I am not unfavorably disposed toward him
and do not want him to dip his hand into the ashes [i.e., let the opportunity
run through his fingers]. Because the maiden pleases him so well and is not
of dissimilar rank, and because she is a fine, pious child of honest extraction,
so it still seems to me that you might be satisfied inasmuch as he has humbled
himself like a child and asked you for [permission to marry] this girl, as
Sampson did. Accordingly, it would be proper for you, as a loving mother,
to give your consent to this. Although we have written that children ought
not to get engaged without their parents' permission, we have also written
that parents should not and cannot properly either compel or hinder their
children in accordance with their own wishes. Therefore, the son should
not bring a daughter to his parents without their consent. But the father
should not force a woman upon his son. Both sides should contribute to
this [decision]. Otherwise, the wife of the son is compelled to become the
father's daughter without his thanks. And who knows what good fortune
God might give him through this girl, which he might otherwise lack,
particularly because the good maiden gives him hope, is not of different
background, and her unhappiness might become a bad prayer. In short, I
ask you not to withhold your decision any longer, so that the good fellow
may emerge out of his unsettled existence. I can no longer hold back but will
have to do something on account of my office. But I ask that you not bring
this letter to your son Johannes's attention, for he should not know until
a decision is reached, so that he does not take matters into his own hands
and become too bold. For I love him, of which he is worthy on account of
his virtue, and I would not want to advise him to do the worst. Therefore,
as his mother, do something and help him to be free of this torment so that
he does not have to do it himself. Herewith be commended to God. [Date]

Martinus Luther D.

To Katharina, the Widow. Metzler in Breslau, from Wittenberg,
3 July 1539, WA BR VIII, no. 3354, p. 485
To the honorable, virtuous lady Catherin Metzleryn, citizen of Breslau, my
kind, good friend.

Grace and peace in Christ! Honorable, virtuous, dear lady! I cannot refuse to write to you and, as much as God enables me, to comfort you. I can well imagine that this cross that God has now laid upon you, in the form of your dear son's passing, presses hard and painfully upon you. It is natural and proper that a person should be grieved, especially in [a case of] such close blood and flesh, for God did not create us without feelings or as stone or wood. Rather He wants us to grieve and lament the dead, for to do otherwise would be a sign that we had no love, even for our own. On the other hand, it must be done in moderation. The dear Father tries us to see whether we are able to love and fear Him both in love and suffering, and also if we are able to return to Him what He has given us, so that He has reason to give us more and better. Therefore, I ask you to acknowledge the gracious good will of God and in order to please Him to bear this cross patiently. Think with heartfelt faith what a cross He himself has borne for you and for us all, in comparison to which our crosses are nothing or are only slight. It should also console you that your son was a pious, quiet person, and that he departed from this shameful world in such a Christian and blessed manner. God intended this well and perhaps even wanted to secure and guard him against greater evil. For this is such an evil and dangerous time that we should all rightly say with Elias and Jonah, "I would rather be dead than live." Let those grieve whose children so shamefully die and go to the devil; that is heartfelt pain, as David had to suffer because of his son Absalom. Your son is with our Lord Christ, in whom he went to sleep. Thank God for the favor of so graciously taking your child to Himself, which is better for him than if he were at the very highest emperor's and king's court. May God, the Father of all comfort, plentifully strengthen your faith with His Spirit, Amen. [Date]

Martinus Luther.

To Frau Ursula Schneidewein, from Wittenberg, 10 July 1539,
WA BR VIII, no. 3357, pp. 492–93

Grace and peace, etc.! Honorable, virtuous lady! I have now, if I rightly remember, written to you twice on account of your son Johannes, who as a pious child has asked you through me to act in a motherly way (as you are obligated to do) and give your permission for him to take the girl as his wife. And thereby he has sufficiently done his filial duty, as Sampson did in relation to his parents. Additionally, I have indicated that I could not hold back any longer, but [I have to tell you] that I regard it as good – for I am well-intentioned toward him – that he remove himself from danger. It is my opinion that his studies will be hindered and that nothing good will follow from this if you were to be so hard. What I do, I also do to honor you. And she is similar to him, an honorable child of good parents. You ought to consider that it is intolerable to move other people's children to love and then without reason to let them sit there, which would be very hard for your own children to bear – and so it is for others too, especially when everything occurs honorably. I have written you and recommended that you should not refuse in this matter, so that we are not compelled nevertheless to proceed. I have written that children should not marry against their parents' wishes, but I have also written that parents should not hinder their children. In sum, I cannot now repeat everything that I wrote to you earlier. It naturally amazes me that I have had no answer at all from you. And it is so hard for me, because my boarder desires the best for our citizen's daughter, that I ask again if you would hurry to give a positive answer. Otherwise, we shall have to do whatever we must to prevent scandal. You have been petitioned enough. When parents are unwilling, the pastor must be willing. If you are worried about how he will feed himself, you should recall that a person has to trust in God, who alone nourishes the marital estate. Nor will I, as long as I live, abandon Johannes, although he himself, God willing, without my action will be able to make his own way. I ask, therefore, that you be accommodating, for I am tired of writing so often, especially on a matter that you have no reason to refuse. You should consider that you force me to fulfil your son's wish, which I would prefer not to do inasmuch as I have always been well-intentioned toward your family. Herewith be commended to God. Amen. [Send] your proper brief reply. [Date]

Martinus Luther D.

[He married the couple on 27 July, without the mother's having replied.]

To Marguerite of Navarre, from Wittenberg, probably 1540,
WA BR IX, no. 3565, pp. 300–1

[There is uncertainty about whether this is actually from Luther.] To the most serene lady, Lady Margaret, Queen of Navarre, Sister of the King of Gaul [*Galliae*].

Grace and peace! Most serene Lady, we have now known, first from the word of many and then from your famous reputation, that Your Highness has been sincerely devoted to true doctrine and the gospel, supporting genuine ministers and preachers of the word of God in various extraordinary duties. The great man and prophet Isaiah says that monarchs will be the ministers of the true church and the saints and elect of Christ. Although many worldly powers will fight bitterly against Christ, nevertheless, [righteous monarchs] will be held in some haven and nest of the kingdom where they will be protected against the will of the devil, as if under the wings of Christ. Moved by your most famous reputation, which has now spread over all of Europe, I thought several times to write to Your Highness, but in truth, I set out a little too hesitantly in my writing lest the hatred and ill will of those whom I cannot please in any way and for whom my writings are not held most dear burden Your Highness and other pious men, and lest by chance a letter sent by me be unwelcome to Your Highness. But since Your Highness has now mercifully deigned to greet me through men both famous and worthy in faith, I began to hope that Your Highness would not be averse to an exchange of letters.

But what shall I write? For all of us here in the churches of Germany, which lay claim to the freedom of the gospel more and more every day against the Roman Antichrist and portent of wickedness, all foulness and sin, and the pope, I believe nothing more desired or necessary than that Your Highness press on, fruitfully employing the gift of the excellent spirit with which God has endowed her. The daughter of kings should continue steadfastly to confess Christ and, for the honor of Christ the Son of God and the highest Lord, to speak before kings about the word and testimonies of God, to assist ministers of the word, to advance Christ's cause, and to defend other pious confessors of the truth, whom at other times the ungrateful world persecutes and spits upon with the stench and harshness of Cain and Satan. And now, when we see that God, against the will of Satan and his minions, the Roman cardinals, carries out in the kingdoms His divine work, which is above both all wisdom of the world and human deliberations and thoughts, we pray for the sake of the illustrious King of France that God preserve, fortify, and, as Paul says to the Colossians, "strengthen with all spiritual vigor" Your Highness, so that the word and truth of God might be extended as widely as possible throughout the churches of France, so that the kingdom of France can truly uphold and lay claim to the title "most Christian." May Jesus Christ our God and Lord preserve Your Highness alive for as long as possible. [Place]

Martinus
Lutherus D.

To a lady M. [name unknown], from Wittenberg, 11 January 1543,
WA BR X, no. 3837, pp. 239–40
The grace of God and peace in the Lord! My dear lady M. Your brother Johannes has indicated to me that the evil spirit has burdened your heart

because the following evil speech came out of your mouth: "I wish that the devil would take all those who advised that my husband become burgomaster," etc. As a consequence, he [the devil] plagues you and suggests that you must remain eternally his.

Oh, dear M., because you feel and acknowledge that it is the evil spirit who has torn such words out of you, and who has also suggested that you should remain his, you need to know that everything he suggests is a lie. For he is a liar. Most certainly this suggestion that you belong to the devil does not come from Jesus Christ inasmuch as he died so that those who were in the devil's power should be freed. For this reason, do the following: spit at the devil and say, "If I have sinned, then alas, I have sinned, and I am sorry; Christ has taken away the sins of the whole world for those who confess this, and so it is certain that my sin, too, has been taken away. Rise up [and depart], devil, I am absolved, as I am obligated to believe." And what would I do if I had committed murder, adultery, or even crucified Christ himself? Despite everything, if I repent and acknowledge [my sin], it is forgiven, as he said on the Cross, "Father, forgive them!"

My dear M., you must not believe your thoughts nor those of the devil, but rather us preachers, whom God has commanded to instruct and absolve souls, for He says (Matt. 18:18): "What you free shall be freed!" You must believe this. We preachers now declare you to be loosed and freed in Christ's name and at his command, not only from this sin but from all sins that are inherited from Adam. These are so great and many that God does not want us to comprehend them all or entirely in this life, much less impute them to us. Therefore, be content and comforted, for your sins are forgiven. Boldly rely on and completely obey what your pastor and your preacher tell you! Do not despise their word and consolation! For it is God Himself who speaks to you through them when He says (Matt. 18:18), "What you free shall be freed," and (Luke 10:16), "He who listens to you listens to me, [and] he who despises you despises me." Believe that, and the devil will stop. Or say, "I would like very much to believe more strongly, and I well know that this is true and to be believed. Whether or not I believe it enough, yet I know that it is the truth." This counts as belief for purposes of salvation.

May Christ, the dear Lord, who suffered for our sins and arose for our justification, comfort and strengthen your heart in the true faith! It is not necessary [for you to worry] on account of sin, Amen. [Date]

Martinus Luther D.

LETTERS FROM WOMEN

Dorothea, Countess of Mansfeld, to Luther, from Mansfeld, 26 August 1543,
WA BR X, no. 3905, pp. 373–74

To the reputable and highly learned, especially kind, dear Martin Luther, Doctor of Holy Scripture in Wittenberg, etc.

Dear lord Doctor, a short time ago one of the servants of my children was with you, by name Mr. Johan Vlia. When he got back here, he reported to me, with regard to your illness, that you had been advised to make an opening in one leg and have blood flow out in order to effect an easing of your head. In this connection, I am not of the opinion, nor do I want to be, that it is somewhat useful to make the blood flow in cases of a headache [*gesonnte heupt*] where there has not been one before. Rather, where you have already had a headache before, you have probably (out of good intention) let the hole heal up. Observe whether a rather thin or watery liquid does not flow out of the leg that you have left open and whether it is inclined to heal. [In this instance] it would be my advice to let it heal in God's name – though not forcibly or too hastily. But if it has not been newly opened but rather a long time ago, and if a thin stream of liquid runs out, then one should be concerned that it might injure you if you let it heal. And as Mr. Johann reports to me, you often experience a dizziness or [a sensation of things] revolving in your head; this is not to be wondered at. For a fast and sharp exertion of the head when there is no physical movement brings such a difficulty. I would gladly give you my advice in this matter, insofar as I understand; and I am sending you herewith a little vial on which is written "for dizziness," together with a sneezing powder that should be used along with it, in accordance with the accompanying instructions. And if your dizziness does not soon disappear, [you may experience] as a result of the dizziness a great weakness, such as a stroke or other incident. Against such an occurrence you should use this. It is ever my hope to God the Almighty that it will preserve you against all such incidents. I have great and much experience of this from God.

For the further strengthening of your body, I am sending you two bottles of aquavit, yellow and white. The white is, with God's help, [to protect you] against unconsciousness or faintness, whether on your deathbed or otherwise. [It is to be] applied with a little feather on the mouth and around the nostrils. You will be amazed – unless God does not want it to happen – how much it strengthens the spirit. Many a person sustains himself with this. The yellow you may take either morning or evening, when you feel discomfort in either chest or stomach. One spoonful strengthens the stomach, the head, and purifies the chest. I do not doubt that if you use it, you will feel its healing power, if the almighty God wills it. I pray to Him that He give His blessing to your good health. And I ask that when you are praying in devotion to God, you remember me as a poor sinner, for the sake of my improvement. And whatever herein promotes your health, I wish, if God wills, to transmit to you free of charge, at your request. Written in Mansfeld with my hand [date].

Dorothea of Mansfeld, widow

Electress Sibylle of Saxony to Luther, Weimar, 27 March (?) 1544,
WA BR X, no. 3977, pp. 546–48

By God's grace Sibylle, Duchess of Saxony, your Most Gracious Lady.

First of all our kindest greeting! Reputable and highly learned, dear devoted one [*Andechtyger*, probably should be translated as servant today]! It is our gracious request to you that you give us to know how you and your dear wife are. For out of Christian loyalty, we could not fail to write to you in order to learn how everything is going with you. For we have not heard about you for a long time. Accordingly, we most graciously request that you inform us how your health is, [and] whether you are still fresh and healthy. It would give us great pleasure to hear this from you. You should provide us with all this information. It could never go well enough with you that I did not wish you many thousand times better besides, and everything good in this transitory world, until that time when we shall all become other than we are now, to which happiness may the dear God help us all, Amen. We do not wish to conceal our gracious opinion from you that we together with our dear children are still in good health, may the dear God bless us long with His grace and all blessedness, Amen. We can also not conceal from you, our kind devotee of the consoling word of God, that we have a sad time here because our heart's very dearest lord and husband is not here. If we were as close to you as we were in Torgau, we would have requested you to come to us, so that we could have been a little bit happy with your presence and you could have comforted us a little, which we would have been heartily glad to hear from you – if this could have been. But inasmuch as it can be no other than it is, we must entrust this matter to the dear God. May He help all things to come to a happy end. We and ours pray to Him assiduously from our hearts for this; and we hope to the dear God that He will graciously hear us and that our heart's very dearest lord and husband and all those with him will return to us with fresh and healthy body. We pray heartily and hard to Him for this and have absolutely no doubt that He will graciously hear us, as He says in [the book of] John: "Whatever you ask of the Father in my name, that will you receive," and in Psalms, "Call upon me in the time of need, and I will save you, and you should praise me." We have fixed our heart on such comforting verses as these, and we certainly do not doubt that the dear God will graciously hear us, if He wills. All of this we have not wanted in haste to keep from you, and we commend you together with your dear wife to the grace of the Almighty God, that He may long keep you healthy in body and soul, and also give you a long life for the sake of His godly word, with which you have consoled me and many other persons. Therewith we want to commend you to the dear God. [Place and date] We ask you most graciously to wish your wife on our behalf very graciously [*sic*] say to her many thousand good nights. And if it was God's will, we would like to be with her once, and with you as with your dear wife... To the honorable and highly learned man, our dear servant [*andechtigenn*], Mr. [*Herr*] Martino lutter, doctor of Holy Scripture in Wittenberg... for his own hands.

[Luther's answer] To Electress Sibylle of Saxony, from Wittenberg,
30 March 1544, WA BR X, no. 3978, pp. 548–49
To the most serene, highborn Princess and Lady, Lady Sibylle, born Duchess of Julich, Cleves, etc., Duchess of Saxony, Electress, Countess in Thuringia, Marchioness of Meissen, Countess of Magdeburg, My most gracious Lady,
    Grace and peace in the Lord! Most serene, highborn Princess, most gracious Lady! I have received Your Electoral Princessly Grace's letter and thank Your Electoral Princessly Grace most humbly for your concerned and diligent inquiry about my health, and about how things are going with my wife and children, and for wishing me all things good. God be praised, it goes well with us, and better than we deserve in the eyes of God. It is no wonder that I occasionally have trouble with my head, in view of my age, and thus it itself [my head] is old, cold, and misshapen, ill and weak. The cup goes to water until it finally breaks. I have lived long enough. May God grant me a blessed hour of death, in which this lazy, useless sack of maggots joins its people under the earth and is divided among the worms. Note well that I have seen the best that I am going to see on earth, for it looks as if the bad is coming. May God help His own, Amen. That Your Electoral Princessly Grace is unhappy because Our Most Gracious Lord, Your Electoral Princessly Grace's husband, is away, I can well believe. But because it is necessary, and because his absence is in the service and for the good of Christianity and the German nation, we must bear it patiently in accordance with God's will. If the devil were able to keep the peace, then

we would have more peace and less to do, and especially less unpleasantness to bear... We have the advantage of having the dear God's word, which comforts and sustains us in this life, and which promises and brings us that life of bliss. And we also have prayer, which we know (as Your Electoral Princessly Grace also wrote) pleases God and that He hears in His time. Such unspeakable treasures as these two the devil, Turk, and the pope and his followers cannot have, and because of that they are much poorer and more miserable than any beggar on earth. We can certainly boast of this and comfort ourselves with it. For this we ought to thank God, the Father of all mercy, in Christ Jesus, His dear Son, our Lord, that He presented us with such a precious, blessed treasure and has called us unworthy people to such a treasure by means of His rich grace. In exchange, it is not only proper that we see temporal evil and gladly endure it, but also that we should take pity on the blind, wretched world, and in particular on such high, great heads in the world, because they have been robbed of this grace and are not yet worthy of having it. May God enlighten them once so that with us they may see, acknowledge, and desire it, Amen. My Kethe prays her poor Our Father for Your Electoral Princessly Grace in all humility and sends her many thanks for Your Electoral Princessly Grace's having so graciously thought of her. Herewith commended to the dear God, Amen. [Date]

> Your Electoral Princessly Grace's
> Humble
> Martinus LuthR D. [*sic*]

LETTERS ABOUT WOMEN

Letter from Luther concerning Rosina von Truchsess, 1544,
WA BR X, no. 3963, pp. 520–21

Grace and peace, my dear Lord Judge [Herr Richter] and good friend! I am told that you have a guest over there in Leipzig who calls herself Rosina von Truchsess. She is the most shameless liar that I have recently seen. With such a name she came first of all to me, as a poor nun from such a high-ranking family. But as I afterward made inquiry, I discovered that she had lied to me. Then I interrogated her and investigated who she might be. She confessed that she was a burgher's daughter from Minderstatt in Franconia, that her father had been beheaded in the peasants' revolt, and that she, a poor child, had gone astray. She begged me for God's sake to forgive her and take pity on her. At that I told her that henceforth she should refrain from such lies with the name Truchsess. But of this I am certain and know no other than that she committed behind my back all manner of knavery and whoring, even in my house, [and] deludes [*bescheust*] all the people with the name Truchsess, so that I know how she came away – can think no other than that she was sent to me by the papists as an archwhore, desperate slut, and sack of lies. She has done me injury in cellar, kitchen, and cupboard, but nobody is to blame for it. Who knows what more she had in mind, for I trusted her completely in my bedrooms and with my children. Finally, she drew a number [of men] to her and became pregnant by one of them. She asked my maid to jump on her body in order to kill the fetus. She got away because of the mercy of my Käthe. Otherwise she would never again have betrayed anybody unless the Elbe had run out of water. Accordingly, it is my request to you that you keep an eye on such a Miss Truchsess and let yourselves be commanded and ask where she comes from. In the end, if it can be no other way, in order to serve the gospel and do me a service, do not tolerate among you this accursed whore, this lying, thieving rascal. In this way [by banning her] you will secure yourselves against her devilish knavishness, thievery, and betrayal. I am almost worried that if one questioned her rightly, she would have earned more than one death sentence, so many witnesses have come forward since her departure. With good intention I wanted to inform you of this so that it does not lie on my conscience that I failed to warn you about such a damned, lying, whoring, thieving slut. Do with her, now, what and how you will; I am no longer responsible. Herewith be commended to God, Amen. [Date]

[No signature]

LETTERS AND OTHER WRITINGS ABOUT THE HORNUNG MARRIAGE

To Margarethe Blanckefeldynn, from Wittenberg, 7 January 1528,
WA BR IV, no. 1205, p. 345

[This has to do with the marriage of Wolf Hornung, the son-in-law of Margarethe B. Luther is trying through the mother-in-law to effect a reconciliation between Wolf Hornung and his wife, but the wife is apparently involved in a relationship with Elector Joachim of Brandenburg, who forbade Margarethe to correspond with Luther.]

To the honorable, virtuous lady Margarethe Blanckefeldynn in Berlin, my kind [*günstig*], good friend,

Grace and peace in Christ! Honorable, virtuous lady! I have received your answer, and although I as an outside person have enough to attend to, so you have to consider that the person whom this matter touches [the addressee's son-in-law] can by no means be satisfied. Such letters give him reason to think many things, especially that the individual who has now often let him be led around (as he complains) by the nose has never yet sent him a written answer from which he might be able to detect her seriousness. It is unbelievable, my dear lady, that if she were serious, she should do no other than to state her position, at least in writing, which she could carry out in secret. Accordingly, it is my friendly request that you consider the distress of the poor fellow and that he neither should nor can endure this any longer. If she does not let her intentions be known, he must behave as though she were dead, or, as Phillip did when his brother Herod took Herodias away from him: provide for himself elsewhere. Would you speak seriously with her about this, or else a farewell will soon result. Herewith be commended to God, Amen. [Date]...

Martinus Luther.

To Katherina Hornung, from Wittenberg, 7 January 1528,
WA BR IV, no. 1206, p. 346

To the honorable and virtuous lady Katherina Hornung in Berlin, my kind [*gonstigen*], good friend.

Grace and peace in Christ! My dear lady Katherin! I have allowed myself to receive advice from several people – assuming that your intentions are good – on how to move that good fellow Wolff Hornung, your wedded husband, again (as others repeatedly have, but in vain, just like the most recent time) to call you back to him in a friendly manner and to resolve the matter in peace. But because you alienate yourself so and, after sending him so many mocking letters, are unable to write him even one friendly, serious letter – which you well could – how can he possibly be such a stone and blockhead and let everything be all right with him and regard it as in keeping with kinship? Accordingly, it is my friendly request that you give him an indication in writing, as you well could, so that he can detect your seriousness. If not, you have to consider that he neither can nor should go on this way, but rather, in accordance with God's word, think about what is best for him and preserve his soul. To this I ask for your proper answer, or I shall have to advise him to do what is his right and what God allows. Herewith be commended to God, Amen. [Date]

Martinus Luther.

To Katharina Hornung in Berlin, from Wittenberg, 1 February 1530,
WA BR V, no. 1526, pp. 230–31
To the honorable lady Katherin Hornungin in Cölln on the Spree.

Grace and peace in Christ! Honorable, dear lady! What I now write to you, you should be sure that I do at the request and desire of your husband Wolff Hornung. Your conscience can well tell you that you cannot be certain of the [validity] of the boobish and worthless contract [of divorce] that Wolff Hornung, compelled and rejected (as he says), has given you. Nor can you look for nor use your prince's protection [enforcement of it], for it is clearly in violation of God's word for married people themselves to arrange a divorce. For that reason, the master who drew up the contract was not fully in possession of his senses and did not consider certain parts of it. Nevertheless, he pulled his head out of the noose and attempted to push the whole matter off on Hornung; he does not see that he has "fallen in backwards" ["got into a legally dubious position"].

For you know that you are perpetrating upon your poor husband such a great and gruesome vice and outrage, that you are robbing him by withholding yourself, his child, his house and yard, his goods and honor, and in addition have hounded him into misery, such that he is a poor beggar who hangs suspended in great poverty and need. In addition, as a young person he has daily had to live in danger to his soul for over four years now. His sin will all too often fall upon your head and neck and will press upon you. What is more you have been requested, entreated, asked, and begged but have nevertheless not come back. Necessity thus compels one henceforward to attack the matter in a different way. I give you to know that I am considering declaring Wolff Hornung to be divorced from you as an adultress, if you do not otherwise conform, so that he can begin a new existence in which he can remain and not have to dwell in perpetual misery.

Accordingly, I am setting a deadline for you, in case you were minded to do something: namely until 27 March. Whatever you want to negotiate, you should do within that time. After that date, if God wills, you will certainly read another letter [from me]. If the poor Wolff Hornung has to bear such robbery – well, so be it! God has more misery than He has ever given out to people. God will probably present him with another wife, child, house and yard, property and honor. Know this and act accordingly! May God help to extricate you from your sins and bring you back to the right way, Amen. [Place and date]

D. Martinus Luther.

[Katharina Hornung did not answer Luther but rather wrote to her husband. Luther took that letter, added a preface, and published it! This is printed with BR V, no. 1526, pp. 232–34. The following are Luther's preface (p. 232) and one paragraph of Katharina's letter (pp. 232–33).

The title of the publication was: Ein antwort // Katherinen // Hornung, auff // D. Marti. Luthers // notbriefe, An Wolff // Hornung...Gedruckt zu Wittem//berg durch Nickel // Schirlentz. Ym Jar. // M. D. XXX. //]

Preface

Luther sent out several emergency letters (as he calls them) to the Margrave, Elector of Brandenburg, etc., and to the communities and estates of the same land, in addition to Katherina Hornung, in order to admonish them to put an end to the shameful, blasphemous matter that stinks throughout the entire empire and causes the whole world great aggravation. She alone answered these letters, but only to Wolff Hornung, and she defends both herself and the Elector and addresses him at the end: "I did not wish to withhold from you this response to your written [instructions?] and Luther's chattering." Because of this answer to such public letters, it would be too bad if this letter itself were not made public, so that everyone could see what sort of answer was made to Luther's letters.

And in truth it is a very female [*weibisch*] composition, such that it is not easy to grasp who may have mastery over such a woman, unless he wears a glove made of deerskin and lined with the skin of misery, as everyone can well notice. [This is referring to a protective glove.] She calls herself Katherina Blanckenfelt, yet Luther wrote to Katherina Hornung. Perhaps this is a matter of which Moses spoke in Genesis 2: "The two are one flesh," although Moses strictly forbade that a man should wear women's clothing. And God preserve every man's wife from *this* lady Katherina Blanckefelden – unless a good pig doctor has come in advance with a sharp knife and castrated him...Phooey and again phooey! What infamous, shameless things whores and knaves are!

The letter follows verbatim.

Wolff Hornung! I have received your writing together with the enclosed copies of several other supposed letters that your idol and advisor, that Luther, is supposed to have written and had sent out to My Gracious Lord the Elector and Prince, also to the three bishops, counts, lords, and knighthood of this electorate, the Margraviate of Brandenburg. Because I have found little truth in these, I do not let them lead me astray or tempt me. I have no doubt that the communities and praiseworthy estates of these lands will by no means allow themselves to be moved to any peevishness, ungraciousness, or disagreeableness by such a man's loose, open, unsealed, untrue invention and printing, and certainly not against their Most Gracious Elector and Prince, but similarly not against me... Luther should not be so concerned on my account but should rather examine himself how good a marriage and faith he maintains with his runaway nun, when at night he sometimes walks in the streets with the lute... The tyrannical, murderous, evil act that you committed against me, unprovoked and cunningly, as I sat at your side at the table, this is known throughout city and land. This can be described and testified to by living witnesses if necessary. I can still prove it by the evidence [a scar?] that I have from you on my body. You cannot deny or contradict the truth and reason of this. . . .

CHAPTER 10

Witchcraft and magic

During the sixteenth and seventeenth centuries between 100,000 and 200,000 people were officially tried, and between 50,000 and 100,000 executed for witchcraft in Europe. Of these, about 80–85 percent were women, though this percentage varied throughout Europe. Both Protestant and Catholic authorities tried and executed witches, with the Holy Roman Empire, Switzerland, and eastern France seeing the highest levels of persecution. The early modern upsurge in witch trials – often called the "Witch Craze" or the "Great Witch Hunt" – is an extremely complex phenomenon which has been the subject of a huge number of studies over the last thirty years; most of these emphasize the ways in which economic, social, political, legal, theological, and intellectual factors all played a role.

Luther did not write a systematic treatise on witchcraft, so his ideas emerge in discussions of Biblical references to witchcraft and in the table talk. These ideas did not break dramatically with those of late medieval Christian thinkers. Most historians of witchcraft note that during the late Middle Ages, Christian philosophers and theologians developed a new idea about the most important characteristics of a witch. Until that period in Europe, as in most cultures throughout the world, a witch was a person who used magical forces to do evil deeds (*maleficia*). One was a witch, therefore, because of what one *did*, causing injuries or harm to animals and people. This notion of witchcraft continued in Europe, but to it was added a demonological component. Educated Christian thinkers in some parts of Europe began to view the essence of witchcraft as making a pact with the devil, a pact which required the witch to do the devil's bidding. Witches were no longer simply people who used magical power to get what they wanted, but people used by the devil to do what *he* wanted. (The devil is always described and portrayed visually as male.) The primary charge became *being* a devil-worshipping witch rather than *doing* specific evil deeds, which meant that many more people could be implicated. Gradually this demonological or Satanic idea of witchcraft was fleshed out, and witches were thought to engage in wild sexual orgies with the devil, fly through the night to meetings called sabbats, which parodied the mass, and steal communion wafers and unbaptized babies to use in their rituals. Some demonological theorists also claimed that witches were organized in an international conspiracy to overthrow Christianity, with a hierarchy modeled on the hierarchy of angels and archangels constructed by Christian philosophers to give order to God's assistants. Witchcraft was thus spiritualized, and witches became the ultimate heretics, enemies of God, a position that Luther firmly accepts. His most dramatic statement of this was in his 1516 sermon on the Ten Commandments, which he considered republishing in 1540 when there was a witch trial in Wittenberg.

This demonology was created by Catholic thinkers during the fifteenth century, and brought together in the *Malleus Maleficarum* (*The Hammer of [Female] Witches*), written by two German Dominican inquisitors, Heinrich Krämer and Jacob Sprenger, and published in 1486, with many editions and translations over the next several centuries. This book was not simply a description of witchcraft, however, but a guide for witch-hunters, advising them how to recognize and question witches. It was especially popular in central Europe, and the questions which it taught judges and lawyers to ask of witches were asked over a large area; the fact that they often elicited the same or similar answers fueled the idea that witchcraft was an international conspiracy. Though witch trials died down somewhat during the first decades after the Protestant Reformation when Protestants and Catholics were busy fighting each other, they picked up again more strongly than ever about 1560. Protestants did not reject Catholic demonology, and the *Malleus* was just as popular in Protestant areas as in Catholic ones; Luther clearly supports the investigation and execution of witches, complaining at one point that the legal system was too slow rather than too summary in its judgments. He and other Protestants may have felt even more at the mercy of witches than Catholics, for they rejected rituals such as exorcism, which Catholics believed could counter the power of a witch.

The Protestant and Catholic Reformations may also have contributed to the spread of demonological ideas among wider groups of the population, for both Catholics and Protestants increased their religious instruction of lay people during the sixteenth century. As part of their program of deepening popular religious understanding and piety, both Protestants and Catholics attempted to suppress what the elites viewed as superstition, folk belief, and more open expressions of sexuality; some historians view the campaign against witches as part of a larger struggle by elite groups to suppress popular culture, to force rural residents to acculturate themselves to middle-class urban values. The fact that women were the preservers and transmitters of popular culture, teaching their children magical sayings and rhymes along with more identifiably Christian ones, made them particularly suspect.

Women were also more likely to be witches, in the eyes of learned theorists, because they were more sexual than men. The authors of the *Malleus* are obsessed with sex (even some of their fellow investigators and demonologists thought that they overdid it), seeing this, and not evil deeds, as the key issue in witchcraft. Female sexual drive was viewed as increasing throughout a woman's life, making the post-menopausal woman most vulnerable to the blandishments of a demonic suitor. Luther's early sermon references to witchcraft focus specifically on women's sexuality, and his stories about witches include ones that focus on older women's lust and on the ways in which young women used magically enhanced sexual allure to tempt men.

Along with learned demonology, Luther's discussions of witchcraft contain many elements that come from popular ideas about witches. The incidents of witchcraft he relates often involved food preparation or the care of animals and children, all areas of life over which women had control and in which misfortune could occur easily, with magic or malevolence the most likely explanation. Witches are the inversions of the good wives and mothers he praises so extensively elsewhere: they destroy, rather than sustain, children; they scold, curse, or cast spells rather than being silent; they are willful, independent, and aggressive, rather than chaste, pious, and obedient. Luther's voice thus added little that was new to discussions of witchcraft, but his authority was such that later authors and compilers of witch treatises included some of his writings to give their arguments extra weight.

SERMONS

Sermon on the Ten Commandments, 1516, WA I
[P. 403] For the devil holds the female sex organ [*organum sexum foemineum*] as his servant, so that he admits it to his holy rites, proclaims his laws and sows his superstitions through it, in every way contrary to God, who has imposed His sacred rites and priesthood and His word on men [*viris*]. For a

long time this feminine priesthood has prevailed and it has filled these lands with innumerable superstitions, charms, and frivolous teachings, which for a long time people have feared more than the laws and rights of the masculine and divine priesthood.

[P. 407] And who can enumerate all the ludicrous, ridiculous, false, vain, and superstitious ideas of this seducible sex? From the first woman, Eve, it originated that they should be deceived and considered a laughing-stock.

Sermon on Exodus, 1526, WA XVI, p. 551

[Sermon on Exodus 22:18, "You shall not permit a female sorcerer to live."] *Concerning the female sorcerer.* Roman law also prescribes this. Why does the law name women more than men here, even though men are also guilty of this? Because women are more susceptible to those superstitions of Satan; take Eve, for example. They are commonly called "wise women." *Let them be killed.* None of them should take advantage of the holy things of Christians. For they say: "I swear to you by the sword that pierces Mary's heart, by the thorns of Christ, by the four Evangelists, etc." To us Christians it is said: "If you lack anything, ask for faith, ask for bodily and external things; if you do not immediately receive them, wait. Do not deal with Satan; do not command God as the witches do." The sorceress establishes a certain time, person, and places, saying: "There in bed you will find a frog, hair, the ones of the dead; unless you take them away, unless you dig them up, your painful leg will not be healthy, you will not see, etc." Here the fool says, "By my soul, I have found it to be so," as if Satan cannot most easily place those things in such a way or take possession of your leg. For just as you believe, so it will seem to you. The law that sorceresses should be killed is most just, since they do many cursed things while they remain undiscovered, for they can steal milk, butter, and all things from the house; thinking about some cow, they can say one good word or another and get milk from a towel, a table, or a handle. And the devil leads milk and butter to their milking instrument. They can enchant a child to cry continually, not eating or sleeping, etc. They can also hide a lesion on someone's knee, so that the body decays. If you should see such women, look away, for they have diabolical faces. Therefore, let them be killed. In truth, medicine is something else; namely nature, not a demon. If you apply herbs to men with your words or a benediction by the Lord's Prayer or an angel, etc., that is a demon. Nature, however, is God's; where the nettle burns, water moistens. Certain herbs are medicinal. But if your words are needed, it is a demon, not nature.

LECTURES AND COMMENTARY

Lectures on Galatians, LW XXVI, p. 190
From *Luther's Works*, vol. XXVI, edited by Jaroslav Pelikan, © 1968
Concordia Publishing Company. Used by permission of Concordia
Publishing House

[Commenting on Galatians 3:1, "Who has bewitched you so that you do not
obey the truth?"] The reason Paul calls the Galatians foolish and bewitched
is that he compares them to children, to whom witchcraft does a great
deal of harm. It is as though he were saying: "What is happening to you
is precisely what happens to children, whom witches, sorceresses, and hags
usually charm quickly and easily with their bewitchment, a trick of Satan."
Paul does not deny that witchcraft exists and is possible; for later on, in the
fifth chapter (5:20) he also lists "sorcery," which is the same as witchcraft,
among the works of the flesh. Thereby he proves that witchcraft and sorcery
exist and are possible. For it is undeniable that the devil lives, yes, rules in all
the world. Therefore witchcraft and sorcery are works of the devil, by which
he not only injures people but sometimes, with God's permission, destroys
them. But we are all subject to the devil, both according to our bodies
and according to our material possessions. We are guests in the world, of
which he is the ruler (John 16:11) and the god (2 Cor. 4:4). Therefore the
bread we eat, the drinks we drink, the clothes we wear – in fact, the air
and everything we live on in the flesh – are under his reign. Through his
witches, therefore, he is able to do harm to children, to give them heart
trouble, to blind them, to steal them, or even to remove a child completely
and put himself into the cradle in place of the stolen child. I have heard
that in Saxony there was such a boy. He was suckled by five women and
still could not be satisfied. There are many similar instances.

Therefore witchcraft is nothing but an artifice and illusion of the devil,
whether he cripples a part of the body or touches the body or takes it away
altogether...

Commentary on 1 Peter, 1522, LW XXX, p. 91
From *Luther's Works*, vol. XXX, edited by Jaroslav Pelikan, © 1968
Concordia Publishing Company. Used by permission of Concordia
Publishing House

It is commonly the nature of women to be timid and to be afraid of
everything. This is why they busy themselves so much with witchcraft and

superstition. One teaches the other, so that it is impossible to tell what kind of hocus-pocus they practice. But a Christian woman should not do this. She must go along freely and with confidence and not be so timid. She should not practice witchcraft and superstition and run hither and thither, uttering a magic formula here and a magic formula there. Whatever her lot, she should let God rule and she should remember that she cannot fare badly. For since she knows how she is faring and that her position in life is pleasing to God, why should she fear? If your child dies, if you become ill, be of good cheer; commit it to God.

Lectures on Genesis, LW II, p. 11
From *Luther's Works*, vol. II, edited by Jaroslav Pelikan, © 1968
Concordia Publishing Company. Used by permission of Concordia
Publishing House

It delights Satan if he can delude us by taking the appearance either of a young man or of a woman. But that anything can be born from the union of a devil and a human being is simply untrue. Such an assertion is sometimes made about hideous infants that resemble demons very much. I have seen some of these. But I am convinced either that these were deformed, but not begotten, by the devil, or that they are actual devils with flesh that they have either counterfeited or stolen from somewhere else. If with God's permission the devil can take possession of an entire human being and change his disposition, what would be so remarkable about his misshaping the body and bringing about the birth of either blind or crippled children?

Thus he is able to delude people who are irreligious and who live without the fear of God; when the devil is in the bed, the young man imagines that he has a girl, and the girl that she has a young man. But that anything could be born from this cohabitation, this I do not believe. Yet in many places sorceresses have been consigned to the pyre and burned for having had commerce with the devil.

TABLE TALK

WA TR II, no. 2529b, pp. 504–5
The devil has sexual relations with the weather witches. It could certainly be true that the devil has sexual relations and copulates with those old whores, the weather witches, that he satisfies their lust; but that he produces a child with them is not possible, for God alone is the creator and maker of human beings and creation is only possible through His actions and not through

those of the devil. But it is true that they [the weather witches] often confuse women who have just given birth, lie down in the place of the child and are more awful than ten children with shitting and eating, screaming, and so on. I know an example of this that occurred in Halberstadt. There the devil lay down in the place of a child, and made himself look exactly like the child; he was so unsettled and cried so much that the parents had no peace at night because of him. He also sucked the mother dry, so that she could no longer nurse him. After the mother had nothing more to give him, the father sent in another wetnurse, whom he also sucked dry, and so on until the fifth [wetnurse]. The parents did not know what they should do with the child, and they were advised to bring it to Hoppelstad, which was a pilgrimage site because it was still Catholic. The father put the child in a basket and left. As he was going on his way, he crossed over some water, and something in the water cried out: "Hilero!" Out of the basket the child answered: "Hoho!" The voice in the water asked, "Where are you going?" And the child in the basket answered, "I am supposed to go to Hoppelstad, so that I will be better able to thrive." With this the man was shocked, and he immediately threw the child and the basket in the water. The two devils then began to laugh and chatter in the water, making fun of the man, etc.

WA TR III, no. 2982b, pp. 131–32

The torments of the devil through witches. Doctor Luther spoke often of witches, of the asthma and nightmares that plagued his mother because of her neighbor, a sorceress, though she had always treated her nicely and with friendship and had tried to reconcile with her. For she shot [a look at] children, so that they cried themselves to death. And she punished a pastor and bewitched him, so that he had to die; he could not be helped with any medicine. She took dirt on which he had walked and threw it in the water; he could not get healthy again without that dirt. After this he [Luther] was asked whether those who fear God and are good Christians can also be bewitched. And he answered: "Yes, because our souls are subject to lying. These [the souls] can be redeemed, but the body must expect the devil's fatal stabs. And I believe that my illnesses are not always natural, but that Sir Satan works his mischief on me through magic. God, however, saves His chosen from such evil."

WA TR III, no. 3601, pp. 445–46

A citizen of B. was bewitched by a witch so that he lost all of his goods and became poor. He asked the devil for advice, but afterwards his conscience troubled him so that he sought consolation and wondered what to do. At this Doctor Martin said, "He did evil and acted against God. Why didn't he follow the example of Job? Have patience, stick with God and entreat Him for His blessing? You should tell him that he should do penance and not seek refuge in Satan, but bear God's will with patience."

WA TR IV, no. 3921, pp. 10–11

About love-potions. Doctor Jonas and Doctor Balthasar told about a case in which a man who was at Leipzig loved a young woman very much and spoke of this to her and promised marriage. But then he found out that she had given him a potion, drink, or soup that had made him fall in love with her. After he went to another woman to be made healthy again, his love disappeared. Then Doctor Luther became angry and said: "Why do you bother me with such stories? My thoughts on this are that he should either take her [in marriage] or else clearly accuse her to the authorities and prove that he was deceived by the love-potion or drink. If we accept this excuse and allow it, then everyone will excuse himself in this way, whenever he regrets [his actions]. One shouldn't joke about such things! If someone feels that he is a man, he should take a wife and not put God to the test. This young woman did what she was accused of having done to help the man, and to avoid uncleanness and adultery."

And then he began to complain about the terrible temptations in the monasteries, about the pollution and nocturnal emissions, with which the devout fathers are almost always tormented, so that they cannot say mass on the following day. "But so many masses that we were supposed to perform would have been omitted because of our needing to be excused, that [the matter] became public and the prior allowed even those who were unclean to say mass. Shame on this! We should just destroy all the monasteries and convents because of shameful pollution, where idle people laze around all day, letting themselves be fed like swine with the best and rarest food and drink, so that they stimulate such uncleanness to increase every day. Dear God, protect us from this abomination and let us stay in holy marriage, so that our weakness may be turned to good."

WA TR IV, no. 3969, pp. 43–44

About a bewitched young woman. Master Spalatin spoke to Doctor Luther in 1538, about a young woman in Altenburg who was bewitched so that she cried blood. When the sorceress was in a place that [the young woman] could not see her, she could still feel her presence and cried. To this Doctor Martin replied. "Such things should be punished. The lawyers always need too many witnesses and testimonies, and don't pay enough attention to these. Recently I handled a marriage case in which the wife wanted to kill her husband with poison, so that he vomited lizards. When she was interrogated with torture, she would not confess. For such sorceresses become dumb and do not pay attention to the pain; the devil will not allow them to speak. But such deeds give proof enough, and one should punish them harshly to serve as an example, so that others are shocked away from such devilish doings."

WA TR IV, no. 3979, pp. 51–52

Of [female] milk thieves. On 25 August 1538 there was much discussion about witches and sorceresses who steal chicken eggs out of nests, or steal milk and butter. Doctor Martin said: "One should show no mercy to these [women]; I would burn them myself, for we read in the Law that the priests were the ones to begin the stoning of criminals. People say that such stolen butter stinks and falls to the ground if you try to eat it, and that afterwards such sorceresses, when they want to do mischief again, are very much vexed and tormented by the devil. Village pastors and schoolmasters have long known about their arts and have harassed them."

And he said: "Once on St. John's Day at a St. John's Day fire an ox-head was lying on a fence, and a huge crowd of sorceresses gathered around it and pleaded to be able to burn candles and lights [in front of it]. But Doctor Pommer's solution was the best: one should harass them with dirt and stir the milk so that their things will all stink. For when milk was stolen from his cows, he instantly took off his pants and, sitting as a watchman, mixed ashes with milk and stirred it around, saying: 'Eat this, you devil!' After this, milk wasn't taken from him any more."

WA TR IV, no. 4646, p. 416

Of two sorceresses. Doctor Martin spoke about two sorceresses who were sitting one night in a tavern with two pails of water that they had prepared near them, discussing whether they should harm the grain or the wine. But the tavern-keeper, standing hidden in a corner, heard them, and took both of the pails. When the women went to bed, he poured the water over them; the water turned to ice, and the two of them died immediately. Dr. Martin said, "The devil is very powerful through sorceresses."

WA TR VI, no. 6836, p. 222

Witchcraft described theologically. "Sins are a falling away from God's work, through which God is angered and offended; because it is so loathsome, witchcraft is correctly described as a crime against God's divine majesty, a rebellion and a depravity, through which one intends to violate the divine majesty to the utmost. The jurists engage in fine scholarly disputations and speak about all types of rebellion and disobedience to higher authorities, and among other things they include leaving one's lord on the field of battle, betraying him, and joining the enemy; for this they all recognize that bodily torture and death are appropriate punishments. Witchcraft is therefore a much more shameful and terrible defection, for through it one turns away from God – to whom one is promised and sworn – to the devil; thus it is also appropriate to punish it through loss of body or life."

Further reading

This list contains only works that refer solely or extensively to Luther. For larger bibliographies of women and the Reformation, see the references in note 12 of the Introduction.

Ahme, Elisabeth. "Wertung und Bedeutung der Frau bei Martin Luther," *Luther* 35 (1964): 61–68.

Arnold, Mattieu. *Les Femmes dans la correspondance de Luther*. Paris: Presses Universitaires de France, 1998.

Bainton, Roland H. *Women of the Reformation in Germany and Italy*. Minneapolis: Augsburg Publishing House, 1971.

Baranowski, Siegmund. *Luthers Lehre von der Ehe*. Münster: Heinrich Schöningh, 1913.

Behrens, Martha. "Martin Luther's View on Women," M.A. thesis, North Texas State University, 1973.

Biel, Pamela. "Let the Fiancées Beware: Luther, the Lawyers and Betrothal in Sixteenth-Century Saxony." In Bruce Gordon, ed., *Protestant History and Identity in Sixteenth-Century Europe*, 2 vols. Aldershot & Brookfield, VT: Scolar Press, 1996, vol. ii, pp. 121–41.

Bluhm, Heinz. "Luther's Translation and Interpretation of the Ave Maria," *Journal of English and German Philology* 51 (1952): 196–211.

Boehmer, Heinrich. "Luthers Ehe," *Lutherjahrbuch* 7 (1925): 40–76.

Boehmer, Julius. *Luthers Ehebuch*. Zwickau: Herrmann, 1935.

Boyd, Stephen B. "Masculinity and Male Dominance: Martin Luther on the Punishment of Adam." In Stephen B. Boyd, W. Merle Longwood, and Mark W. Muesse, eds., *Redeeming Men: Religion and Masculinities*. Louisville: Westminster John Knox, 1996, pp. 19–32.

Brauner, Sigrid. "Martin Luther on Witchcraft: A True Reformer?" In Jean R. Brink, Allison P. Coudert, and Maryanne C. Horowitz, eds., *The Politics of Gender in Early Modern Europe*. Kirksville: Sixteenth Century Journal Publishers, 1989, pp. 29–42.

Brooks, P. N. "A Lily Ungilded? Martin Luther, the Virgin Mary and the Saints," *Journal of Religious History* 13 (1984): 136–49.

Classen, Albrecht and Tanya Amber Settle. "Women in Martin Luther's Life and Theology," *German Studies Review* 14/2 (1991): 231–60.

Cocke, Emmett W. "Luther's View of Marriage and Family," *Religion in Life* 42 (1973): 103–16.

Cole, William J. "Was Luther a Devotee of Mary?" *Marian Studies* 21 (1970): 94–202.

Delius, Hans-Ulrich. "Luther und das 'Salve Regina,'" *Forschungen und Fortschritte* 38 (1964): 249–51.

Douglass, Jane Dempsey. "Luther and Women," *Lutherjahrbuch* 52 (1985), 294–5. "The Image of God in Women as Seen by Luther and Calvin." In Kari Elisabeth Børreson, ed., *The Image of God and Gender in Judeo-Christian Tradition*. Oslo: Solum Forlag, 1991, pp. 229–57.

Duefel, Hans. *Luthers Stellung zur Marienverehrung*. Kirche und Konfession 13. Göttingen: Vandenhoeck & Ruprecht, 1968.

Ebneter, Albert. "Martin Luthers Marienbild," *Orientierung* 20 (1956): 77–80, 85–87.

Fudge, Thomas A. "Incest and Lust in Luther's Marriage: Theology and Morality in Reformation Polemics," *Sixteenth Century Journal*, forthcoming.

Globig, Christine. "Die Frau in der Sicht Martin Luthers." In *Frauenordination in Kontext lutherischer Ekklesiologie. Ein Beitrag zum ökumenischen Gespräch*. Kirche und Konfession 36. Göttingen: Vandenhoeck & Ruprecht, 1994, pp. 23–43.

Gorski, Horst. *Die Niedrigkeit seiner Magd*... Frankfurt am Main: Peter Lang, 1987.

Hampson, Daphne. "Luther on the Self: A Feminist Critique." In Ann Loades, ed., *Feminist Theology: A Reader*. London: SPCK, 1990, pp. 215–24.

Haustein, Jörg. *Luthers Stellung zum Zauber- und Hexenwesen*. Münchener Kirchenhistorische Studien 2. Munich: Kohlhammer, 1990.

Hendrix, Scott. "Luther on Marriage," *Lutheran Quarterly* 14 (2000): 335–50.

Hoffmann, Julius. *Die "Hausväterliteratur" und die "Predigten über den christlichen Hausstand": Lehre vom Hause und Bildung für das häusliche Leben im 16., 17. und 18. Jahrhundert*. Weinheim and Berlin: Julius Beltz, 1959.

Johnson, Susan M. "Luther's Reformation and (Un)holy Matrimony," *Journal of Family History* 17 (1992): 271–88.

Karant-Nunn, Susan C. "The Transmission of Luther's Teachings on Women and Matrimony: The Case of Zwickau," *Archive for Reformation History* 77 (1986): 31–46.

Kawerau, Waldemar. *Die Reformation und die Ehe. Ein Beitrag zur Kulturgeschichte des 16. Jahrhunderts*. Schriften des Vereins für Reformationsgeschichte 39. Halle: Verein für Reformationsgeschichte, 1892.

Kreitzer, Beth. *Reforming Mary: Lutheran Preaching on the Virgin Mary in the Sixteenth Century*. Oxford: Oxford University Press, forthcoming.

Kroker, Ernst. *Katharina von Bora, Martin Luthers Frau*. Berlin: Evangelische Verlagsanstalt, 1952.

Lähteenmäki, Olavi. *Sexus und Ehe bei Luther*. Schriften des Luther-Agricola Gesellschaft 10. Turku: Luther-Agricola Gesellschaft, 1955.

Lazareth, William H. *Luther on the Christian Home.* Philadelphia: Muhlenberg Press, 1960.

Lorenz, Dagmar, ed. *Martin Luther: Vom ehelichen Leben und andere Schriften über die Ehe.* Stuttgart: Kohlhammer, 1978.

Ludolphy, Ingetraut. "Die Frau in der Sicht Martin Luthers." In *Vierhundertfünfzig Jahre lutherische Reformation 1517–1967: Festschrift für Franz Lau zum 60. Geburtstag.* Göttingen: Vandenhoeck & Ruprecht, 1967, pp. 204–21.

Mattox, Mickey. *Defender of the Most Holy Matriarchs: Martin Luther's Interpretation of the Women of Genesis in the* Enarrationes in Genesin, *1535–1545.* Leiden: Brill, forthcoming.

Michaelis, Karl. "Über Luthers eherechtliche Anschauung und deren Verhältnis zum mittelalterlichen und neuzeitlichen Eherecht." In Heinz Brunotte, ed., *Festschrift für Ernst Ruppel.* Hanover: Lutherhaus Verlag, 1968.

Miller, Thomas Fischer. "Mirror for Marriage: Lutheran Views of Marriage and the Family, 1520–1600," Ph.D. dissertation, University of Virginia, 1981.

Mueller, Gerhard. "Protestant Veneration of Mary: Luther's Interpretation of the Magnificat." In James Kirk, ed., *Humanism and Reform: The Church in Europe, England, and Scotland, 1400–1643: Essays in Honor of James K. Cameron,* Oxford: Basil Blackwell, 1991, pp. 99–111.

Mühlhaupt, Erwin. "Sieben kleine Kapitel über die Lebenswege Luthers und Käthes," *Luther* 57 (1986), 1–18.

Preuss, H. D. *Maria bei Luther.* Schriften des Vereins für Reformationsgeschichte 172. Gütersloh: C. Bertelsmann, 1954.

Roper, Lyndal. "Luther: Sex, Marriage and Motherhood," *History Today* 33 (1983): 33–38.

Schaffenorth, Gerta. "Martin Luther zur Rolle von Mann und Frau." In Hans Süssmuth, ed., *Das Luther Erbe in Deutschland*, Düsseldorf: Droste, 1985, pp. 111–30.

" 'Im Geiste Freunde werden': Mann und Frau im Glauben Martin Luthers." In Heide Wunder and Christina Vanja, eds., *Wandel der Geschlechterbeziehungen zu Beginn der Neuzeit.* Frankfurt: Suhrkamp, 1991, pp. 97–108.

Schroeder, Joy A. "The Rape of Dinah: Luther's Interpretation of a Biblical Narrative," *Sixteenth Century Journal* 28 (1997): 775–91.

Siggins, Ian. *Luther and His Mother.* Philadelphia: Fortress Press, 1981.

Smith, Jeanette C. "Katharina von Bora through Five Centuries: A Historiography," *Sixteenth Century Journal* 30, 3 (1999): 745–74.

Stein, Albert. "Martin Luthers Bedeutung für die Anfänge des Evangelischen Eherechts," *Österreichisches Archiv für Kirchenrecht* 34 (1983/84): 29–95.

Steinmetz, David C. "Luther and Tamar," *Consensus: A Canadian Lutheran Journal of Theology* 19 (1993): 135–49.

Suppan, Klaus. *Die Ehelehre Martin Luthers. Theologische und rechtshistorische Aspekte der reformatorischen Eheverständnisse.* Salzburg: Universitätsverlag A. Pustet, 1971.

Thoma, Albrecht. *Katharina von Bora, geschichtliches Lebensbild.* Berlin: Georg Reimer, 1990.

Treu, Martin. *Katharina von Bora.* Wittenberg: Drei Kastanien Verlag, 1995.
"Katharina von Bora, the Woman at Luther's Side," *Lutheran Quarterly* 13 (1999): 157–78.
"Lieber Herr Käthe" – *Katharina von Bora, die Lutherin.* Wittenberg: Stiftung Luthergedenkstätten in Sachsen-Anhalt, 1999.
Wiesner, Merry E. "Luther and Women: The Death of Two Marys." In Ann Loades, ed., *Feminist Theology: A Reader.* London: SPCK, 1990, pp. 123–37.
Williams, Mary Cooper. *Luther's Letters to Women.* Chicago: Wartburg, 1930.
Zarncke, Lilly. "Die naturhafte Eheanschaung des jungen Luthers," *Archiv für Kulturgeschichte* 25 (1935): 281–305.
Zophy, Jonathan W. "We Must Have the Dear Ladies: Martin Luther and Women." In Kyle C. Sessions and Phillip N. Bebb, eds., *Pietas et Societas: New Trends in Reformation Social History.* Kirksville: Sixteenth Century Journal Publishers, 1985, pp. 141–50.

Index

Lightning Source UK Ltd.
Milton Keynes UK
UKOW05f1820270217

295459UK00024B/659/P

9 780521 658843